HEGEL'S PHENOMENOLOGY, Part II

HEGEL'S PHENOMENOLOGY, Part II

The Evolution of Ethical and Religious Consciousness to the Absolute Standpoint

Howard P. Kainz

OHIO UNIVERSITY PRESS
ATHENS, OHIO
LONDON

Library of Congress Cataloging in Publication Data

Kainz, Howard P.
    Hegel's Phenomenology, Part II.

    Bibliography: p.
    1. Hegel, Georg Wilhelm Friedrich, 1770–1831.
Phänomenologie des Geistes.   2. Spirit.   3. Conscience.
4. Truth.   I. Title.
B2929.K283   1982   193   82–22444
ISBN 0-8214-0677-9
ISBN 0-8214-0738-4 (pbk.)

Table of Contents

Preface

This book is a sequel to my *Hegel's Phenomenology, Part I: Analysis and Commentary* and brings to completion my exegesis and interpretation of the text of the *Phenomenology* in its entirety. The writing of this sequel has been accomplished under very different circumstances than had been the case with its predecessor. When I wrote the previous volume, there were only a few "commentaries" available—the most useful of these being, in my opinion, Hyppolite's French commentary. Now the situation is being reversed. To the works of Hyppolite, Lukacs, Wahl, Kojève, and Loewenberg, and Heidegger's commentary on the Introduction, have been added those of Labarriere, W. Marx (both in German and in English translation), Becker, Fink, Scheier, Navickas, Norman, Shklar, Robinson, Lauer, Westphal, Taylor and Findlay, as well as my own commentary on the first half; English translations of Hyppolite and Kojève; and others are currently in preparation. In addition, besides the sort of systematical part-by-part treatment that we usually equate with "commentary" in the strict sense, many useful studies in German—by Pöggler, Bonsiepen, Heinrichs, Gauvin, Fulda, Lim and others—have been published recently.

One could argue that the prospective commentator on the *Phenomenology* who reads too many of these interpretations runs the risk not only of becoming confused by the often divergent opinions expressed or of distancing himself too much from the simple meaning that should stand out from the text, but also of losing his originality and producing a kind of textbook treatment of the *Phenomenology* (if such an entity can be imagined). But such opinions do not seem to accord well with the spirit of the *Phenomenology*, which incorporates so many ideas from other authors that it occasionally—with regard to Diderot and Fichte, for example— borders on plagiarism, but without losing its originality. And so I do not share such fears, and have, in fact, immersed myself as much as possible in the interpretations of others before beginning this book. But in the end, one must get back to the text, deal with Hegel *tête-à-tête* and come to one's own conclusions. A final encounter of this sort was the direct springboard for this commentary.

The format of this book is for the most part similar to that of the previous volume, in which the "Analysis" section, which simply restates as clearly and systematically as possible Hegel's arguments as they proceed in the *Phenomenology,* is almost completely separated from the "Commentary" which is added by way of "footnotes." I have found from my experience with the previous volume that this separation has one disadvantage: that some of my readers have taken the "Commentary" section for footnotes in the usual sense—that is, as somewhat extraneous to the author's main arguments—and bypassed it. But there is still, to my mind, a decisive advantage to such a separation with regard to Hegel and in particular with regard to this particular book by Hegel: Interspersing philosophical ramifications, historical references, cross-references, literary allusions, interpretive applications, etc., etc., in the course of one's exegesis of the text—especially in the most complex texts, such as the sections on Insight and Enlightenment in the *Phenomenology*—can (and, for the reader less versed in Hegel, almost certainly must) distract the reader from Hegel's main arguments and keep him from following that dialectical *movement* which is, after all, the most important thing in that unique book concerned precisely with the *development* of consciousness and Spirit. And so by means of this separation I hope to be able to convey more clearly both the structure of these movements and the additional information about interpretative nuances, historical and cultural allusions, etc., that are necessary for a fuller appreciation of Hegel's book. Fortunately, the editors have positioned notes together with text in this volume, thus facilitating use of the commentary.

In the present volume structural diagrams are utilized to recapitulate the developments in Part I and also to give an overall view of the movements in Part II and the *Phenomenology* as a whole; references to the Miller translation, which features a paragraph-by-paragraph numbering based on Hoffmeister's German edition, are included; and an Appendix offers summaries of certain literary works that Hegel, presuming in his nineteenth-century readers an extensive familiarization with ancient and modern literary works, draws upon extensively in certain sections of the *Phenomenology.*

All the quotations from the *Phenomenology* are my own translations. Since the various parts of the *Phenomenology* are so closely tied contextually, terminologically and grammatically with their surrounding parts, it is difficult to excerpt quotations which are clear and autonomously meaningful, and so my translations tend to be freer than one would expect to find in a straightforward translation of the whole book; but for these excerpts the corresponding German texts are added in the Commentary section, to assist the reader in his own textual analysis. In using quotations from other works of Hegel and other German or French writers and secondary sources in the Commentary, I have used published English translations wherever usable ones were available; otherwise, I have translated these quotations rather literally in English.

The title of this book is meant to give as much an indication of its *contents* as is possible within the space of a few words. In spite of possible and unwelcome overtones of "natural selection," I use the word "evolution" instead of "phenomenology" in order to emphasize the difference of Hegel's *Phenomenology*, which is concerned primarily with *movement* (see K45 ff.), from contemporary phenomenologies, which seem to be concerned primarily with the eidetic and/or linguistic *structures* of subjective, intersubjective and/or objective experience. "Part II" is merely a reference to Hegel's own distinction between the "forms of consciousness" in the earlier sections of the *Phenomenology,* and the "forms of the world" which become paramount in chapters VI–VIII; it is *not* meant to indicate any sharp division between the two parts, as suggested by e.g. Theodore Haering. Also, "ethical consciousness" and "religious consciousness" are simply two of the more important developments of "Spirit" discussed in the second half of the *Phenomenology*. Anyone familiar with Hegel's holistic orientation in philosophizing will not be surprised to learn that Hegel also devotes considerable space in these pages to detailed discussion of legal consciousness, economic and political consciousness, Catholic and Protestant forms of religious consciousness, revolutionary consciousness, moral consciousness, a supra-moral type of consciousness ("Conscience"), and an ultimate stage of consciousness which functions as a kind of "set of all sets" with regard to the other stages—i.e., "Absolute Knowledge." But perhaps I may be allowed to point out, to paraphrase Hegel in his Preface to the *Phenomenology,* that titles and introductions to philosophical works will be useless and even misleading, unless one immerses himself in the content which they briefly allude to and anticipate.

Erhard Lange in *Hegel und Wir* calls the *Phenomenology* "an immortal work." I agree with this not so much because of its extraordinary range of content or the genius of its insights, but simply because it is a great example in philosophy of serious, sustained and powerful creative *thought*—that *sine qua non* of philosophy which is less common than one would expect, but welcome in any form, school or style of philosophizing, and in Hegel's philosophical work shines forth in spite of (or perhaps even because of) those incredible successive and cyclical and interwoven concatenations of triads for which he is noted.

I am very grateful to the National Endowment for the Humanities for their 1977-78 grant which enabled me to complete most of this commentary; and also to Louise Henderson, Tom Michaud and Ken Pirsig for their expert help in proofreading its semi-final versions.

Conventions

B Hegel, G.W.F., *Phänomenologie des Geistes,* Bonsiepen, Hsgb., Hamburg, 1980.

B Hegel, G.W.F., *Phenomenology of Mind,* Baillie tr., London, 1961.

M Hegel, G.W.F., *The Phenomenology of Spirit,* Miller tr., Oxford, 1977.

H Hegel, G.W.F., *Phänomenologie des Geistes,* Hoffmeister Hsgb., Hamburg, 1948.

K Kainz, H.P., *Hegel's Phenomenology, Part I: Analysis and Commentary,* Tuscaloosa, Ala., 1976.

For other works, abbreviated forms of longer titles will be used. Complete titles are given in the Bibliography.

Introduction to the Analysis of Part II of Hegel's Phenomenology

It would be possible, in the case of many philosophical books, to open the book at the middle and begin to follow the arguments of that book in a somewhat satisfactory and creditable fashion. Unfortunately, the *Phenomenology, of Spirit* is not this sort of book. Like a Russian novel whose plots and subplots get more and more intricately interwoven as the novel progresses, the *Phenomenology* at midpoint (i.e., the section on "Spirit" with which we begin) already presupposes an immense number of movements or developments which function after the manner of "premises" for the dialectical climaxes and denouements which will emerge in Part II. Diagram 1 which follows should help to put the presupposed preliminary developments of Part I into perspective. Diagram 2 will then sketch out the relationships between the two halves of the book and, in doing so, present a summary overview of the whole. Then, finally, Diagram 3 will offer a kind of map of the progressions of Spirit to be charted in the "Analysis" segment of my interpretation.

DIAGRAM 1. RECAPITULATION OF "PART I" OF HEGEL'S PHENOMENOLOGY.

1

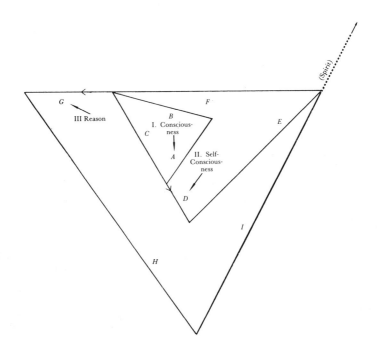

Explanation of Diagram 1 and the Symbols

The three paralleloid but continuous triangles in Diagram 1 represent the three major stages of the "Phenomenology of Consciousness": I. Consciousness Proper, II. Self-Consciousness, and III. Reason. Each of these stages is subdivided into its own triads, and often these triads are further subdivided into subordinate triads. The *major* outlines of the dialectical developments are as follows. (For further structural analysis see K34f., and K161ff. and the diagrams for specific sections in K *passim*.)

I. The Phenomenology of Consciousness

A. Sense-Certainty. Consciousness proceeds from a state of relative immersion in an objective "here" and "now" to a final comprehension of the "here" and the "now" as a reciprocity of subjective and objective factors.

B. Perception. The perceptual object becomes the primary locus of multiple "heres" and "nows" (i.e., various coexistent properties), which are seen at first as a multiplicity unified by the ego, then as a unity differentiated by the ego, and finally as a subjective–objective synthesis of both unity and multiplicity.

C. Understanding. The relationship of one perceptual object to another is similarly seen as an alternation between a unifying Force and multiple determinate expressions of Force. This process of alternation is then itself codified in laws formulated by the human understanding. Finally, Understanding comes to view its own process of lawmaking as a manifestation of the more fundamental "law" that self-conscious Life must strive somehow to objectify itself—and with this insight the transition is made to Self-Consciousness as a stand or attitude radically contrasted with Consciousness.

II. The Phenomenology of Self-Consciousness

Self-Consciousness, as is indicated schematically in Diagram A, is an extension of the basic insight into the "law" of Life, attained at the culmination of Understanding. The drive of Self-Consciousness to fulfill its "law" and the Desire to find a suitable objective expression for its Life leads it through the following distinguishable sub-stages:

D. Self-Certainty, which is discovered to require a new and special type of "object," namely another self-consciousness. And thus the essence of Self-Certainty is finally seen in terms of intersubjective unity with one's "alter-ego," and recognition of and from the alter-ego.

E. The Master–Slave Dialectic: The drive for recognition *from* one's alter-ego proceeds from a state of primitive imitativeness to a "Life and Death" struggle for preeminence, to a compromise "Master–Slave" relationship, which reverses itself as the Master becomes overly dependent on the work of the Slave, and the Slave by being forced into creativity becomes the superior, in spite of himself.

F. Stoicism, Scepticism, and the Unhappy Consciousness: As the antithesis between Master and Slave resolves itself, Self-Consciousness becomes aware of more individual, albeit abstract, ways of attaining recognition: through Stoical conceptual transformation of reality; through the negative, critical, manipulative power of Scepticism over reality; and finally in the passionate struggles of the Unhappy (Self-)Consciousness to find a stable and unchanging absolute Reality within *itself.* These struggles terminate in an all-too-meager, but important, glimpse into the essential *union* of Self-Consciousness with "objective reality"—a union which in Hegel's technical terminology is called Reason (*Vernunft*).

III. Reason

As may be seen from Diagram 1, Reason is an extension of that "meager glimpse" that was attained at the culmination of Self-Consciousness. This basic insight into the union of the ego with reality, or thought and being, now needs corroboration and explication, and the search for such corroboration and explication takes place in the following three stages:

G. Rational Observation: Here Reason looks to inorganic and organic Nature, to the human psyche, and to the mind-body composite for external evidence of the basic identity between thought and being, between thinghood and selfhood.

H. Rational Self-Actualization: Having failed to find the identity of thinghood and selfhood, Reason desists from trying to *find* this identity and attempts something which seems to be more within its power—*making* the self into a thing, i.e., objectifying the self and thus fulfilling the insight that thought is one with existence.

I. Subjective/Objective Individualization: Being similarly unsuccessful in its attempts to *create* the identity of thought and being, Reason finally hits upon the proper sense in which it both finds *and* creates the union of the self with reality—namely, in its immediate relationship with *society,* which is at one and the same time (*a*) a real *"ethical substance"* which gives rise to and nurtures the individual self, and (*b*) a result or *product* of self-consciousness, without which it could not exist at all. Thus with this final insight we begin to focus no longer on the individual consciousness, or on Reason trying to validate its subjective-objective synthesis through individual ingenuity, but on the more universal reciprocity of thought and existence, or self and other,—a reciprocity which in Hegel's technical terminology is called "Spirit," and which is manifested in its most immediate and objective fashion in intersubjective union, i.e., society or community as an ethical entity.

DIAGRAM 2. RELATION OF PART I TO PART II.

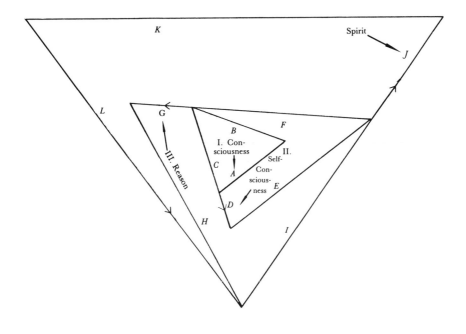

Explanation of Diagram 2 and Symbols

The designation of the two halves of the Phenomenology as "Part I" and "Part II" is not Hegel's own designation, but it is convenient for emphasizing Hegel's different focus in the two sections: on the "Forms of Consciousness" in the first half, but on the "Forms of a World [of Spirit]" in the second half (see K17 f., K164, K180, M§441).

As consciousness proceeds through its exploration of Consciousness Proper, Self-Consciousness and Reason (from *A* to *I* on Diagrams 1 and 2), the parameters of its experience are gradually widened until it begins to understand that these experiences themselves are conditioned by larger developments taking place in the world as a whole, and that, in fact, the progress of the "world-Spirit" is the indispensable context which gives direction and meaning and teleology to the progressions of individual consciousness (see K163 f., K174 f., K181 f., M§28, M§357, *Logic* §25).

But this wider, overarching context of Spirit, like consciousness itself, manifests the necessary progression of dialectical movement from the in-itself, to the for-itself, and to the in–and-for-itself (see K23 ff), and this progression is symbolized in the diagram as the movements from *J* through *K* to *L*, the latter being an ''absolute'' movement which encompasses and supersedes the previous movements, but is based on them, and is in inseparable continuity with them, in the same sense that science both supersedes and depends on the its experiential bases.

DIAGRAM 3. DEVELOPMENTS IN PART II, SCHEMATIZED IN GREATER DETAIL

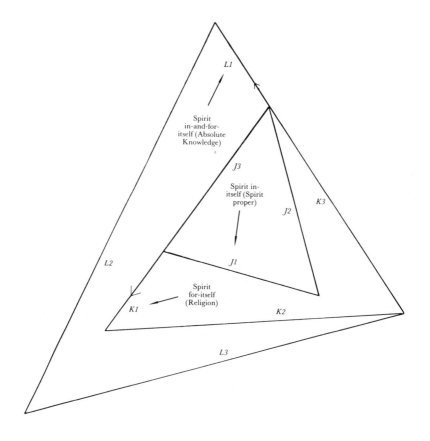

Explanation of Diagram 3 and Symbols

Spirit is the explicit manifestation and continuation of Reason (see Diagrams 1 and 2), which is the union of the self with the otherness of being. Since the otherness primarily proportioned and suited to a *self* is another *self* (see K85), Spirit in its immediate stage, or "in-itself," is a fundamental relationship of intersubjectivity which is susceptible to dialectical development. This development proceeds in three stages:

J1. The "Ethical substance": This is a direct rapport and reciprocity between individual and society, and vice versa, which reaches its culmination in the creation of the legal "person" who is a repository for both natural individual right and socially guaranteed rights.

J2. Culture: This is essentially a breakup of the harmony and rapport which characterized the previous state; and the quest of the former legal person to overcome the state of alienation which results, leading to rebellion and absolute *freedom,* which turns into its opposite: oppression and terrorism.

J3. Morality: This is the final solution to the alienations of Culture—the manful attempts of the disillusioned bourgeois citizen to establish the groundwork *in himself* for harmonious intersubjective relationships. But contradictions appear in the concept of morality, and finally lead to an emphasis on "Conscience" as a state of subjective self-certitude. Conflicts develop, however, in the interpretation of this latter, and the resolution of these conflicts is found only in mutual forgiveness and reconciliation—an atmosphere approximating to the religious spirit, which is characterized as "Spirit *for*–itself" because through it a *self*-conscious fusion with otherness counterbalances the "*conscious*" (Hegel uses "conscious" in contrast to "self-conscious" often to indicate an objective and antithetical orientation) thrusts in society, culture and morality towards intersubjectivity. Spirit for-itself, or *Religion,* then evolves through the following three stages of self-consciousness:

K1. Nature-Religion: Aesthetic "transcendence" is induced through objects in Nature: light, plants, animals, great and sublime spaces, etc. This development reaches its zenith as man begins to imitate nature, and express himself, i.e., becomes an artist.

K2. Art-Religion: A simultaneously religious and artistic enhancement and intensification of communal self-consciousness is produced by a wide variety of classical arts. The culmination of this development is in *literary* art, especially tragedy and comedy, through which the human actively meets and wrestles with the otherness of the divine, and temporarily wins the laurels in the contest.

K3. Revealed Religion: This is the final and irreversible stage in the encounter of the human Self-Consciousness with the divine—a final equalization or homeostasis in which God becomes man and man becomes God. In Revealed Religion, at least on the level of symbol and imagination, the self-conscious communal fusion with otherness is complete. The only thing that still remains is for this fusion to be recaptured and stabilized on the *conceptual* level. And this final need leads to the development of *Absolute Knowledge,* in three final stages:

L1. Absolute Knowledge of Spirit in-itself: Commemorative intellectual assimilation, synthesis and enshrinement of the oppositions occurring in Spirit-as-Consciousness (see *J1, J2,* and *J3,* above). In this assimilation, the ultimate dialectical reconciliation of consciences is recognized as supplying the *formal* conditions for Absolute Knowledge.

L2. Absolute Knowledge of Spirit for-itself: A similar conceptual synthesis and enshrinement of the pictorial-mythical oppositions occurring in Spirit-as-Self-Consciousness (see *K1, K2,* and *K3,* above). The ultimate development of Revealed Religion is recognized as supplying the primary *content* of Absolute Knowledge.

   L3. Absolute Knowledge of Spirit in-and-for-itself, which signifies all of the following: (1) A final synthesis of the two previous moments (*J* and *K*); (2) the special character of Absolute Knowledge as a distinct stage of Spirit *in its own right,* i.e., not just as a recapitulation or summary of previous stages; and (3) the paradoxical state through which the knowledge held *by* Spirit (because it is now in-*and*-for-itself) is simultaneously Spirit's knowledge *of itself.*

Analysis
of
Part II

VI.
Spirit

Introductory Remarks:

Up to the present we were engaged largely in the phenomenology of individual consciousness, and now we embark upon the phenomenology of the world-spirit. The abstract essence of spirit which had already become manifest in the examination of the earliest stages of consciousness is what we twentieth-century readers of Hegel might call the "power of reflection," the ability to distinguish oneself into an in-itself which is reflected upon and a for-itself which does the reflecting, while simultaneously remaining the in-and-for-itself which does both. The continual experience of fixing upon some aspect of consciousness which seems to abide as an alien in-itself; then negating this alienation or negation to reveal it as properly assimilated or for-itself; then (as with one final comprehensive grasp of both spiritual hands) holding both negation and negation-of-negation together in some overarching synthetic and often paradoxical insight—this is the personal empirical basis upon which the individual consciousness rises to the notion of Spirit. This notion becomes transformed into Reason: the unity of opposites, the at first theoretical and eventually practical synthesis of subject and object, thought and being, self and otherness, inner and outer, consciousness and self-consciousness. But a particular consciousness as particular *can be no more than the notion or concept of Spirit, i.e., Spirit in a still abstract state, for the simple reason that it would be a contradiction in terms for actual Spirit to exist as particular. For Spirit, if it is to be truly concrete, must be expressed as the unity-in-distinction of* particular *and* universal, *of the "I" and "we." The subjective preparation for this expression took place in the immediately preceding chapters, in which* die Sache selbst *(paraphrased in K126 ff. as the* "Subjective/Objective Indi-

11

viduality"*) brings to a culmination the long process of intersubjective develop-*
ment which began with the "Life and Death Struggle" and the "Master-Slave
Dialectic" (see K87 ff.). As we end the first half of the Phenomenology *(see*
H306 ff., M§256 ff.), the Subjective/Objective Individuality finally realizes
itself as inherently, essentially united with the "others" who constitute its spir-
itual horizons. The objective result of this subjective preparation is that con-
sciousness will become explicitly *united with these "others," i.e., with the*
universal—*and thus no longer just a (particular) consciousness, but Spirit, the*
"I" that knows itself as a "We" or the "We" that operates only in and through
the "I" (i.e., community and communality existing after the fashion of an indi-
vidualized entity in the world). Part II of the Phenomenology, *which begins*
now, is thus no longer a phenomenology of consciousness but a phenomenology of
the dialectical vicissitudes of what at this point has become the essential thing, the
important thing, namely, actual "Spirit" in the sense just adumbrated.

In the preceding sections[1] we have considered *forms of consciousness,* and
seen how consciousness abstracts itself from the object to which it is
immediately united (in sense certainty, perception, and understanding); then finds itself as object (self-consciousness); then comes to find
the implicit unity of subject and object (Reason); and finally by pass-
ing through a series of attitudes in observation and experimental activity, comes to the point where it is a *de facto* unity in and with the
world[2]—i.e., instead of just finding the paradox of the subjective-
objective category, it *exists* as such a category. The individual is inti-
mately united with the world, and its spirit is his spirit.

In this present phase, we are now situated at the vantage point of "ethical substance"[3]; the point at which spirit exists in its truth, but is

---

1. See B147–453, M§90–437, K62–133, H79—312, B63–237.

2. This state of immediate unity with one's world had been the earmark of the
culmination of the development of *die Sache selbst* in the immediately preceding section.

3. *Die sittliche Substanz.* This is not "substance" as opposed to, or outside of, the
thinking subject, but substance immediately permeated with subjectivity, i.e., human
social consciousness as externalized and perpetuated in solid communal and customary institutions. There is no awareness of the state as something standing over and
above "the people," at this point. Rather, there is such a complete immersion of
individuals in their communality, and such a complete assimilation by the communality of its constituent individuals, that no effective and meaningful distinction between
the two sides obtains here, at least in the beginning, before some latent contradictions
begin to appear. The archetype for the type of consciousness described here seems to
be Greece at its acme, concerning which Dickinson says "it was the aim, conscious or
unconscious, and, in part at least, the achievement of the Greeks to maintain an essential harmony. The antitheses of which we in our own time are so painfully and increas-

uncertain of its nature. The individual has come to an immediate awareness of his participation in universal law-making, and the ethical substance reaches out to reduplicate that degree of self-consciousness which the individual has attained, and, in this stage of immediacy, *is* an individual in its own right. But spirit, which both as goal and as starting point causes all processes, has not yet come to its own with its world. It projects itself as an ultimate state of self-hood still to be reached, as ethical self-consciousness which must rise out of this ethical substance. And to see how this latter state is brought about, we must pass through various *forms of the world-Spirit*, just as we previously passed through the various forms of consciousness. We must follow spirit as it bifurcates into the present world of culture, and the "beyond" of faith; then arrives at an uneasy synthesis in Insight, Enlightenment and the concept of revolutionary freedom; and finally attains self-consciousness in the stages of morality and conscience.[4]

A. Spirit as "True."[5] Objective Ethicality
[Ethical and Legal Consciousness]

---

ingly aware, between Man as a moral being and Nature as an indifferent law, between the flesh and the spirit, between the individual and the state, do not appear as factors in that dominant consciousness of the Greeks under whose influence their religion, their institutions, and their customary ideals had been informed. And so regarded, in general, under what may fairly be called its most essential aspect, the Greek civilization is rightly described as that harmony" (G. Lowes Dickinson, *The Greek View of Life*, p. 157). Hegel sounds like an ethical relativist when he says (*Natural Law*, p. 115), "as regards ethical life, the saying of the wisest men in antiquity is alone true, that 'to be ethical is to live in accordance with the ethics of one's country'," but in saying this he was only emphasizing—against Kant and others who tried to derive morality from subjective excogitations—that true morality or ethics was *absolutely* related to, and dependent on, one's social environment. Thus to Hegel's mind the Greeks, having managed in a paramount way and *without sacrificing* individuality, to harmonize their personal lives with the spirit of their country, represented an acme of ethical consciousness, taking into account the special and limited character of their political and historical situation.

4. As we will see in the later stages of Religion (M§672ff.), Hegel speaks about Religion also as the attainment of "self-consciousness" by Spirit. The ambiguities connected with these remarks and their possible interpretation will be discussed later (see pp. 108, 123–4, 129–30, *infra*).

5. The reader should recall the constant contrast of "truth" with "certitude" in the earlier sections of the *Phenomenology*. In the first half of the Phenomenology, the movement was from the rather tentative and falsifiable "certainties" about objectivity found in "Consciousness," to the rather abstract and ivory-turreted "truths" of Self-Consciousness, to the gradual reconciliation of certainty and truth by Reason.

Self-consciousness,[6] which is a kind of model of self-generating oppositions, and also of the transcendence of opposition, acts as a middle
term in developing the potentialities of this phase of "immediate"
spirit: The ethical substance is "opposed" to individuality and, as a
massive consciousness, splits itself up into opposed elements (divine
and human law)—a spiritual opposition which is also manifested in
exemplary individuals who ally themselves with one or the other of the
two laws, and also begin to manifest a parallel subjective split between
consciousness and unconsciousness, knowledge and ignorance. Eventually, this ambivalence of self-consciousness leads the individual, who is
raising the particular to the universal (acting ethically) and bringing the
universal likewise into the particular, to realize the inherently
contradictory nature of these two opposed laws, and ultimately to arrive
at the realization that there is a difference between what is "objectively"
right and what he "knows" to be right.[7] This latter realization, which is
"higher" in a dialectical sense,[8] will lead to a transendence of the
immediacy, spontaneity and beauty of that stage of spirit which is characterized here as "the ethical substance."

a) The Ethical World. Human and Divine Law. Man and Woman
    [Ethical Consciousness]

   "Individuality," at the present stage of Spirit, is a socio-ethical self-

---

Now in the second half, we witness a converse movement from the Objective Ethicality of Spirit, a more concrete state of truth than was found in Self-Consciousness, to
Religion, a less tentative and falsifiable certitude about the most essential and important
realities of Spirit, to Absolute Knowledge, which synthesizes the conceptual grasp of
spiritual truth attained in the Ethical Spirit with the imagination-bound certainty about
spirituality attained in religion.

   6. In using the term "Self-Consciousness," here, Hegel seems to be thinking primarily of certain exemplary self-conscious individuals—certain heroes, certain artistic geniuses—who presided at the birth of (Western) ethical consciousness or acted as
catalysts bringing it about.

   7. This is a pristine emergence of the attitude akin to "conscience" in our modern
subjective sense, i.e., a moral orientation that bespeaks some personal maxim or nostrum which can be, and sometimes is, at odds with publicly "accepted" ethical values.

   8. "Personhood" emerging in section B below is inferior to the ethical conscience
discussed here, insofar as it leads to alienation; but it is superior in a dialectical sense,
insofar as it is the mark of a movement towards moral self-consciousness which is necessary for the development of the "Absolute Knowledge" described in the last section of the *Phenomenology.*

consciousness *in general,*[9] i.e., not any particular concreẗe consciousness. *Absolute Spirit* is expressed through this socio-ethical self-consciousness in manifold ways: It is in-itself through its members, but for-itself through transcending these members. Insofar as it is actual, it is a *Nation*; insofar as it is actually conscious, it is the *Citizens*; insofar as it is in the form of publicly recognized universality, it is *human law*; and insofar as it gives this universality a distinctive, individualized form,[10] it is *government.* It results in acts which break up into moments of particularity and universality, just as perception breaks up into moments of unity and multiplicity, universality and particularity.[11] And there develops within it a curious opposition, insofar as the immediate ethical substance (embodied especially in the family) stands over against the universal and public element and opposes its own transcendent "divine law"[12] to the other's "human law."[13]

The Family is the side of Spirit which expresses the ethical order in its immediacy of mere "existence." It is the stem from which emerge all the more public manifestations of the Ethical Substance. In the family there is an immediate consciousness of oneself in the other. The goal of one's actions is always the family itself, and at the same time the conscious intent is always focused on an individual *member* of that family. The ethical element flourishes here, precisely insofar as the members deal

---

9. The individual as a kind of conscious monad is not meant here. The emphasis here is on individuality as an adjunct of one of the most intense states of intersubjectivity imaginable. The individuality which is extolled here in the context of the Ethical Substance is that state of committed self-conscious *participation* in one's world which is a necessary concomitant of ethical consciousness as described here.

10. The government which creates and fosters individuality is itself an "individuality," capable of giving a single, consummate expression of selfhood to the disparate selves who make it up.

11. See the earlier chapter on "Perception" in Part I of the *Phenomenology.*

12. As Judith Shklar observes (*Freedom and Independence*, p. 76), for Hegel the family is not just an economic basis for the polity as it was for Aristotle, but something far more important: the sacred guarantee of, and cherished retreat for, individuality. "By insisting on the religious functions of the family in a free city, Hegel separated the household and the polity as completely as did those modern critics of the patriarchical monarchy, Locke and Rousseau" (*Ibid.*, p. 77).

13. Jean Hyppolite (*Genesis and Structure,* p. 340) equates "human law" with what we call "positive law," i.e., the specific enactments made by those in authority. This would seem to imply that "divine law" which is contrasted with human law is very similar in concept to "natural law" in one of its more important contemporary connotations—as a kind of unwritten law of human nature which applies to all men everywhere and at all, times.

with one another as universal, i.e., not for some particular contingency or to fulfill this or that particular need, or *merely* under impetus of some sentiment or even of the relationship of love.[14] (We have a general and *connatural* commitment to the members of our family, just because we belong to them, and they belong to us.) The "universality" of the action of a family towards its individual members does not really become manifest through distribution of property, or education of the young, or service on behalf of the members or satisfaction of their needs—because all such acts are concerned with civic existence, or preparation for civic existence, i.e., with activities regulated by the human law, and thus outside the peculiar ambit of family existence, which is controlled primarily by divine law. If we would define more precisely the truly *universal* activity of the family on behalf of its members, we would have to say that this activity is concerned at this stage with each member only *insofar* as he or she is an idealized universal, not insofar as he or she is a sensuous, breathing individual. In other words, the individual within the pale of the family is not just another human being, but is divinized, and thus we could say that family activity in its *highest* sense

is oriented no longer towards the *living*, but towards the *dead* individual,[15] i.e., the one who out of the long succession of his constantly interrupted existence finally gathers himself together into a single Consummate Configuration, and out of the restlessness of the circumstances of life has broken through to the calm of simple universality.[16]

But this Configuration, in spite of its universal significance, lacks the actuality of civic existence, and thus is, in comparison with the latter,

---

14. The family transcends mere "need-relationships," such as are found in the politico-economic realm (what Hegel calls "bourgeois" society). The family, though a union based on love, also transcends relationships based on "love-as-need."

15. The logic behind this rather startling idea seems to be the following: To universalize or idealize someone is to elevate him beyond the contingences and actualities of this present life. In some cultures or in certain circumstances this may involve ascribing eternal existence or an afterlife to him, so that he becomes truly universal only after, and by means of, death. Jacob Loewenberg (*Hegel's Phenomenology*, p. 191) offers some further observations: Because any actual self at this stage is inseparable from the larger community, it is only as dead that an individual can belong wholly to the family, and the family can possess him solely as an individual.

16. *B*244, H321: "*Die Handlung . . . betrifft nicht mehr den* Lebenden, *sondern den* Toten, *der aus der langen Reihe seines zerstreuten Daseins sich in die vollendete Eine Gestaltung zusammengefasst, und aus der Unruhe des zufälligen Lebens sich in die Ruhe der einfachen Allgemeinheit erhoben hat.*"

merely an unreal marrowless "shade."[17] This shadow-universality, which, in its *static* being and elemental isolation, is brought on by a natural event (death), must be spiritually transformed through the conscious deeds of the individual family members, so that in some way the irrationality and opacity of nature may be overcome. Thus

consanguinity makes up for the deficiencies of the abstract natural process of death, by interposing the process of consciousness, interrupting the operations of nature to rescue one's kin from disintegration; or better, since such dissolution, or transformation into pure being is necessary anyway, consciousness takes upon *itself* the rite of disintegration. . . . The dead person, having freed his *being* from his *acting* (which had been the source of unity through negation), survives only as a contentless individuality, a passive being-for-others, at the mercy of every subrational individuality and all the forces of dissevered elements, the former of which now are mightier than he because of the life they possess, the latter because of their connatural negativity. But the family obviates the dishonoring of the dead individual by such subrational appetites and dissevered entities by substituting its own initiatives: it binds the kinsman to the heart of the earth, the deathless elemental Individuality,[18] and simultaneously incorporates him into a Fellowship which prevails over and disarms those sundry elemental forces and lower life forms which otherwise would be unleashed against him and destroy him.[19]

This action fulfills the divine law (personified in the influence of the "Penates[20]"), and accentuates the significance of the individual to the na-

---

17. The idea of the universal individual as a "shade" or ghost reflects an inchoate and imperfect and excessively abstract concept of the "eternal" significance of the individual. The implication would be that a culture that idealizes the individual more fully, and ascribes greater significance to him than is ascribed at the stage considered here, would not conceive of him even in the afterlife as someone deficient in clarity or luminosity, but just the opposite. The Christian idea of the self-conscious disembodied soul in heaven contrasts markedly with the Greek idea of the melancholy "shade" in the realm of Hades.

18. For Hegel's depiction of the Earth as another kind of "Universal Individual," see M§296, B327, K109–10, H220, *B*166.

19. *B*244–5, H322–3: "*Die Blutsverwandtschaft ergänzt also die abstrakte natürliche Bewegung dadurch, dass sie die Bewegung des Bewusstseins hinzufügt, das Werk der Natur unterbricht, und den Blutsverwandten der Zerstörung entreisst, oder besser, weil die Zerstörung, sein Werden zum reinen Sein, notwendig ist, selbst die Tat der Zerstörung über sich nimmte . . . Der Tote, da er sein Sein von seinem Tun oder negativen Eins freigelassen, ist die leere Einzelheit, nur ein passives Sein für anderes, aller niedrigen vernunftlosen Individualität und den Kräften abstrakter Stoffe preisgegeben, wovon jene um des Lebens willen, das sie hat, diese um ihrer negativen Natur willen jetzt mächtiger sind als er. Dies ihn entehrende Tun bewusstloser Begierde und abstrakter Wesen hält die Familie von ihm ab, setzt das ihrige an die Stelle, und vermählt den Verwandten dem Schosse der Erde, der elementarischen unvergänglichen Individualität; sie macht ihn hierdurch zum Genossen eines Gemeinwesens, welches vielmehr die Kräfte der einzelnen Stoffe und die niedrigen Lebendigkeiten, die gegen ihn frei werden und ihn zerstören wollten, überwältigt und gebunden hält.*"

20. Hegel's reference to the Roman household gods, the "Penates," in a context

tion in virtue of the immortality and divinity of his immediacy, that natural immediacy which is acknowledged as the indispensable spring of all the conscious accomplishments of a nation.

The human law, as one expression of ethical consciousness,[21] splits asunder into the moments of (*a*) negative unity (which must oftentimes be maintained through government by means of the unifying power of war[22]) and (*b*) the subsistence (*fürsichsein*) of individual members and individual associations—which is the whole reason, or purpose, for the universal community. It should be noted, however, that a government in periodically utilizing war as an instrument of unification is drawing on the power of Death, the sovereign of the netherworld—and thus is implicitly coming into alliance with the divine law, which alone grants jurisdiction and sovereignty to Death.

The divine law, as another expression of ethical consciousness,[23] causes the family to distinguish itself into husband and wife, parent and child, brother and sister:

---

where all other references and allusions are typically Greek, is curious. It is unthinkable that this was a mistake, since Hegel was so thoroughly familiar with ancient Greek and Roman religion. There are a few other cases of "lapses" like these in later phenomenological stages, and we will point these out in the Commentary on these later sections. If they were intentional "lapses," what was the motivation for making them? Perhaps Hegel inserted these historical anomalies to emphasize the fact that the historical allusions are used as universal archetypes; in other words, that in these sections he is not discussing *either* the Greeks or the Romans, but a state of social consciousness which is universal and perennial, and which can best be exemplified by references redolent of a certain culture, but is not limited to, or constrained by, the historical contingencies pertaining to that culture.

21. Here, as often in the *Phenomenology*, a contrast of Consciousness with Self-Consciousness is intended. Ethical *Consciousness*, as Consciousness, is characterized by an emphasis on external objectivity, a sense of immersion in one's object, and a disconcerting tendency of one's apparently unified objects to polarize and manifest unmediated oppositions as one proceeds to examine them.

22. The simple negation of the Ethical Substance leads to the expression of individuality in the polity, and this state of differentiation must be counterbalanced by the negation of negation, i.e., war, which serves the function of reasserting unity amid individualities. The idea that war is a necessity for maintaining or restoring the unity and integrity of a given political society is a recurring idea in Hegel's writings. Compare *Natural Law*, p. 93 and *Philosophy of Right*, §324 *Zusatz*.

23. Findlay sees the two "laws" here as symbolic of two complementary aspects of morality—intensity of interpersonal concern and altruistic extensivity—both of which are necessary and inseparable. According to Findlay, the divine law is noted for its depth, the human law for its breadth; but the truly moral life "will be as deep in its care for individual problems and circumstances as it is wide in its concern for anyone and everyone" (M, p. xii).

The husband–wife relationship is the immediate natural form of consciousness in which one comes to recognize himself in another;[24] and
thus it is a figurative representation of Spirit, which is essentially conditioned by mutual self-recognition. And as a representation, it finds its
reality, its reference point, in the child which is generated.

The wife in this initial stage in which nature and spirit are so inter-
mingled, becomes the "natural" embodiment of the "immediate"
para-conscious divine law; while the husband, conversely, becomes
the "natural" embodiment of the mediations of consciousness. Thus,
in respect to their general ethical significance, the wife manifests an
ability (in her relationship to her home and family members) to view and
act upon the particular always in terms of the "divine" universal. In the
case of the husband, on the other hand, these two sides—universal and
particular—tend to get separated, so that distinctively male activity,
consequently, is concerned in great part with either maintaining or mediating the opposition thus produced between his life as a citizen and his
personal desires, and other related aspects of the tension between universal and particular.

The parent–child relationship is based on the natural devotion which results when one finds his conscious realization in a being external to himself (or, in the case of the child, finds the source of his life to be an external being of this sort).

The sister–brother relationship is a unique unmixed and intransitive relationship in the family, insofar as it does not feature the mutual externality and subjection to particular desires and stages that are to be found in
the husband–wife and parent–child relationships. The sister finds in the
brother a pure immediate ethical reflection unperturbed by admixtures

---

24. In the stage of "recognition" immediately preceding the Master-Slave dialectic
(see M§178 ff., B229 f., PG141 f., K87, *B*109), we find that recognition of oneself (self-
consciousness) is inseparable from recognition of the other. This theme is repeated in
various parts and contexts in the *Phenomenology*—e.g. in the section on the "Unhappy
Consciousness," the chapter on "Pleasure and Necessity," and later chapters on "The
Beautiful Soul" and "Revealed Religion," as well as in the present context. Here the
emphasis is on the fact that the differentiation of the sexes by Nature is geared to
facilitate the attainment of self-consciousness by human beings. As Hegel observes in
The Philosophy of Mind §398, the ability to find oneself in the other naturally promotes the
emergence of the consciousness of otherness within oneself—which is the essence of what
we call "self-consciousness." There is also emphasis here on the fact that the recognition
is *mutual*, no longer one-sided as in previous instances. It is only where recognition is
mutual and reciprocal that it can qualify as an explicit representation of Spirit.

of sensual desire[25] or genetic externality. They exist as two completely free moments in a kind of stable equilibrium.

The sister, as the immediate feminine element who is also free, is signalized by an intuitive rather than mediated (conceptualized) awareness of the ethical. She is the picture of ethical resignation upon encountering the various vicissitudes of life (such as the death of the parents or husband) but tends to feel absolutely lost in her immediacy if her brother (her immediate and irreplaceable source of self-recognition) dies.[26]

The brother is the member of the family in whom the family spirit becomes individualized in a social and political life essentially external to the Penates and its divine laws. Thus, in a sense, the self-contained life of the family eventually reaches its natural limit at the life and activity of the brother, and thence gives way to the outer sphere of the polity, i.e., publicly expressed Spirit.

Spirit in these early stages, characterized by the differentiation of human and divine law, thus causes a parallel differentiation which is at the same time natural *and* conventional, substantial *and* deliberated—the differentiation into male and female, each with its own specific nature, and capabilities, and tasks, and accomplishments. In the woman, man finds the "object" which is immediately and obviously the result of his own self-consciousness as a man, a "fact" which is immediately and obviously his own doing, a pleasure which is virtue, a free association which is necessity. The woman, as constituted on the side of the divine, immediate,

---

25. While the various other interfamilial relationships, as has already been observed (*supra* n. 14), transcend particular desires or needs, they still include these elements, unlike the sister-brother relationship.

26. Various motivations have been ascribed to Hegel for his extraordinary emphasis on the ethical strength of the sister–brother relationship: (1) From an autobiographical point of view, Hegel had a remarkably close relationship with his sister Christiane, who committed suicide shortly after Hegel's death; (2) as Shklar points out (*Freedom and Independence*, p. 78) Hegel's emphasis on the purity of the sister–brother relationship may betoken a reaction against Montesquieu's suggestion (in *Persian Letters* XLVII) that nothing should keep brothers and sisters from marrying each other; and (3) Antigone, whom Hegel takes as a model of sisterly fidelity in this chapter, is also a paradigmatic case of inconsolability upon loss of a brother. In reflecting upon her reasons for flouting the edict of Creon by burying her brother, she represents brotherly love as more irreplaceable than love for husband or child: "never, had I been a mother of children, or if a husband had been mouldering in death, would I have taken this task upon me in the city's despite. . . . The husband lost, another might have been found, and child from another, to replace the first-born; but father and mother hidden with Hades no brother's life could ever bloom for me again" (Sophocles, *Antigone*, l. 138).

unconscious, netherworld element, naturally tends toward her complementary fulfillment in the conscious "light of the day," i.e., in the social
world of human law where she is able to find herself and see herself. Spirit in the man, on the other hand, as constituted on the side of human law,
consciousness, and mediation, naturally returns continually to its roots
in immediacy, in order to bring about with the help of woman the perfection of the *individual* (the divine "immediate"), and to exert conscious
control over the cycles of natural existence and death, which stand in irrational opposition to the human spirit. The interaction and union of the
two sexes must also be seen in this larger context as furthering, in a manner that is simultaneously natural and conscious, the interaction of the
human and divine laws and their constant tranquil metamorphosis one
into the other:[27]

---

27. Loewenberg (*Hegel's Phenomenology*, p. 194) observes that the woman is essentially
subordinate to the man in the interrelationship developed here. Because of the close parallel drawn here between the human and divine laws on the one hand, and male and
female on the other, the relative subordination of women would seem necessarily to entail, and be entailed by, a corresponding subordination of divine law to human law. In
the dramas of Sophocles and Aeschylus, which Hegel draws upon in developing the idea
of the interrelationship of the two laws, there does seem to be a subordination of the divine law of home, family and individual to the human law of society at large. For as Glen
Gray observes (*Hegel and Greek Thought*, p. 57), "in these dramas in relation to the demands of the larger society the claims of the family were less rational, because less universal, and in the case of conflict the lower claim must yield." One is also reminded of
the somewhat analogous, but less harmonious, relationship between the Knight of Virtue and the Course of the World [*Weltlauf*], in which the Course of the World attained a
tentative victory because it had public power and human laws on its side (see K124).
And in a later section on "Faith and Insight" (infra, pp. 54 ff.), in which "Faith" is a
more sophisticated reappearance of the divine law and Insight of the human law, we
also find that it is Insight that eventually wins as it evolves into Enlightenment. All of
these observations would tend to corroborate Loewenberg's contention. Nevertheless,
it is also noteworthy that Hegel does not put any emphasis in the present section on the
relative superiority of man or woman, human law or divine law. This may be because
Hegel is reading Sophocles and Aeschylus from the vantage point of one who has been
influenced by the post-mediaeval emphasis on romantic and courtly love, in which both
woman and individuality are placed on a pedestal and divinized, as Denis de Rouge-
mont (*Love in the Western World*) and others have pointed out. One must also not fail to notice that in the struggle between the Knight of Virtue and the Course of the World, the
Course of the World, while conquering, is also conquered in the sense that it must acknowledge the necessity for that sort of transcendence of individual aspirations which
the Knight had championed; and that, although Enlightenment will be victorious over
Faith, it will also be vanquished in the sense that it will have to reconstruct the idea of a
supreme being borrowed from Faith, and transplant the other-worldly heavenly happiness sought by Faith to the more mundane quarters provided by the philosophy of
Utility; and finally that, in the present section, although the polity, as we shall see, man-

Through the individuality of the man, the one extreme, the fully conscious universal spirit [of the *human* law], becomes interfused with its own counterpart, the unconscious spirit[28] which is man's strength and his primordial environment. On the other hand, the *divine* law finds its individualization [or the unconscious (divine) Spirit of the individual attains its determinate existence] in the woman, who acts as the "middle term" through whom the unconscious spirit emerges from unreality to actuality, and breaks forth from the state of being unknowing and unknown to the sphere of consciousness. The union of man and woman thus functions as the effective middle term in the entirety of this realm of immediate spirit. . . .[29]

Justice in the ethical polity is attained by the constant restoration to equilibrium of the two sides: universal unity on the one hand, and the aspirations of individual members and classes on the other. The former receives impetus from human exigencies,[30] the latter from divine preroga-

---

ages to offset the influence of woman by "man's occupation" of waging wars, it ends up subverted by the young men groomed by their women to take the place of those who die or of those whose fortunes take a downswing because of the eventualities of war.

28. I.e., the spirit of the divine law, which is prior to all the conceptual determinations and enactments elaborated by human beings, and is epitomized in the "unconscious consciousness" of woman, i.e., her intuitive or instinctive way of thinking which is the opposite of man's mediated and reflective manner of thinking.

Kierkegaard seems to have taken over this "metaphysical" way of distinguishing the sexes in a number of writings. For example, in *Sickness unto Death* (N.Y., 1954), p. 183n., Kierkegaard points out that "Woman has neither the selfishly developed conception of the self [being-for-self] nor the intellectuality of man, for all that she is his superior in tenderness and fineness of feeling"; and in *Stages on Life's Way* (N.Y., 1967), the "married man" observes that "A feminine soul has not and should not have the sort of reflection a man has" (p. 162), and "Frater Taciturnus" reflects that "Infinite reflection is not essentially a thing for women." For a discussion of the way in which Kierkegaard applies the Hegelian categories of "existence-for-self" and "existence-for-another" to man and woman, respectively, see my article, "The Relationship of Dread to Spirit in Man and Woman, According to Kierkegaard," in *The Modern Schoolman* XLVII, 1 (Nov. 1969), pp. 7 ff.

29. B250, H330: *Das eine Extrem, der allgemeine sich bewusste Geist, wird mit seinem andern Extrem, seiner Kraft und seinem Element, mit dem bewusstlosen Geiste, durch die Individualität des Mannes zusammengeschlossen. Dagegen hat das* göttliche *Gesetz seine Individualisierung oder der bewusstlose Geist des Einzelnen sein Dasein an dem Weibe, durch welches als die* Mitte *er aus seiner Unwirklichkeit in die Wirklichkeit, aus dem Unwissenden und Ungewussten in das bewusste Reich herauftritt. Die Vereinigung des Mannes und des Weibes macht die tätige Mitte des Ganzen.*

30. Human law is a necessity for maintaining social unity, and cannot take into account the exceptional and the anomalous. Creon sums up the philosophy of human law in Sophocles' *Antigone*, l.136, insisting that "Whomsoever the city may appoint, that man must be obeyed, in little things and great, in just things and unjust"; and Creon's words are echoed by the Chorus, which says (*ibid.*, l.138), "An offence against power cannot be brooked by him who hath power in his keeping." (For notes on the plot of Antigone, see Appendix, #1.)

tive.[31] The former is concerned with the inevitable inequalities that emerge in the polity, and in righting these it is affirming the universal will of all to maintain a balanced whole. The latter is concerned with maintaining the rights of the individual, and, in restoring these, actually works through concrete individuals. Thus, when Agamemnon was murdered by his wife and her lover, and his son Orestes was saved through the mediation of his sister and eventually avenged his father—this was at base the action of the spirit of the wronged individual (Agamemnon) wreaking vengeance (personified in the Erinys) through the immediate factor of consanguinity (found in Orestes).[32] So that in a real sense it is not Orestes who is doing the deed, but the divine element of nature, constantly setting aright the imbalances caused by human mischief; or, from another point of view, it is individual human consciousness constantly trying to bring the most irrational manifestations of natural existence and death into rational control.

b) Ethical Action. Human and Divine Knowledge. Guilt and
     Destiny.

Self-consciousness in the stage of immediate opposition of the human and divine (dealt with in the preceding section) has not yet come to the moment of the *realization* of individuality. Individuality is realized through the performance of *acts*, by which mutual interpenetrations of the individual and social spheres take place. These acts, however, will result in paradoxical self-negations and self-destructions in both spheres.

---

31. The divine law, which keeps the individual from being smothered by the universal, is *naturally* prior to human law, and to the mind of its proponents should be given actual priority by those in power. Thus Antigone objects to Creon that his edict forbidding the proper burial of her brother was an unseemly transgression of divine prerogatives: "It was not Zeus that had published me that edict; not such are the laws set among men by the Justice who dwells with the gods below; nor deemed I that thy decrees were of such force, that a mortal could override the unwritten and unfailing statutes of heaven. For their life is not of today or yesterday, but from all time, and no man knows when they were first put forth" (*Antigone*, 1.135).

32. A partial account of these mythological developments is found in Aeschylus' *Eumenides* (see Appendix, #4). In his reference to Orestes' avenging of Agamemnon, Hegel curiously leaves out the fact that Agamemnon had offered up his daughter Iphigenia at Aulis to appease the anger of Artemis. Perhaps the fact that Artemis prevented the sacrifice from taking place nullified the ethical import of this event in Hegel's interpretation of the tragic plot.

Consciousness at this stage must be understood as transcending those prior abstract stages where it was caught between the particularity of commands and the tautological universality of laws.[33] It now takes refuge in a special kind of duty, in which the universal and particular, form and content, are united in concrete decisions.[34] In those earlier[35] and more abstract moments, it was possible that an excessively formal idea of morality could be applied haphazardly to various kinds of duty—giving rise to the spectacle of the inexorable conflict of duties, which has supplied so much grist to the mills of comic playwrights. (Even passions or inclinations can be transformed into the character of a "duty" with the magic of a purely formal "morality," because duty as a formal universal is indifferent to *external* content and applicable to almost anything if one has sufficient ingenuity.) Consciousness is here beyond such formal abstractness and is not caught up in any ambivalent type of decision-making. The consciousness allied to the divine law is not concerned about whether the human law may be equally or more important; neither is the agent of the human law plagued by intimations that perhaps right is on the side of the divine law. Nevertheless the harmony and

---

33. See M§419–435, B439–451, K129–133, H301, *B*228.

34. This is to contrast the notion of duty which characterized the "Ethical Substance" with the (largely Kantian) idea of duty which prevailed in Hegel's time and, to a great extent, still prevails in our own. While the latter notion of duty involves a conception of an "ought" which is in conflict with "the way things are," this contradistinction between the "ought" and the "is" is lacking at the inception of Western ethical consciousness, discussed here. Dickinson's remarks concerning the Greek spirit are relevant in this context: "It is a distinguishing characteristic of the Greek age that the ideal formulated by thought was the direct outcome of the facts. That absolute separation of what ought to be from what is which continues to haunt and vitiate modern life had not yet been made in ancient Greece. Plato, idealist though he be, is yet rooted in the facts of his age; his perfect republic he bases on the institutions of Sparta and Crete; his perfect man he shapes on the lines of the Greek citizen.

35. "Earlier," not necessarily in a chronological or historical sense, but as regards the dialectical progress from abstract to concrete in the earlier sections of the *Phenomenology*, in which the progress of individual consciousness towards constitution of the Ethical Substance was considered. (On the ahistorical nature of transitions in the *Phenomenology*, see K10, K117–118, K164.) The abstract idea of morality and duty associated with the earlier stage in which moral values or laws were tested for logical self-consistency, is exemplified in the ethics of a Kant or a Fichte, but also in the systematic cross-examinations of a Socrates, whom Hegel calls "the *inventor* of morality" (*Philosophy of History*, p. 269), and who is considered by Hegel to have been at the forefront of the sad but necessary breakup of the harmonious pre-"moral" ethical Spirit of the Greek world. Note that both Socrates and later moralists appeared historically after the Grecian era which best exemplifies the spirit discussed in this section.

simplicity which *seems* to grace such decision-making is only apparent. For there is a latent but nevertheless real contradiction[36] in the behavior of the ethical champion of either the divine or human laws: Both types of consciousness are in immediate unity with the ethical substance, which in turn is initially characterized by an immediate unity of divine and human laws; but in the very act of deciding for one side the acting individual must take sides against the other, thus contradicting his natural state of "immediate unity" by his explicit decisions and consequent deeds.[37]

Since the consciousness which allies itself with the divine law sees only right on its side and wrong on the other, the other side takes on the aspect of "arbitrary human authority"[38]; the consciousness which furthers the human law, on the other hand, being affected with a similarly one-sided ethical perspective,[39] sees only stubbornness and willful disobedience in the opposite consciousness.[40]

The ethical substance, which inexorably gives rise to such contradictions, thus takes on the aspect of "pathos"[41] for dutiful individuality at this stage. For the dutiful individual, as soon as he engenders any concrete ethical actuality, is bound to come into conflict with one of the two "laws." Thus Oedipus in killing Laius was expressing legitimate human indignation, and in marrying Jocasta was exercising a human right.[42] But in doing so he was breaking the divine laws which command honor to one's father, and forbid incest. And in general, when the individual immersed in the ethical substance posits any act on the basis of human laws, he comes into conflict with the dark, overtly weak, divine

---

36. Here Hegel begins to explicate the moment of antithesis which was merely latent in the immediate state of harmony of the Ethical Substance.

37. The conflict between divine and human law subtly and almost imperceptibly inculcated the necessity (and the ability) for making personal moral decisions, the sort of deliberation that eventually led to the disconcerting and disruptive criticisms of a Socrates (see M§746). But in the beginning, the decision-making is manifested only in one's taking sides with the divine law against the human, or vice versa.

38. See n. 31 *supra*, and Appendix, #1.

39. See n. 30 *supra*, and Appendix, #1.

40. *B*252, H332: *Indem es das Recht nur auf einer Seite, das Unrecht aber auf der andern sieht, so erblickt von beiden dasjenige, welches dem göttlichen Gesetze angehört, auf der andern Seite menschliche zufällige* Gewalttätigkeit; *das aber dem menschlichen Gesetze zugeteilt ist, auf der andern den Eigensinn und den* Ungehorsam *des innerlichen Fürsichseins. . . .*

41. "Pathos" because there is really no villain, and no hero, just inevitable mutual infliction of suffering. "The protagonists . . . are each a personification of a social necessity: Creon is not a tyrant . . . Antigone is neither a criminal nor a martyr to conscience" (Shklar, *Freedom and Independence*, p. 83).

42. See Appendix, #2.

laws, rooted in nature and the unconscious, which are the opposite of the one-sided formulations framed in "man's world." But because law is the essential reality of ethical substance, and because the ethical substance is his *own* substance, which he is trying to affirm, the dutiful individual, in coming into radical conflict with divine or human law, in effect alienates himself from his *own substance*. Thus every act of duty results in *guilt*—something which one must suffer because of the finite one-sided character of his acts.

We should note that the guilt we are discussing here is not the sort of guilt that is said to accrue to the individual conscience which has gone astray. This is a more modern, subjective concept of guilt. This guilt we are discussing here has cosmic proportions: there is no possibility for making a fine distinction between personal responsibility and the neutral acts of innocent bystanders. And so those witnessing the predicament of the guilty individual are not just an audience which weeps or thrills empathetically, but fellow participants who perceive the woes of the guilty individual as their own common woes.[43] It should also be noted that there are dialectical gradations of guilt. Oedipus' guilt is of the minor degree, since he was unconscious of the laws he was flouting. The highest degree of guilt is manifested in Antigone, who was fully cognizant of the existence and importance of the laws she was breaking. In this case the actual commission of crime has the effect of wrenching the individual into an absolute division, because in the aftermath she learns even more clearly than prior to the crime the significance and the equal validity of the laws she broke.

But as the two laws enter into conflict in and through the mediation of certain paradigmatic individuals, the ancient harmony that used to prevail gives way to a "new" negative force which appears on the scene and replaces the ancient harmony—namely, Destiny or Fate [*Schicksal*], which consists *formally* in that conflict between self-consciousness and unconscious nature which presents itself as a contingency to self-consciousness, and *materially* (i.e., as regards *content*) in the conflict between the two laws. Thus, when Oedipus became the individuality (Ruler) of the community, his two sons, Eteocles and Polynices, had equal divine

---

43. The Chorus, which was an integral part of the production of Greek tragedies, was not just a group of specialized singers or recitativists, but representatives of, and participants in, and explicators of, the feelings and reactions of people at large.

right to the possession of the community in spite of the contingency that one was born prior to the other. When the younger son, ruler by lot for one year, refuses to entrust the throne to the firstborn at the end of his term, he is affirming the human rights of actual possession, but compromising the divine law, which gives them equal shares in their father's blood. When the firstborn then attacks the community which expelled him, he is only flouting human law. When the community "does honor to the one who is found on its side" and dishonors the elder, exposing his corpse in some foreign land,[44] the universal divine law is only temporarily superseded by the *human* law. But by refusing to deposit his body in the ultimate individuum (the earth), they have incited the divine law (manifest in the individual *qua* concrete natural object) to assert a self-conscious actual universality. A foreign nation[45] seizes upon this divine incentive, and destroys that community which has thus dishonored its own divine roots.

And thus, in general, Destiny or Fate is the absolute ethical force,[46] through which the divine law is continually nullifying the human, and unconscious natural forces continually superseding conscious enactments.

The drama in which this nullification becomes particularly epitomized is the war between the sexes.[47]

---

44. The background for these dialectical examples is developed in Sophocles' plays, *Oedipus at Colonus* and *Antigone* (see Appendix, #1 and #3).

45. Argos, with the help of Athens. See Euripides' play, *The Suppliants*.

46. Destiny is analogous to "Force" (see the chapter on "Understanding" in Part I), insofar as it involves an essential bifurcation into poles which are constantly cancelling each other out (see K74), and also insofar as, just as Force was an objectified form or *projection* of the Infinite *Concept* which was going to be revealed through it, and would be the basis for the transition to Self-Consciousness, so also Destiny is an objectified form or projection of the restless nullifying activity of Self-Consciousness itself, which will gradually appear (in the sections on Culture) in more explicit form. In regard to this latter aspect, it should also be noted that now while the negativity of Self-Consciousness appears externally as Destiny, it appears as threatening and ominous. Hyppolite cites a relevant remark from Hegel's *Early Theological Writings* which brings out this aspect: "Destiny is consciousness of oneself, but consciousness of oneself as enemy" (*Phenomenologie de l'esprit*, Hyppolite tr., p. 353).

47. It is not just an accident that the ethical drama of the conflict between divine and human law, as it is concretized, is acted out as a conflict between women and men. For there is a kind of proportion set up from the beginning of this section:

$$\frac{\text{Nature}}{\text{Spirit}} = \frac{\text{Divine Law}}{\text{Human Law}} = \frac{\text{Woman}}{\text{Man}}$$

One cannot separate the mutual misunderstandings of the sexes from the larger ethical

Womankind, as the personification of the divine law, and the guardian of the *Penates*, is the constant enemy-behind-the-scenes, who thwarts the universal purposes of the manhood of the community:[48]

The woman—community's everlasting irony—manages through intrigue to alter the universal goal of government into her own private aims, transforms its activity into the accomplishment of some particular individual, and perverts the universal property of the state into a possession and adornment of the family. She makes the serious wisdom of experienced elders—who, indifferent to individualization through pleasure, enjoyment, and active participation, think and care only about "the universal"—into an object of ridicule and scorn for petulant and enthusiastic youth; and in general extolls the value of the power of youth—of the son as the innate master of his mother, of the brother as a sexual equal for his sister, of the young man as facilitating the escape of the daughter from dependence to the enjoyment and respect of married life.[49]

And in her estimation of the value of youth, woman has put her finger

---

conflict taking place. Shklar carries this reasoning one step further by suggesting (*Freedom and Independence*, p. 80) that Hegel's perception of the war between the sexes as a result of the degenerative struggle between divine and human law, seems to be a prevision that this "war" is a necessary concomitant of democratic societies (in which the conflict between "divine" individuality and "human" universality and socialization is institutionalized). But of course this necessity is dependent upon the prior necessity that at this relatively simple stage of democratic consciousness the woman should be the "divine" agent for the protection of family life and individuality and the man should be the appropriate agent for the expression of human consciousness in citizenship, lawmaking and governing.

48. This is a recurring theme not only in tragedies like *Antigone*, but in the comedies of Aristophanes, e.g., the *Lysistrata*, in which the women subvert the plans of the men to continue fighting the second Peloponnesian war, by refusing to sleep with their husbands. And the same idea is found in the Homeric epics. For example, Odysseus in Hades, upon encountering the shade of Agamemnon who was murdered by his wife, Clytaemnestra, cries out: "Mercy upon us! Indeed there is no doubt that Zeus All-seeing has been the deadly foe of the house of Atreus [cf. the previous tragic history of Agamemnon's family] from the beginning, and he has always used the schemes of women. For Helen's sake how many of us fell! And for you Clytaemnestra was laying her plot while you were far away."

49. B259, H340–341. *Diese—die ewige Ironie des Gemeinwesens—verändert durch die Intrigue den allgemeinen Zweck der Regierung in einen Privatzweck, verwandelt ihre allgemeine Tätigkeit in ein Werk dieses bestimmten Individuums und verkehrt das allgemeine Eigentum des Staats zu einem Besitz und Putz der Familie. Sie macht hiedurch die ernsthafte Weisheit des reifen Alters, das, der Einzelheit,—der Lust und dem Genusse, sowie der wirklichen Tätigkeit— abgestorben, nur das Allgemeine denkt und besorgt, zum Spotte für den Mutwillen der unreifen Jugend und zur Verachtung für ihren Enthusiasmus, erhebt überhaupt die Kraft der Jugend zum Geltenden, des Sohnes, an dem die Mutter ihren Herrn geboren, des Bruders, an dem die Schwester den Mann als ihres gleichen hat, des Jünglings, durch den die Tochter, ihrer Unselbständigkeit entnommen, den Genuss und die Würde der Frauenschaft erlangt.*

on something that the state can by no means ignore, no matter how concertedly hostile it is to the devastations of womanly influence. For the state, as a self-conscious entity, asserts its freedom and character of (national) individuality by *war*; and it wrenches youth (immature manhood, in the condition of particularity) away from their provident and protective females to wage its wars. By this means it hopes both to nullify the designs of womankind and also to attain its own practical purposes (national unity and conquest). But ironically, in entrusting its future to youthful physical strength and the chances of fortune, i.e., to raw individuality and contingency, it *eo ipso* sacrifices the ethical life which gave it character in the first place. The universality of this character now devolves into a merely formal universality loosely holding together the particular elements on which it has come to *depend*,[50] and on the uncertain shoulders of these "particulars" it must now pursue a new destiny and take on a new character:

The *living* spirits of the people are now broken down through their own individuality and reabsorbed into a "universal" commonwealth, whose unvariegated [*einfache*] uni-

---

50. This process can be illustrated by the example of Greece, as analyzed in Hegel's *Philosophy of History* (pp. 256 ff.): The victories of the Greeks against the Persians in the Median wars were not just great exemplifications of valor, but immortal victories which assured the supremacy for centuries to come of the Greek spirit of free individuality over the Oriental spirit of unity under a supreme lord. But Greece's subsequent freedom from external threats was accompanied by an intensification of the natural rivalry between Athens (representing the subjective and individual side of the Greek spirit) and Sparta (representing the orientation of the Ethical Substance to communal unity). Because all the emphasis in the Greek spirit was on closely knit city-states, they would have had to sacrifice their essential spirit to subsume such rivalries into the overarching unity of a Greek "state." This was unconscionable for a Greek; and, as a matter of fact, the Greeks did not have any understanding of the state as we know it (*ibid.*, pp. 252–3). Thus, in lieu of any strong and lasting overtures to political unity, the rift between Athens and Sparta continued to widen, and the Peloponnesian war was the result. The defeat of Athens in the Peloponnesian war was hastened by the decline of the Greek principle of democratic participatory unity. In spite of spasmodic attempts to reinstate this principle, disintegration continued over the next few centuries until the time was ripe for a new and stronger spirit—the Roman spirit—to overtake the scattered remnants of previous cultures and mold them into a new political unity. One of the distinguishing features of this new political unity, however, would be the fact that, because of its size and other factors, participatory government in the Greek sense would no longer be feasible. In its place we have the characteristically Roman emphasis on the "person," not in our contemporary psychological sense, but as a standardized unit of self-consciousness which facilitated the legal cooperation and governmental federation of the vast Roman Republic—that superimposed unity which began to approximate our modern idea of the "state" as something abstract from and independent of the people.

versality is spiritless and dead, and whose life force is epitomized in the single individ-ual, *as* single. . . . In its immediate ethical stage a people or nation is an individuality de-termined by nature and hence severely limited; and thus it looks to another for its trans-formation. But as its former status of natural determination . . . begins to disappear, the former life of spirit in all of its self-conscious substantiality is forfeited. This life re-emerges now as a *merely formal universality* subsuming the people, rather than as a living spirit dwelling within them, and the simple compactness of their former individuality is fragmented into multiple disparate points.[51]

Thus ethical consciousness in its disrupted immediacy shows forth the full effects of the latent contradiction with which it was laden from the start: the contradiction between the peace of unconscious "natural" existence and the unpacific peace, the unresting rest of self-conscious, self-subsisting spirit.[52]

c)   The Condition of Right or Legal Status
     [Legal Consciousness]

Introductory Remarks:
The condition of unity, harmony and stability that characterized the stage of Ethical Consciousness (developed in the preceding section) was dependent upon the ingen-ious and relatively unconscious interpersonal cooperation to be found in certain rela-tively homogeneous and limited communities such as the Greek city-states. With the disintegration of this unity and sense of community through civic rivalry and war, a situation of social atomicity and chaos results, a pre-Marxian variety of alienation. To restore unity in the world at this particular stage, a stronger force than the Ethi-cal Substance is required. This stronger and supervening force is Legal Conscious-ness, which because it can mold much larger and heterogeneous groupings into effec-tive spiritual unities by means of an organized system of laws, must be considered

---

51. *B*260, H341–2: . . . *so gehen die* lebendigen *Volksgeister durch ihre Individualität jetzt in einem* allgemeinen *Gemeinwesen zu Grunde, dessen* einfache Allgemeinheit *geistlos und tot, und dessen Legendigkeit das* einzelne *Individuum, als einzelnes, ist. . . . Ist überhaupt dieses sittliche Volk eine durch die Natur bestimmte und daher beschränkte Individualität und findet also ihre Aut'. 'ung an einer andern. Indem aber diese Bestimmtheit . . . verschwindet, ist das Leben des Geistes und diese in allen ihrer selbst bewusste Substanz verloren. Sie tritt als eine* formelle Allgemeinheit *an ihnen heraus, ist ihnen nicht mehr als lebendiger Geist inwohnend, sondern die ein-fache Gediegenheit ihrer Individualität ist in viele Punkte zersprungen.*

52. The great harmony of Nature and Spirit which was the hallmark of the genius of the Greeks, of their art and culture and political life, was also their downfall. For Spirit can never remain in repose with Nature. It must break forth to show its independence of Nature, even if this means producing the rather contrived, artificial and sometimes in-humane monuments to the progress of civilization and greatness that characterized the Roman spirit.

dialectically superior to mere Ethical Consciousness. This spiritual benefit, however, cannot be attained without sacrificing one prized possession of Ethical Consciousness, namely, that natural stamp of individualization which people formerly received from their nation and/or their ethnic background. For, if law is to prevail equally everywhere, this *sort of distinctiveness must be henceforth minimized; the various populations must be metamorphosed into homogeneous units (legal "persons") which have the same significance and value everywhere and are more easily manipulated by laws of the most general and functional sort. The clearest historical embodiment of this level of consciousness would seem to be the Roman Empire, which, in the aftermath of the repeated failures of the Roman Republic to achieve the ideal of supranational unity, began to rely on strong rulers and an elaborate and ingenious code of laws to guarantee stability and unity both in domestic territories and among conquered peoples. From the time that Caesar Augustus was enthroned in 23 B.C., the extension in the "spiritual" sphere of the Pax Romana throughout the Empire relied heavily on the constant enactment and codification of laws, and the process of lawmaking was furthered with genius during the first few centuries of the Christian era. But as Socrates observes in Plato's* Republic *(425C ff.), the need of rulers and ruled to resort more and more to laws to keep order among themselves can itself be a telltale sign of spiritual disease and disintegration. And as Hegel will argue in this section, the growth of legalism as a state of consciousness produces such an extreme of disintegration and alienation that it prepares the way for its own reversal.*

Although Roman law is widely considered a foundation for legal traditions of equal rights, constitutionality, and the supposition that an accused person is "innocent until proven guilty" in Western civilization, Hegel here and also in his Philosophy of History *presents Roman civilization as rather repressive, a sort of "lowest common denominator" of political slavery, comparable in some respects to the ancient Chinese unity through uniform and customary subservience to an Emperor. In this outlook he voices a rather typical German reaction against Roman law, as Peter Viereck shows in* Metapolitics *(p. 22 and passim). There is no doubt that Roman law, in granting power to Emperors to circumvent constitutional guarantees, and in countenancing slavery, was autocratic in orientation; but Hegel seems to give unusually scant attention here to the undeniable role of Roman law in grounding the conception of the* equality, *if not the freedom, of citizens in modern political consciousness. Hegel's general opposition to some aspects of political equality (see the later section on "Absolute Freedom" in the* Phenomenology, *and also* Philosophy of Right, *§200, Remark) was intensified also by his reaction to the Rousseauan concept of equality prevalent in his day.*

We have just seen how the intensification of the struggle between the divine and human laws in and through the female and male principles, respectively, led through the ironic eventualities of war to the seizure of the universal power by contingent elements,[53] and the consequent dissolution of the previously harmonious unity of the ethical substance. This ultimate accomplishment of Destiny is in a sense negative, in a sense positive. It is negative just insofar as it makes that former harmonious societal union of individual and social consciousness a thing of the past, to be recaptured only as a beautiful memory[54] of the distant origins of a new, more intense certainty of self-conscious unity. But it is also positive, insofar as the universal significance which used to pertain only to the ethical substance now devolves upon the individual himself, whose self-consciousness is correspondingly enhanced: Man and Woman discover, to their amazement and delight, that Destiny unmasked is only an aspect of their own ego.[55] When this realization becomes rampant, the immediate un-self-conscious unity of the ethical substance breaks up into the myriads of its atomic constituents; and the result is the emergence of the notion of the "person," in a very abstract, formal, *legal*[56] sense. The person, thus construed, is the heir of the previous concept of

---

53. The "contingent elements" here would be exemplified by the various factions and individuals that came to power by legitimate or illegitimate means in the final days of the Greek era and in the subsequent era of Roman ascendency.

54. In addition to the ancient example of the sad but necessary destruction of Greek social harmony by Roman legalism, Hegel was most probably also thinking of the more modern example of the subordination of various European nations including Hegel's own Prussia to the Napoleonic Empire, and the substitution of the post-revolutionary *Code Napoleon* for the systems of Roman law and customary law that had previously prevailed in the conquered regions.

55. Just as the participants in ancient Greek tragedy (see M§743 ff., B745 ff.) eventually came to perceive that they themselves were their own "Destiny" and began to doff their masks in Comedy and make light of the various human and divine laws that had previously appeared as Destiny; so also in the more practical realm of ethical activity the partisan proponents of the divine ("female") role or the human ("male") role begin to discover now that these roles are simply two disparate aspects of the "destiny" of personhood of each and every individual self-consciousness.

56. It is only as an *abstract* unit denuded of national or ethnic "natural" characteristics that the person can serve as the supranational unifying factor required at this stage of Spirit. If we keep this in mind, it is easy to understand the parallel between the idea of the person and the philosophical position of stoicism which Hegel draws up in this section. See Joseph Navickas, *Consciousness and Reality*, p. 217: "Just as the stoical consciousness has failed to link its independence 'to anything that exists,' so legalism has failed to link the right of the person to the inner, substantial nature of the individual."

universal "individuality" which, as we saw, attached primarily to the dead family member, the "shade." But now this shade shakes off its character of other-worldliness and unreality, and enters into the limelight of public consciousness as "personality." We must still emphasize, however, that the person, at this stage, is nevertheless in an absolutely undeveloped, abstract condition;[57] and this concept will have to undergo a long process of cultural development before it can boast a more concrete formulation.

The initial and primitive stages of development which we are concerned with here run parallel to some degree with the much earlier development of self-consciousness from the Master-Slave dialectic to the Unhappy Consciousness:[58] Just as the domination of the Master resulted in the emergence of the stoical self-consciousness as a flight from both domination and servitude, so also the dominion of the ethical substance has now led to the affirmation of the self-conscious unit or "person" as an escape from the extrinsic necessitations of Destiny.[59] Then again, just as stoicism in its emphasis on the negative power of self-consciousness developed into scepticism, in which the mind feels its power to create and annihilate determinations of reality, so here the emphasis on the abstract person leads to the assumption that the individual can impress his own form on any arbitrary content—whether external possessions (property)[60] or internal possessions (character traits, etc.)—in such a fashion that the nature of the person's "rights" (i.e., the content on which the form of the "mine" is impressed) seems to make very little dif-

---

57. Not a "person" in the more concrete and nonlegal sense of modern usage.

58. See Section B (Ch. IV) of the *Phenomenology*.

59. Parallel with the liberation of the Stoic from the Master-Slave dichotomy, the liberation of the "person" from the rigid divine-human, female-male polarities that earlier held sway, would also be implied. For now the previous limited insight into the interrelationship of the "divine" female principle of protection of individuality and family rights with the "human" male principle of maintenance of public order is superseded, and in its place appears a new insight into the value of the (legal) person as a unique synthesis of *both* these former principles. For the person is legally defined *both* as an individual with certain inalienable (divine) rights including property rights and as the basic unit of civic life who has a (human) right as well as a duty to contribute to the public order.

60. Under the influence of the new legal set of attitudes, "possessions" become transformed into "property," with all the network of stipulated limits and guarantees attached thereto. Thus the groundwork is laid for the system of relations that will much later be called "bourgeois society," and some of the problems that will develop in that later society are anticipated here, as Lange points out in *Hegel und Wir*, p. 37.

ference at all.[61] Finally, just as the state of Scepticism led to the utter self-contradiction and alienation of the Unhappy Consciousness,[62] which is resolved only after the suprahuman Unchangeable, which seemed to be alien and other, is recognized as merely a projection or creation of the self; so also here the contemptibly abstract notion of person as *mere* property owner and as *merely* equal with every other ego[63] leads first to the necessity for an external and alien super-individual human being, the Lord and Master of the world, to hold together by force this infinite and potentially chaotic multiplicity of spiritual units; but then his "unifying force" proves itself to be unsubstantial chaos and disunity, and his minions recognize[64] that

> his might is nothing like that spiritual unity wherein each component person comes to realize his own self-consciousness. Rather, the "persons" here are strictly for-themselves, and exclude any effective connection with others because of their absolutely stubborn atomicity. And thus they find themselves in a merely negative relationship both to one another and to him who alone *is* their bond of continuity and interrelationship. True, he in this "unifying" capacity *is* their "essence" and a "content" for their purely formal existence, but a content which is estranged, and a hostile essence, who despoils them of the very thing that they thought to be their essential significance— namely, their purely formal existence-for-self; and who also in supposedly supplying the interconnection of one personality with another utterly destroys personality itself.[65]

---

61. "Just as stoicism leads to scepticism, so also the emphasis on abstract right leads to a scission between the abstract guidelines which are supposed to protect individual rights, and the concrete respect for persons that is presumably the basis for these guidelines in the first place" (Navickas, p. 217). The excessive formalism of law which expressed a confidence in the ability of legal consciousness to transform any sort of content into property or rights is the legal counterpart of the attitude of Scepticism, which expresses a similar confidence in its ability of negating any external content and transforming it into its opposite.

62. The Unhappy Consciousness is the state of consciousness particularly associated with Christianity (see M§751 f., B752 f., H522 f., *B*401), which emerged within the Roman Empire prior to the stage of legalism discussed here.

63. In *Natural Law*, Hegel quoted Gibbon's *Decline and Fall of the Roman Empire*, I, Ch. 2, to the effect that the notion of "personal equality" in Roman legalism gradually destroyed the public courage and sense of national honor that were the keys to the greatness of Rome. This notion, says Hegel, had a leveling effect which gradually transformed the whole Empire, aristocracy and commoners alike, into commoners, so that they could be more easily manipulated and mastered by the imperial authority (*op. cit.*, pp. 101–102).

64. As in the case of the Unhappy Consciousness, which returned to itself only after the shocked realization that it had been projecting its self-consciousness onto an *un*substantial "Absolute" (K95 ff.), so also here the hapless "legal persons" begin to return to their senses after the shocked recognition that they have given rise to a "personality" who is the utter dissolution of personality itself.

65. *B*263, H346: . . . *seine Macht ist nicht die* Einigkeit *des Geistes, worin die Personen ihr*

The stark realization by the ethically developing world that it has produced this utter monstrosity, this personification of chaotic self-schism,
is the necessary and sufficient impetus for beginning the groundwork
that is required for understanding and dealing with the unavoidable
alienations of personhood which gave rise to such a monstrosity in the
first place.[66]

B. SELF-ALIENATED SPIRIT. CULTURE.
[CULTURAL CONSCIOUSNESS].

Introductory Remarks:

*"Culture" (Bildung) has a special and technical meaning in Hegel's writings. It
is the sphere in which man rises above his nature and his natural social institutions
and fills his world with more or less lasting reflections of, and monuments to, the
independence of Spirit from Nature. The term "Culture" is somewhat cognate in
Hegel to our term "civilization," except that in Hegel the idea of Culture necessarily implies a high degree of "alienation"* [Entfremdung]. *The cause of this alienation is pinpointed very well by Josiah Royce, in his analysis of this section of the*
Phenomenology:

> *The world of the "self-estranged social mind" of Hegel's definition we might, to use a current phra-
> seology, characterize as the world of the imperialistic sort of national consciousness, or simply as the
> world of imperialism. In such a world, as Hegel skilfully points out, the individual comes to regard
> himself as in relation to the social powers, which, in the first place, he cannot understand. The fact
> that, as in our present civilization, he is formally a free citizen, does not remove his character of self-
> estrangement from the social world in which he moves. Furthermore, since such a society is so vast as to
> be no longer easily intelligible, not only its political, but also its other social powers, appear to the
> individual in a similarly estranged and arbitrary fashion. In Hegel's account stress is laid upon the in-*

---

*eigenes Selbstbewusstsein erkännten, vielmehr sind sie als Personen für sich und schliessen die
Kontinuität mit andern aus der absoluten Sprödigkeit ihrer Punktualität aus; sie sind
also in einem nur negativen Verhältnisse wie zueinander so zu ihm, der ihre Beziehung oder Kontinuität ist. Als diese Kontinuität ist er das Wesen und der Inhalt ihres Formalismus, aber der
ihnen fremde Inhalt, und das feindliche Wesen, welches gerade dasjenige, was für sie als ihr Wesen
gilt, das inhaltsleere Fürsichsein, vielmehr aufhebt;—und als die Kontinuität ihrer Per-
sönlichkeit eben diese zerstört."*

66. From a psychological point of view one might say that the requirement that there
should be some supreme concrete personality as a unifying focus and source for all the
artificially created legal personalities throughout a vast empire, and the strain of trying
to *be* such a supreme personality, led of itself to such arrogant pretentiousness and excesses—as in a Nero—that the charisma of the "Lord and Master of the World" waned
and no longer blinded recently created personhood to its actually alienated condition.

evitable conflicts between wealth and governmental authority, between corporate and political digni-
ties, —conflicts which characterize the imperial stage of civilization in question."
(See The Philosophy of Loyalty, *p. 950 in Royce's* Basic Writings *II.)*

But while Royce is merely resigned to such alienation as the "inevitable" by-
product of larger civilizations, standing in the way of that mutual communal
loyalty which is paramount in true social progress, Hegel is more sanguine. For the
process of alienation was considered by Hegel to be an indispensable stage in educa-
tion (Bildung *means "education" in German, as well as "culture"). In other*
words, the development of negative or alienated relationships between man and his
environment, man and fellow man, or state authorities and their subordinates, is the
necessary catalyst that leads to the maximal manifestations of Spirit in the socio-
political realm and even to the maturation of philosophical wisdom (see Faith and
Knowledge, *p. 189). Needless to say, Hegel is at odds with most educational*
theories of his day (such as the theory exemplified in Rousseau's novel, Émile,
which depicted education as the spontaneous and harmonious development of
natural psychic forces) as well as those of our own day. *

The historical setting with which the discussion of cultural consciousness begins
is feudal Europe, in the aftermath of the breakup of the Roman and Carolingian em-
pires. Hegel seems to pass over the Dark Ages and much of the Middle Ages; but we
must attach no special significance to this, since in a phenomenology of Spirit, as
contrasted with a philosophy of history, one is concerned more with selecting arche-
typal examples of socio-cultural evolution than with maintaining chronological,
historical continuity. The evolution discussed here is from feudal Europe up to and
including pre-revolutionary imperial France. This is the period during which one
might say that modern European civilization emerged—complete with all its dis-
tinctive alienations.

The harbingers of the progress of spirit who produced the "Lord and
Master of the World," and who lived through the reign of this monstrosity, are now a bit wiser. They may now be less likely to allow their freedom to be so utterly alienated as to end up by default in the possession of
a single individual. But they are not beyond alienation. It is not possible
to return now to that earlier state of the Ethical World in which there was
such a signal harmony between spirit and world, between consciousness
and its own ethical substance. And now also the development of free-

---

*Dewey's educational theory, however, which was affected by Dewey's early inter-
est in Hegel, and which emphasizes the dynamic and motivating function of the tensions
with environment that a developing child feels, may be an exception.

dom and personality has progressed to the point at which consciousness
on its side, and the cultural environment (which is both the womb and
the offspring [67] of consciousness), engender a certain dilemma: Actually
to assimilate an alienated world is to become alienated oneself; but to re-
sist the development of the cultural world and the expansion of self-
consciousness (with inevitable alienations) implied in such development is *also* to become alienated. The first horn of this dilemma becomes
epitomized successively in various "alienated" types that are described
in this long section on Culture, including the Base or Ignoble Consciousness, the "Distraught Consciousness," and finally "Insight," a lineal
descendant of the "Distraught Consciousness"; the second horn of the
dilemma becomes epitomized initially in the noble or aristocratic proponents of State Power (before they begin to compromise with their ignoble inferiors) and eventually in the advocates of Faith, who look for
stability and harmony in *another world*. The choice finally presented to us
will be a choice between (*a*) rational mediation of the present, actual cultural world, which is now recognized as being fraught with contradic
tion; or (*b*) non-mediated immersion in the thought of a world beyond,
still resplendent with the essential unity of person and objectivity. The
former choice, the position of Insight, involves a complete betrayal of
the former ideal of essential ethical harmony in favor of a dialectic expansion of consciousness through satire, wit, etc. The latter choice, the
position of Faith, opts for a consciousness of ideal harmony at the expense of actual consciousness of this world. The resolution of this split
can be compared to the development of Personality, discussed in the
preceding section: Just as the conflict between divine and human law,
which took on the aspect of Destiny, was dissolved by the evolution of the
"Person" as the primordial divine goal of all human lawmaking (or as
the individual consciousness which takes Destiny upon itself), so also
the alienations between rational mediation and simple immediacy
which develop out of the cultural consciousness will eventually be dissolved in a universal, enlightened Insight which explicitly makes these
alienations its *own* conscious possession (and thus, in the strict sense, no
longer alienations at all). But this latter will find itself in natural and in-

---

67. As Loewenberg's "Meredy" puts it, we have passed from the ingenuous society
(the Ethical World) through the ingenious society (the world of Right and Legality) to
the artificial society (the external world of Culture produced by man). See Loewenberg,
Hegel's Phenomenology, p. 209.

evitable conflict with Faith; and as this conflict develops into full-blown hostility and spiritual war, Insight will become metamorphosed into a more advanced stage of Enlightenment, which will counter the other-worldly "essence" recognized by Faith not only by infecting Faith with this-worldly concerns, but also by doing away with essentiality in one clean sweep by coupling its own version of an *un*-knowable and hence unsubstantial Supreme Being with an all-pervasive "philosophy of utility." This double-faceted affirmation of the immanent and the subjective will bring about an ultimate state where freedom revolves solely around itself, and

> this latter revolution produces the state of Absolute Freedom,[68] wherein the formerly alienated spirit, having now returned full-circle to itself, entirely takes its leave of the land of Culture [69] [the birthplace of Insight] and passes over into the land of moral consciousness.[70]

I. The World of Self-Alienated Spirit

The end result of the development of Culture will be, as we have indicated, a bifurcation into (a) the self-alienated present actuality mediated and also manifested by Insight; and (b) Faith, or pure consciousness of essential unity, which erects a new species of alienation by ascribing this essential unity to "a world beyond." (Before proceeding any further, we should point out that Faith, which involves a psychic flight from the world, is not to be confused with Religion,[71] which is the positive self-possession of the Absolute manifested in self-consciousness. This latter concept is attained by Faith only in a negative and implicit manner.) The processes *leading up* to the above-mentioned bifurcation will now be described.

a.   Culture and its Realm of Actuality
     [Economic vs. Political Consciousness]

---

68. Exemplified in the French Revolution.
69. France.
70. The "land of moral consciousness" is Germany, the birthplace of Kantian moral philosophy. The quote here is from H350:,B266 . . . *diese Revolution bringt die absolute Freiheit hervor, womit der vorher entfremdete Geist vollkommen in sich zurückgegangen ist, dies Land der Bildung verlässt und in ein anderes Land, in das Land des moralischen Bewusstseins übergeht.*
71. See M§672 ff., B685 ff., H473, B363, for the phenomenology of Religion proper.

Introductory Remarks:

The alienations implicit in Cultural Consciousness become manifest in the present section as (a) an antithesis between economic and political motivations and, in the next section, as (b) an antinomy between worldly Insight and other-worldly Faith.

Hyppolite (Genesis and Structure, p. *394) mentions that a few years before writing the present section Hegel had read Adam Smith's* Wealth of Nations, *and had been impressed by the dialectic manifested in that work. Hegel seems to have Smith's theory of the "invisible hand" (which brings unity and order out of selfish interests) in mind as he shows here how desire for wealth and the satisfactions it provides brings about a continual alliance with, even amalgamations with, the contrary cultural thrusts towards political unity and power. The amalgamation of the two dialectically opposite tendencies of Spirit finally produces an extreme state of alienated ("Distraught") Self-Consciousness. But this extremely negative experience—like the mystic's "dark night of the soul" or Kierkegaard's "despair"— will provide the necessary and sufficient impetus for an ascent to more refined and stable levels of self-consciousness (Insight and Enlightenment), in the following sections.*

Self-consciousness, as it advances beyond the concepts of right and personality, does not just incorporate natural forms of character and existence into the spiritless formal universality of *Juridical Right.* Rather, starting out from the in-itself of a particular nature with such-and-such talents and character, which is now less important than it was before,[72] it rises above such particular aspects to further the designs of Spirit; it makes explicit what was implicit, and thus makes it into something objectively *universal,* but also gives it specific, definite, stable form and thus makes it into something concrete and actual (i.e., not merely formal). In doing so, it (1) makes the individual to *be* an individual; (2) alienates itself from itself in the very act of externalizing itself; (3) thus makes itself actual; and (4) establishes its power over the world, which

---

72. In the Greek and Roman world, where Spirit still operated in relatively close conjunction with Nature, temperament and talent were more important than they are in the more recent stages of Spirit, dominated by aristocratic ambition and/or bourgeois competitiveness. From this more modern vantage point it seems, at least to an observer like Adam Smith, that "the difference of natural talents in different men is, in reality, much less than we are aware of. . . . The difference between the most dissimilar characters, between a philosopher and a common street porter, for example, seems to arise not so much from nature as from habit, custom and education" (*The Wealth of Nations,* I, 2.).

has now assumed the form of *culture*: a stable edifice of thoughts and deeds and artifacts and objects which, although starkly separate from self-consciousness, gives purpose and content to the individual, and supplies the measure of his reality and power. The world of culture breaks up in various ways into forms of standard opposition—such as good vs. bad[73]—in which one pole gives meaning to the other and comes to exist precisely by being transmuted into its opposite. As this process progresses, alienation will alienate itself, and we will return once more into the ultimate concept activating the whole.

The moments which we will have to deal with here can be profitably paralleled with the classical distinction of nature into the "four elements": according to the classical theory, *air* is something of a universal, unchanging factor; *water* is forever being transmuted and shifted; *fire* is continually making opposition into unity and unity into opposition; and *earth* stands as the articulated whole. And thus likewise the spirit of culture splits up into various spheres or elements.

1) In its first element, spirit is the universal in-itself, a self-identical spiritual essence; 2) in the second element it is the essence which runs away from and dissolves itself, as self-sundering being-for-self; 3) in the third, it is the self-conscious subject which possesses the force of fire immediately within itself. In its first state, it is conscious of itself just as an in-itself; 2) in the second case it comes into possession of being-for-self through the sacrifice of universality. 3) But spirit in its most advanced state is the existence in-*and*-for-self of the whole, which sunders itself into a stable substance on the one hand, and the same substance as sacrificing itself, on the other, but also [4] restores both sides to unity—a rapacious fire which consumes the substance, but at the same time is the permanent form of that substance.[74]

---

73. In Hegel "bad" (*das Schlechte*) has a much more general and less moral connotation than "evil" (*das Böse*, as used, for example, in the later section on Revealed Religion). A similar preference of "bad" over "evil" in contrast to "good" is found in Nietzsche's *Genealogy of Morals*.

74. *B*269, H353-4: *[Er legt sich aus]* . . . —*in die erste Masse, das* an sich allgemeine, *sich* selbst gleiche *geistige Wesen,* —*in die andere, das fürsichseiende, in sich* ungleich *gewordene, sich* aufopfernde *und* hingebende *Wesen,* —*und in das* dritte, *welches als Selbstbewusstsein Subjekt ist und die Kraft des Feuers unmittelbar an ihm selbst hat; im ersten Wesen ist es seiner als des* Ansichseins *bewusst, in dem zweiten aber hat es das Werden des* Fürsichseins *durch die Aufopferung des Allgemeinen. Der Geist aber selbst ist das* Anundfürsichsein *des Ganzen, das sich in die Substanz als bleibende und in sie als sich aufopfernde* entzweit *und ebenso sie auch wieder in seine Einheit* zurücknimmt, *sowohl als die ausbrechende sie verzehrende Flamme, wie als die bleibende Gestalt derselben*—

The basic idea in this extended simile seems to be that the former unmediated opposition between the in-itself (the ethical community) and the for-itself (the family as a locus

However, we can consider these final developments (*a*) as implicitly and immediately conceived by thought, and (*b*) as objective realities.

a) The simple life of spirit in its inchoate *concept* initially breaks up into two opposite poles: the good and the bad. (1) The *good* is the ever-present reservoir of spiritual power inherent in the social essence, the foundation and substratum for all the sallies of self-consciousness. (2) The *bad* is the universality of spirit insofar as it departs from the context of universality, and transfers (*preisgibt*) itself to individuals to heighten their awareness of their own particularity. This conceptual break-up into opposite members is a stable, permanent transition.

(*b*) As an *objective reality*, this conceptual permanence-of-transition passes from an abstract and subjective dichotomization into a quite factual flux and process of self-alienation. (1) The good *qua* objective reality becomes the *State Power*, the simple social substance which is the "Work" of all its members, their absolutely accomplished universality, an objectively accomplished spiritual fact (*die Sache selbst*) which no longer takes on the character of something-to-be-done. Thus it has the appearance of an external reality, existing as being-for-another. But (2) this very appearance fades into its opposite—*Wealth, or Resources*[75]—the *passive* universal which is consumed by all, and which is continually coming from universal activity as "work-produced," or entering back into a kind of "immediate" universality[76] as a *common* object of enjoy-

---

of property, privacy and individuality) is now to be replaced by a mediated opposition (between State Power as an in-itself and Bourgeois society as a for-itself) existing as a constant interchange (an in-and-for-itself, fire-like), and that this set of developments seen not as historical "moments" but as the present totality of Spirit in-and-for-itself is comparable to the Earth, a "Universal Individual."

Note that Hegel begins with the idea that otherness is already implicit in the in-itself, and must simply become expressed as a for-itself. The process by which the in-itself contains the seeds of dialectical differentiation is described in more detail later in the *Phenomenology* with special reference to the Christian dogma of the Trinity (see M§769 f., B766 f., H534 f., *B*410 f.).

75. The antinomy here between State Power and Wealth is somewhat similar to the antinomy between the Crown and the Estates that Hegel will comment on in §304 of his last published work, *The Philosophy of Right* (1831). Marx reinterpreted this and other more latent antitheses in his *Critique of Hegel's Philosophy of Right* (1843), the work that marked Marx's transition to communism.

76. Hegel has used the terms "universal" and "universality" with so many different nuances of meaning in this section, that it may be well for us to pause to recall the general meaning of "universal" in Hegel. It is any sort of spiritual dynamism which draws discrete determinacies into some higher unity. The social essence or substance is a "universal" because it pervades and defines the individuals who contribute to it and even create

ment. Wealth is "bad," insofar as it is continually assuming the character of particularity, and drawing people into a consciousness of their particularity. But it should be noted also that as a passive *universal*, it is also continually relating to the universal: one who produces a particular work is producing for all; one who has a particular enjoyment is implicitly sanctioning and willing this enjoyment for all.[77]

A process of *judgment* brings the individual consciousness into *actual relationship* to these objective realities, such that they become good *for him* or bad *for him*,[78] and in this process assume their true value (for it is only that which is good for consciousness which is good in itself[79]—although we may distinguish in an abstract way the Essence in-itself as "good" and the Essence for-another as "bad". Judgments of goodness are precisely those in which consciousness finds itself in the object, while judgments of badness are those in which it fails to find itself. But as these judgments are made, consciousness finds that it must abandon

---

it; individual talents and characteristics enter into "universality" when they are expressed externally as something which receives meaning in, and contributes to, a public context; Wealth is a "passive universal" insofar as it is a kind of external by-product of the universal social activity (human work) that gives it its value (cf. Adam Smith's theory of value-created-by-work, which is reflected also in the thinking of the later Marx); and the enjoyment of wealth creates a kind of "immediate universality" by uniting consumer with co-consumer, producer with co-producer, and consumer with producer.

77. The argumentation here is reminiscent of Adam Smith. Consider, for example, the following passage: "It is his own advantage, indeed, and not that of society which [each individual] has in view. But the study of his own advantage naturally, or rather necessarily [!], leads him to prefer that employment [of his money] which is most advantageous to the society" (*The Wealth of Nations*, IV, 2). Adam Smith, like Karl Marx, presents the evolution of wealth as a series of dialectically progressing stages, and his theory of "the invisible hand" is also ready-made for the sort of dialectical interpretation that Hegel gives it here. Erhard Lange in *Hegel und Wir*, p. 39, observes that in H357 (M§497, B522–3, *B*272) expressions such as "universal enjoyment" (*allgemeinen Genuss*), "universal beneficence" (*allgemeines Wohltun*), and "thousand-handed provider" (*tausenhändiger Geber*) are derived directly from Adam Smith.

78. Cf. Diderot's *Rameau's Nephew*, p. 51: "One must be whatever self-interest requires, good or bad, wise or foolish, decent or ridiculous, honest or vicious."

79. The insight arrived at here is that "good" is essentially subjective. In other words, it is unthinkable that there could be some objective good, which was not good *for* somebody, and which was not considered good *precisely insofar* as it was good for somebody. The proponents of the philosophy of self-interest, of course, will interpret this to mean that only that is good which contributes to their (selfish) enjoyment or enrichment, but the idea is also capable of more altruistic interpretations, such as the interpretation given to it by the "Beautiful Soul" in the later chapter on "Conscience."

the clear-cut distinctions which first appeared (state-power "equals" good, resources "equals" bad), since as spiritual realities in consciousness these objective distinctions must now be explicitly related to subjectivity.

Implicit consciousness (*Bewusstsein als ansichseindes Wesen*) sees state-power as the expression of its essence, such that the laws of the state are the substance of consciousness, and the processes of government give it life and sustenance; on the other hand, it sees the enjoyment of wealth as something which is continually drawing man away from his inherence in universality to the particular.[80]

Self-contained conscious mind (*das an-und-für-sich seinde Bewusstsein*), however, finds state-power and civic order to be a threat to its own power, and wealth or property to be a means toward actuating its consciousness.[81]

Conscious life as it becomes more sophisticated, comes to look for goodness or badness in neither of these attitudes (both of which present a bad and a good aspect), but rather in the process of *judgment itself* which can capitalize on the "good" aspects in both attitudes. Within the two attitudes, then, those two judgments which implied agreement with subjective interests are now called "good," and those two judgments which implied disagreement are deemed "bad".

The Consciousness which manages to make double judgments *of agreement-with-self* takes on the aspect of *Nobility*:[82] this is the con-

---

80. It is hard to think of any historical example that precisely embodies this pure position, unless, like Shklar (*Freedom and Independence*, p. 153), one is willing to go all the way to Plato's idea of a perfect, patriotic and property-less class of bureaucrats in *Republic V*; this has the appearance of an anachronism, but as was mentioned above regarding the reference to the "Penates" in an otherwise Greek context, it is not necessarily an anachronism from a *phenomenological* point of view. Closer to our own time, Leninism and Maoism show an affinity with the concept of the "Implicit Consciousness" as here defined, provided that one is willing to substitute "dictatorship of the proletariat" for "state."

81. This position expresses an extreme form of *laissez faire* philosophy that goes beyond Adam Smith's capitalism, and seems to be summed up by Rameau in the following excerpt from Diderot's *Rameau's Nephew* (p. 78): Diderot: "There are people like me who don't consider wealth the most important thing in the world—queer people." Rameau: "Very queer . . . It's unnatural . . . Everything that lives, man included, seeks its well-being at the expense of whoever withholds it."

82. The aristocratic or "noble" consciousness here is typified in the feudal lord, who was dedicated not only to his own aggrandizement but also (especially in later feudalism when marauding invaders and robbers became a problem) was such a devoted advocate

sciousness that perceives the public authority as being in accord with its essence, and wealth as contributing to its consciousness of self-existence.

The consciousness which manages to make double judgments *of disagreement-with-self* has the attribute of *Baseness*: it sees the public authority as suppressing its separate existence, and wealth (which it ambivalently loves and despises) as something evanescent which never quite does justice to the demands of its permanent nature.[83]

Mutual cancellation occurs at this point, since state-power and wealth, which are not yet *an-und-für-sich*, but are still objective to consciousness, give rise to such contradictory attitudes, like predicates for which a fitting *subject* has not been found. We must, therefore, search for an instrument for imparting inner unity to them. And this we find in inferential (syllogistic) judgment, which supplies us with a suitable "middle term."

The process of "syllogistic" mediation:[84] The noble type of consciousness

---

of strong central state power that, as we shall see in this section, he will first alienate himself through the "heroism of service" to foster a monarchy, and then alienate himself even more through the "heroism of language" to produce absolute monarchy, which will have the effect of weakening his own power—although in many cases promoting his wealth. Guy Planty-Bonjour thinks that Hegel received inspiration from Montesquieu for his description of the "noble consciousness" in the present section: "Granted that Montesquieu is not mentioned by name in the *Phenomenology of Spirit*, it is quite clear that in Hegel's descriptions of the 'noble consciousness', the 'haughty vassal', the 'sentiment of honor,' etc., he is profoundly inspired by Montesquieu's *The Spirit of the Laws*" (Planty-Bonjour, *L'Esprit general*, p. 8).

83. The base or ignoble consciousness (*niederträchtige Bewusstsein*) hates the rulers, obeys only with malice, is disenchanted with the benefits and satisfactions of wealth, and is ever prone to revolt against the powers-that-be. Hegel seems to have in mind here the type of disaffected prerevolutionary bourgeois who, given the proper circumstances, would become a leftist Jacobin and even a Robespierre.

Some (e.g. Wolfgang Bonsiepen, *Der Begriff der Negativität*, p. 173 and Hyppolite, *Genesis and Structure*, p. 398) have observed that the Noble–Base relationship here is a kind of repetition of the earlier Master–Slave dialectic. One must qualify this observation by noting that Hegel does not *present* the dialectic development here explicitly and clearly as a simple antithetical interaction between the two types of consciousness. However, the Noble Consciousness does eventually become *disaffected with* wealth and power, and the "Distraught Consciousness" appears later as a Base Consciousness who wants to *ally himself with* wealth and power—so a dialectical development and reversal similar to that between Master and Slave is to be found here.

84. A "syllogistic" mediation is one in which a "middle term" connects two antithetical extremes. In the earlier stage of the Unhappy Consciousness, asceticism and obedience functioned as "middle terms" connecting consciousness and the Unchangeable

now takes up a positive relation to state power, as bringing about perfection of consciousness for it and a negative relation to itself,[85] a self which must be rescued from *mere*-existence, by the state. Thus it takes on the attitude of *Service*, and acquires honor for itself (and gets honor from others).[86] The state, on its side, needs such service if it is to become *universal in fact* (not just in thought). Thus the haughty vassal at this point gives *factual existence* (bare existence) to his state, without going so far, however, as to sacrifice consciousness to it, i.e., to give the animation of consciousness to the state, making it into a *personal will* (not just an essential will). Thus there is no absolute monarch at this point, and the language of the vassal only gradually takes the form of advice or *counsel* (as the State Power emerges from its confusion and weakness and begins to be concretized in this or that weak and indecisive monarchical exponent).

The noble in his attitude of (dumb) service may go so far as to sacrifice his life for the state.[87] Or else he undergoes the *possibility* of death, and attains as a result a fuller realization of the implications of his "service". As a result, he comes to realize that the "sacrifice of death" is deficient, insofar as individuality at death merely passes into the unreconciled opposite (the state).[88] If the individuality, in sacrificing itself, is to *preserve* itself at

---

(see K97); here, first "service" and then "language" will function as "middle terms" connecting the opposite extremes of state power and wealth.

85. The feudal "Lord and Master" over a manor here begins instinctively and hesitatingly to seek for some kind of central and supervening state power, and offers limited loyalty and service to some sovereign.

86. Cf. Montesquieu, *The Spirit of the Laws* III, 6-8: "Honour, that is, the prejudice [social discrimination] of every person and rank . . . is capable of inspiring the most glorious actions . . . A monarchical government supposes, . . . pre-eminences and ranks, as likewise a noble descent. Now since it is the nature of honour to aspire to preferments and titles, it is properly placed in this government. Ambition is pernicious in a republic. But in a monarchy it has some good effects . . . honour sets all the parts of the body politic in motion, and by its very action connects them; thus each individual advances the public good, while he only thinks of promoting his own interest. . . . "

87. Cf. Montesquieu, *ibid.*, 8: "[Honor] glories in the contempt of [i.e., willingness to sacrifice one's own] life."

88. The realization here has parallels in other parts of the *Phenomenology*: The prelude to the earlier Master–Slave relationship was the realization that a warrior must enslave his adversary rather than kill him, to gain recognition from him. In the later section on "Absolute Freedom", the realization that sacrifice of life is an imperfect means of securing freedom will lead to a supersession of that viewpoint. And in the section on "Revealed Religion," the realization that the physical death of the God-Man is insufficient and must be continued by a spiritual death, leads to emphasis on love and the (Christian) religious community.

the same time, it must establish conscious unity (reconcilation) with its opposite as a condition before any species of sacrifice is made. In other words, it must *estrange* itself actively and continually and self-consciously into the permanent substance, if it wishes its individual sacrifice to have permanence.

The means through which consciousness has been able to sacrifice its natural being differ sharply from the means through which it must now sacrifice *self-consciousness* itself. The proper, and indeed the only, means or "middle term" for the latter sacrifice is to be found in *language*:

> This alienation of self-consciousness takes place only in *language*. (We are using the term "language" here in its original and unqualified denotation). Language as *law* and *command* in the ethical world, or as *advice* in the initial stages of the world of self-estranged actuality which has just been discussed, has the essence of the ethical or cultural substance as its content and provides form for this content. But in the present case language holds fast to its very *form* as a *content*, and its value lies precisely in the fact that it *is* language. Language is now the power of speech as that which accomplishes what is to be accomplished. For language *is* the determinate existence of the pure self as a self; and through its agency the *individual* being-for-self of self-consciousness as such emerges into existence, so that it becomes "for-another." Outside the domain of language, the ego in its pure form cannot be present *here* or *there*; for in every nonlinguistic mode of expression the ego is engulfed in an actualization or a configuration from which it can always extricate itself—from its deed or its physiognomic appearance the ego reflects back upon itself, and in so doing abandons such incomplete types of existence (which express simultaneously too much and too little,[89] to their own lifeless isolation. But language retains its grip on the ego in its purity, and language alone announces the presence of the very self of the ego. Precisely insofar as it has determinate existence this ego is an objectivity which has its own veridical nature within it: the ego [as presented in language] is *both* "this" ego *and* the universal [pure, essential] ego, whose "appearance" is directly and simultaneously its alienation and the *dis*appearance of the "thisness," so that the ego remains all the while in its [pure] universality. The ego which expresses itself is "taken in" or "caught"—it is an "infection," in the sense that it has passed directly into unity with those to whom it is presented, and is universal self-consciousness, whose particular presence [*Dasein*] fades away in the very process by which it is "taken in" by others, while the otherness which attaches to this particular presence reverts to itself. For the *real* "particular presence" of the pure ego, as a self-conscious Now, consists in *not*-being "present" in the usual sense, or, in other words, consists in existing through the very process of *dis*appearing. This "disappearance" of the ego through language is *ipso facto* its perdurance; it constitutes the ego's knowledge of itself—a knowledge of a self which has passed over to, and been taken in by, another self, and is universal.[90]

---

89. This idea was expressed earlier in the context of Rational "Observation." See K112, M§312.

90. *B*276, *H*362-3: *Diese Entfremdung aber geschieht allein in der* Sprache, *welche hier in ihrer eigentümlichen Bedeutung auftritt. —In der Welt der Sittlichkeit* Gesetz and Befehl, *—in der Welt der Wirklichkeit erst* Rat, *hat sie das Wesen zum Inhalte und ist dessen Form; hier aber erhalt*

Thus it is through language that the self-conscious ego will be able both to inject selfhood and personality into the essence or state power, and simultaneously to enter into the arcanum of state power itself. But the evolution of the sort of language which makes this possible takes place in three distinguishable stages: heroic flattery, base flattery and the language of distraught consciousness.

[1. *The heroism of flattery*] The noble consciousness, at last disillusioned concerning the possibility of constituting actual existent power through service, now seizes upon language as the appropriate instrument for creating an individual, personal seat of essential power. Through the hyperbolic excesses of flattery, the multiplicity of nobles effectively transfer their own self-consciousnesses to a single focal point of individuality, the unlimited[91] monarch, whose permanence as a kind of infinite personality[92] is made contingent on a continuous influx of flattering recognition from the nobility which surrounds him.[93] Aware of his utter

---

sie die Form, welche sie ist, selbst zum Inhalte, und gilt als Sprache; *es ist die Kraft des Sprechens als eines solchen, welche das ausführt, was auszuführen ist. Denn sie ist das* Dasein *des reinen Selbsts, als Selbsts; in ihr tritt die* für sich seiende Einzelheit *des Selbstbewusstseins als solche* in die Existenz, so dass sie *für Andre ist.* Ich *als dieses* reine Ich *ist sonst nicht* da; *in jeder andern* Äusserung *ist es in eine Wirklichkeit versenkt, und in einer Gestalt, aus welcher es sich zurückziehen kann; es ist aus seiner Handlung wie aus seinem physiognomischen Ausdrucke in sich reflektiert und lässt solches unvollständiges Dasein, worin immer ebensosehr zu viel als zu wenig ist, entseelt liegen. Die Sprache aber enthält es in seiner Reinheit, sie allein spricht* Ich *aus, es selbst. Dies sein* Dasein *ist als* Dasein *eine Gegenständlichkeit, welche seine wahre Natur an ihr hat.* Ich *ist dieses* Ich—aber, ebenso *allgemeines; sein Erscheinen ist ebenso unmittelbar die Entäusserung und das Verschwinden dieses Ichs, und dadurch sein Bleiben in seiner Allgemeinheit.* Ich, *das sich ausspricht, ist* vernommen; *es ist eine Ansteckung, worin es unmittelbar in die Einheit mit denen, für welche es da ist, übergegangen und allgemeines Selbstbewusstsein ist.* —*Dass es* vernommen *wird, darin ist sein* Dasein *selbst unmittelbar* verhallt; *dies sein Anderssein ist in sich zurückgenommen; und eben dies ist sein Dasein, als selbstbewusstes* Jetzt, *wie es da ist, nicht da zu sein, und durch dies Verschwinden da zu sein. Dies Verschwinden ist also selbst unmittelbar sein Bleiben; est ist sein eignes Wissen von sich, und sein Wissen von sich als einem, das in anderes Selbst übergegangen, das vernommen worden und allgemeines ist.*

91. The empire to be ruled is too vast and the individualities to be organized are too discrete and self-seeking for the old-style monarch (the paternal king for the patrimonial kingdom); but we have not yet reached that point (at least in the archetypal French model which Hegel draws upon here) at which a *constitutional* monarch in the modern post-revolutionary sense is possible. In the interim, the only type of monarchy which could exercise absolute and effective sovereignty over such unwieldy spirits is an absolute monarch, exemplified *par excellence* in Louis XIV (1638-1715).

92. Louis XIV is renowned for his boast, "I *am* the State" (*L'État, c'est moi*).

93. This situation is well exemplified in the court of Louis XIV at Versailles.

dependence upon this recognition for his existence[94] as a personification of state power, the monarch in turn endeavors to stabilize and guarantee the continuance of this influx by judicious redistribution of the "passive universal" (wealth) which has been put into his control.[95]

This transfer of wealth to the nobility, however, has two ironical effects: *a*) it brings with it a transference of *actual* power away from the monarch into the hands of the nobility (so that the monarch, the source of power, has power only in name, and in fact is *just* a name)[96]; *b*) it compromises the noble consciousness, which now finds itself dependent for its own self-conscious satisfaction on the external *contingency* of the monarch's whim in distributing wealth (so that wealth becomes a kind of alien object, with an existence-for-self that can be withdrawn at any time). Because of this latter development, the noble consciousness finds itself now in the same camp as the base consciousness, sharing a mutual disenchantment with the transitory nature of wealth and the capricious-

---

94. The existence of the monarch as a kind of infinite personality needs constant bolstering from the hyperbolic praises of his courtiers and admirers. Rameau in Diderot's *Rameau's Nephew* satirizes the sort of input that is necessary to create such an inflated ego in the following passage (p. 17) where he fantasizes himself as a "great man": "You would be told at breakfast that you are a great man, you would read in *Three Centuries of French Literature* that you are a great man, by nightfall you would be convinced that you are a great man, and that a great man, Rameau the Nephew, would fall asleep to the soft hum of praise buzzing in his ears. Even while asleep, he would look sated, his chest would rise and fall with bliss, he would snore like a great man."

95. The relationship between the unlimited monarch and the credulous, devoted and flattering public opinion that actually *creates* him, is, to say the least, a symbiotic relationship. Loewenberg offers us a pertinent example of such symbiosis, and at the same time underlines its universality, by applying it to the contemporary relationship between business and industry, which achieve reputability and power through advertising, and the advertising agencies who are richly rewarded for their indispensable excesses of praise: "The method of flattery, in the form of commercial advertising, has become an integral part of our economic life, having in fact assumed the status of a separate industry with its own captains in command. What is salesmanship if not a name for the various devices involved in plethoric praise of every product of every industry, not excluding the products of the laudatory enterprise? . . . and salesmen are available in profusion whose artificial smiles and artificial voices can be bought to promote the absurdly magnified claims for every possible commodity and every possible nostrum" (Loewenberg, *Hegel's Phenomenology*, p. 225).

96. The monarch indeed exercises power, but he is increasingly dependent upon those who create him as unlimited, and give him his "name" (universal recognition). Carrying Loewenberg's simile (see preceding note) one step further, we could say that the monarch is like the indifferent product that would be nothing without the national instant name-recognition conferred upon it by a massive and continuous advertising campaign.

ness of state power. The former distinction between the noble consciousness and the base consciousness has now disappeared: the noble
consciousness takes on the attitude of the base consciousness, and, in
fact, the so-called ''base'' consciousness has proven itself to be the *truth*
of the noble consciousness.[97]

[*2. Base flattery*] As has been mentioned above, the Wealth which for the
noble-consciousness-turned-base is a source of self-conscious self-satis-
faction, takes on the aspect of an independent object with its own capricious existence-for-self. As a moment of Spirit, Wealth breaks up into
the two complementary poles of wealthy patronage and the impover-
ished client. The wealthy patron, insofar as he is sacrificing his wealth
and imparting it to others, attains a certain universality or essentiality;
but at the same time, conscious of the control he is achieving over the self
of his clients, he becomes the epitome of arbitrariness and contingency,
and reaches a state of arrogance that absolutely blinds him to the inner
rebellion festering in the client consciousness. This latter, in his imperfect stage, maintains himself in a kind of alienated equipoise with his
patron through the language of base flattery.[98]

---

97. As the ''Master'' much earlier became an object of contempt rather than recognition for his industrious slave, and thus became a true ''Slave'' himself, so also in the
present situation the Noble who strains all the powers of language to create a monarch
who can say ''I *am* the State'' ends up depending on the capricious financial patronage of
the monarch for his noble rank and privileges, so that he should really be saying, in contrast to the monarch, ''I (i.e., my nobility) *am* Wealth.'' Insofar as the noble consciousness becomes *aware* of its essentially alienated predicament, it becomes indistinguishable from the Base Consciousness, which was characterized by an essentially negative
relationship to both wealth and power. Niel (*De la mediation,* p. 150) sees in this latter
development the eventual identification of the nobility and the bourgeoisie—the nobleman who uses his status to secure wealth and the bourgeois who uses his wealth to attain
status.

98. Cf. Diderot's *Rameau's Nephew,* p. 35: ''What difference whether you hold a position or not, provided you have means, since you only seek a position in order to get
wealth? Discharge one's duties—what does that bring you?—jealousy, worries, perse-
cution. Is that the way to get on? Nonsense! Pay court, pay court, know the right people,
flatter their tastes and fall in with their whims, serve their vices and second their mis-
deeds—there's the secret.'' And *ibid.,* p. 44: ''There are holders of the military Cross
[an example of the ''heroism of service'']who go without bread—hence the folly of
seeking the cross at the risk of life and limb. Why not go after a position [that of the professional flatterer] absolutely free of danger and invariably rewarded?'' It is perhaps not irrelevant to these observations that Diderot himself played up to Louis
XV and to Frederick II of Prussia, and received preferments from them.

[*3. The language of distraughtness*]

Introductory Remarks:

The model for the type of consciousness described here is Jean François Rameau, a character in Diderot's posthumous novel Rameau's Nephew, *which is presented as a dialogue between a "philosopher" (Diderot himself) and Rameau. Unlike many other posthumous works,* Rameau's Nephew *is far from unfinished or imperfect. Diderot apparently wanted to publish it, but refrained from doing so because of his fear of censorship (the novel is full of satirizations of public officials, artists, musicians, writers, and journalists contemporary to Diderot). The novel was translated by Goethe into German, and published in 1805, before the French edition was made available to the European public.* *

Erhard Lange, in commenting on this section, remarks (Hegel und Wir, *p. 41) on the extraordinarily frequent and extensive use of* Rameau's Nephew *in the development of the dialectic here: "Next to the allusions to Goethe's work (especially* Faust*), Diderot's story,* Rameau's Nephew, *is the only contemporary work that Hegel interprets so profusely in a dialectical sense in the Phenomenology." And as Königson points out, Hegel's extensive use of Diderot's dialogue in the Phe-nomenology is not just for literary or rhetorical effect, but because of his profound conviction of its philosophical importance: "For Hegel, as Lukacs also notes, Diderot's dialogue is not only a masterpiece which characterizes its time in conscious fashion. From the moment that Hegel contradistinguished his own dialectic from that of Fichte and that of Schelling, he recognized in Diderot a veritable precursor"* (Königson, Hegel, Adam Smith et Diderot, *p. 64).*

In Hegel's description of the "Distraught Consciousness" (das zerrissene Bewusstsein*), the consciousness which, like Rameau, is completely given over to mediating contradictions and alienations (although neither Diderot nor his dialogue or its characters are mentioned by name), there are not only long quotations (foot-noted in both the Baillie and Miller translations) from* Rameau's Nephew, *but also multiple allusions to ideas or topics considered in that dialogue: to the idea of a "type" [espèce], to Diogenes' tub, to Rousseau's theory about the "original condition" of man, to the "musical note which surfaces and masters everything." And in the preceding parts of this section on Culture there were not only many ideas reminiscent of Diderot's dialogue (I have offered some examples of these above), but*

---

*Hegel had in his library at his death a copy of this edition: *Rameau's Neffe: Eine Dialog von Diderot*. Aus dem Manuskript übersetzt und mit Anmerkungen begleitet von Goethe (Leipzig: bey G. J. Goschen, 1805).

*also as Bonsiepen (*Der Begriff der Negativität, *p. 231n.) notes, constant use of terms or concepts found therein: the concepts "base," "noble," "nobility," "talent," "character," and "useful"* [nützlich]. *There is also a long paragraph (M§489) towards the beginning of the section on Culture which discusses, as also do Rameau and his philosopher friend, the proper connotation of the French term* espèce.

What is the special philosophical significance that Hegel finds in the character of Rameau? Two things come to mind: Rameau's dialectic, and his universality. If wit (see Philosophy of Mind *§455) essentially involves the dialectical connection of opposites, Rameau's exceptional and overwhelming wittiness offers us a paradigmatic example of this dialectical ability and facility—a sort of natural example of dialectic that would appeal to Hegel as he rebelled against the excessively formalistic concepts of dialectic found in Fichte and Schelling. Rameau is also universal in the sense that he sums up both the strength and the weaknesses of the pre-Enlightenment type of consciousness considered in this section—as Diderot himself seemed to realize: "Diderot: 'Is there anybody in that house with the strength of mind to agree with you?' Rameau: 'What do you mean by "anybody"? Mine's the opinion and the common speech of society at large' " (Diderot, p. 47).*

At a certain point, however, the client consciousness, itself combining the attributes of goodness and badness, and perceiving the perverse interrelationships between wealth and power, and realizing its own utter dejection amidst all the contradictions of the cultural world, nevertheless breaks through to nobility out of the depths of base flattery in a new master-stroke of self-conscious adaptability: the language of distraughtness [zerrissenheit]. The rebelious client consciousness, comprehending its own state of contradiction in depending for consciousness and independence on an agency which is completely alien and other, is shocked by its circumstances into making an "infinite judgment,"[99] a judgment which transcends contradiction by negating it. This transcendence of contradiction, or the artistry of retaining the unity and resiliency of self in the face of distraughtness, is embodied in a correspondingly caustic, sarcastic, sardonic new form of language. This "language of distraughtness" is not just a supervening fashion of speech, but is the Spirit itself which now takes it upon itself to mediate all the alienations

99. Hegel generally uses the expression "infinite judgement" in a non-traditional sense, to signify the power of consciousness to comprehend the dialectical unity of opposites.

and contradictions which the evolution of Culture has given rise to. As a consequence of this mediation, we see that

> what we learn by experience in this world is that neither the actualities of State Power or Wealth, nor their corresponding concepts, Good or Bad, nor the consciousness of these two concepts as embodied in the Noble consciousness and Base consciousness, respectively, possess any truth; but that, rather, all these sundry moments transmute themselves into their inversions, and that each one is the opposite of itself.[100]

Only the Distraught Consciousness, however, really assimilates this dialectical truth. Another type of consciousness—which we shall call the Honest Consciousness[101]—still stands on the side of old-fashioned essentiality, and wants at all costs to maintain the validity and stability of first-order truths about the good, the bad, and so forth. We now end our analysis about the beginnings of culture with a comparison of these two paradigmatic products (and producers) of the cultural world.

[*4. The confrontation of the distraught consciousness and the honest consciousness*]
The Distraught Consciousness does not just recognize the various contradictions of culture, but literally thrives on them. The antitheses connected with good and bad,[102] power,[103] and wealth[104] are the constant

---

100. *B*282, H371. *Was in dieser Welt erfahren wird, ist, dass weder die* wirklichen *Wesen der Macht und des Reichtums, noch ihre bestimmten* Begriffe, *Gut und Schlecht, oder das Bewusstsein des Guten und Schlechten, das edelmütige and niederträchtige, Wahrheit haben; sondern alle diese Momente verkehren sich vielmehr eins im andern, und jedes ist das Gegenteil seiner selbst.*

101. Exemplified by "the philosopher" in Diderot's *Rameau's Nephew.* As Shklar observes (*Freedom and Independence*, p. 162), the philosopher (Diderot's alter-ego?) here speaks for "pure" culture, and for the "republic of letters" freed from the constraints of the social institutions of wealth and power. (As *die Sache selbst* [M§410] reappears in Culture as participation in "State Power [M§494]," so also the "Honest Consciousness" [M§412] reappears as simple-minded theorizing [M§521]).

102. Consider, for example, the following passage (Diderot, pp. 31–32), in which Rameau proposes a kind of language-game theory of morality: "I know well enough that if you apply to my case certain general principles of morals which they all talk about and never put into practice, it will turn out that white is black and black is white. But, Master Philosopher, it is with universal morality as with universal grammar: there are exceptions [idioms] in each language. . . . Each profession makes exceptions to universal morality and those I'd like to call *trade idioms.* . . . In Nature all species live off one another; in society all classes do the same. We square things up with one another without benefit of the law. . . . The exceptions to universal ethics, or moral idoms—about which people make so much fuss under the name of mutual depredations—don't amount to anything, really, . . . "

103. E.g., Diderot, p. 51: "[Rameau:] There is no fitter role in high society than that of a fool. For a long time the King had an appointed fool. At no time was there an appointed

subject of his discourse; but his discourse is the *raison d'être* of his existence and even his vocation. and thus he *needs* the contradictions that constitute the cultural milieu, and so he not only preserves and perpetuates them but does what he can to create them anew. He is like the wild musician depicted in Diderot's *Rameau's Nephew*, who

> . . . piled one upon the other and stirred together thirty arias—Italian, French, tragic, comic, featuring every sort of character; at one time he would be plunging into the infernal regions with a deep bass, at another he would narrow and hoarsen his throat and would be penetrating the ethereal heights with a falsetto note; in rapid succession he was raging, or soothing, or imperious or mocking.[105]

In the very act of creating and engaging in this frenzied recital, Diderot's musician displays a certain artistry and an advanced sense of harmony; and so also, the Distraught Consciousness, in his own explication of the disharmonies, attains a certain degree of conscious universality, albeit of an extremely subjective variety.

But the Distraught Consciousness, who observes and demonstrates the contradictions and disunities of culture, because of his very role and attitude and vocation must be alienated from the substance of the ethical world which formerly[106] united these discordancies at their roots. In contrast, the Honest Consciousness still hearkens back to the social and ethical harmonies of yore, and tries to recapture and salvage the unities and univocities that are still to be found in the sophisticated world of Culture. He points out concrete, but hopelessly contingent, examples of goodness and simplicity; admits the necessity of the Bad and its function in conditioning the Good, although he is impotent to make the next logical step of comprehending the necessary transition of Good into Bad and vice versa (i.e., their dialectical identity); and fantasizes a return to the

---

sage . . . A real sage would want no fool; hence he who has a fool is no sage; and if no sage, must be a fool.''

104. Cf. *ibid*, p. 84: ''[Rameau:] I find that it is no part of good order to be sometimes without food. What a hell of an economy! Some men replete with everything while others, whose stomachs are no less importunate, whose hunger is just as recurrent, have nothing to bite on. The worst of it is the constrained posture in which need holds you. The needy man doesn't walk like the rest; he skips, twists, cringes, crawls. . . . ''

105. *B*282-284, H372 [quoted from Diderot's *Rameau's Nephew*]: ''*der dreissig Arien, italienische, französische, tragische, komische, von aller Art Charakter, häufte and vermischte; bald mit einem tiefen Basse stieg er bis in die Hölle, dann zog er die Kehle zusammen, und mit einem Fistelton zerriss er die Höhe der Lüfte, wechselweise rasend, besänftigt, gebieterisch und spöttisch.*''

106. Before the stages of Legal Consciousness and Cultural Consciousness.

simple immediacy and innocence of nature,[107] without realizing that this oversimplified solution would involve the rejection of the Spirit of Culture itself, and reversion to a more primitive state of the Ethical Substance in its unadulterated harmony.

Thus the aspirations of the Honest Consciousness are insufficiently universal.[108] Although he is propounding a precious value in holding fast to unity and harmony, he fails to realize that the unity that is to emerge must emerge from this world in its present stage of sophistication, i.e., from the world of Culture.

Thus a certain division obtains within the "Cultural Consciousness." On the one hand, the Distraught Consciousness is actively engaged in subjectively mediating and perpetuating the oppositions in the cultural world. On the other hand the Honest Consciousness, which is aware of what is going on, nevertheless stands on the sidelines as a theorizer and tries to reduce the apparent novelties and contradictions to intelligibility of a rather traditional sort.

b). Faith and Pure Insight
   [Catholic vs. Secular Consciousness]

Introductory Remarks:

*The "Faith" that Hegel characterizes in this section is Catholicism, and Hegel uses the word "Insight" (*Einsicht*) to sum up a variegated group of opposing tendencies—Renaissance humanism, empiricism, some strains of rationalism, individualism, freethinking deism—the residues of which become tied together not too neatly in the 18th century "Enlightenment." These latter tendencies were often coupled with a concomitant opposition to supernaturalism and/or dogmatism and/*

---

107. This suggests Rousseau's theory of the emergence of political forms from a "state of nature."

108. The impasse that exists between the Honest Consciousness and the Distraught Consciousness is illustrated by the following passage from Diderot, in which, as Rameau is finishing up a skillful pantomime in which he shows how he knows how to win success by flattery, Diderot comments: "I listened to him, and while he was acting . . . , his soul divided between opposite motives, I hardly knew whether to burst with laughter or with indignation, I was in pain . . . I was overcome by so much cunning and baseness, by notions so exact and at the same time so false, by so complete a perversion of feeling, by such turpitude and such frankness, both equally uncommon. He noticed the conflict raging within me. 'What's the matter?' he asked . . . 'What do you advise me to do?' Diderot; 'To talk of something else.' "

or authoritarianism and/or ritualism as manifested especially in the Catholic Church.

Lauer (A Reading, p. 202) suggests that "Faith" in what follows is modeled on the Protestant Pietist movement, but fails to harmonize this suggestion with the considerable number of allusions to aspects or accoutrements of Catholicism in M§§541ff. Findlay (Mxxiii) suggests more modestly that the "tranquil" or "honest" consciousness in M§522-4 and §539 may be modeled on the typical German Pietist, but the multiple references to Diderot's Rameau's Nephew *in M§522-4 lead one to suspect that Hegel has "the philosopher" in that book, or one of similar orientations, in mind when he makes these allusions. And thus, even if one disagrees with Erhard Lange (*Hegel und Wir, *p. 41) that the Protestant Church is not touched on at all in these sections, it seems clear that Hegel's references to "Faith" here do not envision the Protestant faith, even fideism. The reason for this seems to be that, as Hegel elaborates in* Philosophy of History, *p. 422, the great genius of Protestantism is its ability to synthesize the religious or divine with the secular. In "Romanic" countries like France, however, where the "Catholic principle" prevails, alienation is predominant: Taking a position strongly reminiscent of Rousseau's* Social Contract *IV, 8, Hegel remarks, "This is the leading feature in the character of these Catholic nations—the separation of the religious from the secular interest, i.e., from the special interest of individuality; and the ground of this separation lies in their inmost soul, which has lost its independent entireness of being, its profoundest unity. Catholicism does not claim the essential direction of the secular; religion remains an indifferent matter on the one side, while the other side of life is dissociated from it, and occupies a sphere exclusively its own"* (Philosophy of History, *pp. 421-2).*

The "Catholic" Faith portrayed here must also be further differentiated from (a) the sort of faith which is the lot of the Unhappy Consciousness and (b) that which is the ground for Revealed Religion. In his later section on Revealed Religion (see infra, *pp. 154 ff.), Hegel will show how the subjective devotional aspirations of the Unhappy Consciousness (see K95 ff.) have an affinity with Stoicism, take root in the legalistic-Romanic type of consciousness, and provide the subjective "birthplace" for Christianity. The very subjective attitude of faith of the Judaeo-Christian Unhappy Consciousness contrasts with the very objective "Catholic" type of Faith described in the present section—a Faith which does not seek the Unchangeable in its own consciousness, but is assured of finding the divine in an ecclesiastical hierarchy, in external sacraments, objects of devotion, etc.—the sort of thing Hegel sums up in his early theological writings as "positive" religion. Contrasted with both the subjective legalistic-stoic type of Christianity and the objective, "posi-*

tive'', ''Catholic'' type of religion that emerges in (Romanic) countries still affected by the alienations resulting from the breakup of the world of legal consciousness,
is the more harmonious and perfected (Christian) ''religious community'' described
towards the end of the later chapter on ''Revealed Religion'' (see M§768, B766)
and bearing an unmistakable resemblance to the pictures that Hegel draws elsewhere of (Lutheran) Protestantism as the final synthesis of subjective and objective
aspects of Christianity.

It should be emphasized that both (Catholic) Faith and (secular) Insight here are
products of, and attempts to solve, the alienations (detailed in the preceding section)
produced by Culture. But while Insight, taking its inception from the paradoxical,
ironic, insightful language of the Distraught Consciousness, gradually rises to
conceptual mediation of the contradictions in its cultural environment, Catholic
Faith, decidedly less optimistic about the worth and salvageability of this alienated
world, tries to solve the problem by recognizing, fostering and continuing to construct a supposedly divine nonalienated world right alongside, or even in the middle
of, this fallible and disintegrating cultural world. The orientation of Faith to this
supernatural environment is not a completely unmediated or thought-less orientation, but embodies thought of a special sort, thought of a non-self-conscious sort,
which is directed towards a nonalienated absolute Essence conceived as objectivity of
Being, and mediates its objects in a relatively immediate way, i.e., by imaginative
representations (Vorstellungen) rather than by full-blown concepts.

Both Insight and Faith manifest a disenchantment with the world. Insight masters its disenchantment by its full utilization of the power of
self-consciousness to ''mediate'' the conflicts and contradictions in the
world. Faith flees from the world in a more open manner. Faith would
like, as the Gospels prescribe, to be ''in, but not of'' the world; but it ends
up being both in and of two worlds (see M§572) which come necessarily into
conflict with each other at this stage. The alienation of Insight will only eventually
be overcome in the later chapter on ''Conscience,'' in which reconciliation between
consciousnesses facilitates reconciliation of consciousness and the world. The alienations of Faith will only finally be overcome in the ultimate state of religious community, probably typified by Lutheranism as Hegel idealized it—a religion of love
which so successfully synthesizes the secular and divine spheres that it will no longer
be necessary to make a choice between being in or not in, of or not of, that world,
although it will still be necessary to transcend the imaginative representations of religion.

Whom did Hegel have in mind in drawing up this contrast between Insight and
Faith? Hyppolite (Genesis and Structure, p. 428) suggests, plausibly, that

Insight is especially exemplified in Montesquieu, who in his Persian Letters
*(1721) offers witty critiques of French morals, ecclesiastical superstitions and dog-
mas, and political tyranny through the eyes of two fictitious Persian tourists. It is
more difficult to discern whom Hegel might have been thinking of as the typical
"man of Faith," if indeed he had any particular individual in mind. A possible can-
didate, although several generations prior to Montesquieu, is Blaise Pascal
(1623–1662), whom Hegel considered to be a deep, if overly popularizing, philosopher. In Pascal's philosophy, we are never left in any doubt as to the relative superiority of Faith over "natural," unaided intellect or insight: for "God prefers rather
to incline the will than the intellect. Perfect clearness would be of use to the intellect
and would harm the will"* (Pensée 581). *And if we ever have any doubts about
Faith, Jesus tells us, says Pascal, "Ask thy confessor, when My own words are to
thee occasion of evil, vanity, or curiosity"* (Pensée 553). *And in Pensée 294,
as if cognizant of the anti-establishment forces already gaining momentum in
France, he warns about the futility of the ideal of revolutions doing away with positive laws and institutions (whether ecclesiastical or civil) to arrive at some "natural
foundation" of justice.*

As the successors to both the Distraught Consciousness and the Honest Consciousness stand *Insight and Faith.*

The believing consciousness, or Faith, goes one step beyond the Honest Consciousness, which insisted on harking back to the pristine
harmony, unity and reconciliation found in the past, as if these former
standards might supply guidelines for the present. Since the world of
Culture is *so far removed* from these standards, Faith (perhaps with more
logic than the Honest Consciousness) makes a clean break with Culture
and posits another higher, heavenly, ideal world (mystically but only
partially encapsulated in the sensible actualities of this world) as the
proper substantial "object" of its aspirations.

Before proceeding any further, we should take pains here to emphasize that Faith is not something unconscious or instinctual, but a type of
consciousness:

Faith is pure consciousness of essence, i.e., of simple interiority. And thus it is *ipso facto* thinking. In fact, thought is the most important aspect in the nature of Faith [109]—
albeit the aspect that is usually overlooked.[110]

---

109. Regarding Hegel's later rebuttal of Jacobi's notion that faith is a type of instinct,
see Reardon, *Hegel's Philosophy of Religion*, pp. 80, 84. See also *Philosophy of Mind*, §554
and *Logic* §63, Remark.
110. B289, H379: *Er ist hiemit zwar reines Bewusstsein des* Wesens, *d.h. des* einfachen

As a type of consciousness, however, the most notable quality of Faith is that it holds fast to essential *Being*[111] (i.e., the essence that was at first[112] characterized as the Good although it was not at that time portrayed as a thought-actuality) in a relatively *immediate* and direct manner, i.e., through imagination rather than through ratiocination and conceptualization.

Both Faith and Insight are double negations, rebellions against the pure negative rebelliousness of the Distraught Consciousness, attempts to reassert stability within a dialectic running wild, affirmations of the vanity of such mere dialectical vanity. Faith, however, accomplishes its double negation by turning away from the sharp sallies of self-conscious thought to a simple awareness, unruffled by conflict, of its absolute object. Insight, at least initially, accomplishes its double negation by pointing out and mastering the alienations of the Cultural World, while trying (vainly) to avoid being itself contaminated by such alienations. Thus Faith takes on a positive aspect, as that which simply posits and *affirms* an Absolute Essence transcending this world; while Insight assumes a negative aspect, as that which more openly mirrors that which it is fleeing from, namely, the restless processes of mediation through which the various "good" and "bad" elements of the world of Culture become constantly transformed into each other.

This latter negativity, this consciousness of the transformation of one actual moment into the other, in the actual world, is "insight" in a very special, paradigmatic sense: It is concerned with showing conceptually that the essential is unessential, the good is bad, that everything that pretends to subsistence in the Cultural World can be subsumed in one way or another into the restless mediating activities of the ego, which wants to establish itself as *the* universal.[113] Thus we have grounds here

---

Innern *und* ist *also Denken,* —*das Hauptmoment in der Natur des Glaubens, das gewöhnlich übersehen wird.*

111. Cf. Pascal, *Pensée* 277: "The heart has its reasons, which reason does not know," leading it to love "the Universal Being."

112. See preceding section, p. 41.

113. While Faith as the attempt of Consciousness to maintain its integrity in Culture is oriented to unity and Being, Insight as the response of highly individual *Self-Consciousness* to Culture is oriented towards thought-conditioned Universality. This is a usual pattern in Hegel's dialectic: Inner-oriented and reflective Self-Consciousness emphasizes the mediation of particulars through universal concepts, while object-oriented Consciousness emphasizes a relatively immediate relationship to Being in its state of unity "prior to" any differentiations that will be disclosed in it (see *Philosophy of Mind,*

for the struggles that eventually will have to take place when the simple repose of Faith is disturbed, challenged and attacked by the more self-conscious and intellectual attitude of thought manifested by Insight.

(1) Faith and (2) Insight each can be considered in terms of the three following "moments": (a) in itself; (b) in relation to the Cultural World; and (c) in relation to the opposite attitude.

[1(a) *Faith considered in itself*] is oriented toward essential Being, and marks a progression beyond the devotion of the Unhappy Consciousness and the piety of the family of a departed Shade, in earlier stages. But although Faith both here and in the Unhappy Consciousness is an alienated attitude, nevertheless, in contrast with the Unhappy Consciousness, which was a subjective and *unsubstantial* type of consciousness, (Catholic) Faith proceeds from the very substance of the Cultural World; and in contrast to familial piety, which proceeded in a positive way from the Ethical Substance, (Catholic) Faith bears a rather negative or antithetical relationship to the actual World, and is positively oriented only to the essential being-in-and-for itself, as a "beyond" which pervades and transcends the actual world. If we examine this being-in-and-for-itself more closely, we find that it is not the mere universality of thought-forms which characterized the earlier stage of Stoicism, nor is it the mere Ideal that was sought by the Virtuous Consciousness, nor is it the universal Law which was the prized object of Legislative Reason. Rather, it appears as a real content, just as real as the actual world of Culture, and as emerging from this actual world rather than from the intellectual discriminations of consciousness. In order to understand *how* this notion of Absolute Being can be both a negative Beyond and a positive present content; a universal which is continually dissolving the opposed distinctions of the World and yet a static and stable essential content; a historical and factual reality which nevertheless *transcends* all determinate facts—we must analyze the special (Trinitarian) character that attaches to the Absolute at this point: In the Trinity, Faith encounters (*i*) an absolute self-comprehending Spirit; which (*ii*) becomes objectively for-another, and thus sacrifices its self-identity; and (*iii*) returns from this self-alienation into its primal simplicity.[114] To

§455). However, no hard and fast distinction is implied. The Being that is the object of Faith is a *universal* Being, and the Universal produced by Insight manifests the existence or *Being* of Spirit.

114. The inner interrelationships of the Trinity are examined by Hegel in more detail in

the believing consciousness, this means that the transcendence of spirit has "emptied itself out" in the sphere of concrete actuality, entered into the world and history (through the Incarnation), and yet has returned, and is continually returning, to itself (through the Holy Spirit). Those of us who observe the development of this notion as just one phenomenological stage will naturally have questions about the possibility of maintaining the personhood of the triune spirits simultaneously with their disappearance into, and union with, one another, and we will also tend to interpret the triune relationship as a dialectically necessary apprehension for this type of consciousness at this stage.[115] But for the consciousness which is actually involved in the standpoint of Faith, the distinction into three divine persons is seen as distinct from the overall unity, and the presence of the Absolute is an immediate and quasi-empirical "fact" rather than a developmental necessity.

[1 (b) Faith in relation to the actual world of Culture.] The believing type of consciousness sees conceptual determinations in the practical and theoretical spheres as a squandering of its thought-energy. It tries to attain unity with the essential source of this thought-energy, by means of *service* and *praise*.[116] From its lofty spiritual vantage point, it looks down on the *esprit* and wit of the estranged self-consciousness, and sees his world of culture as a soulless world. But *qua* individual self-consciousness, it can never succeed in comprehending the absolute unity it seeks after—especially in the spatial and temporal forms which that absolute unity

---

the later section on "Revealed Religion" (see below, p. 161ff.). See also *Philosophy of History*, p. 324.

115. This distinction between the viewpoint of us phenomenological observers and the viewpoint of the consciousness being examined (see K42 ff.) is implicit throughout the *Phenomenology*, and sometimes pointed out explicitly, as is the case here and also later, in the chapter on Revealed Religion, in which the ways the believer and the philosopher who goes beyond belief to conceptual synthesis differ. The main distinction in the two points of view is that while the philosophical phenomenologist sees the Christian dogmas such as the Trinity as necessary developments out of a certain maturity of consciousness, the believer sees them as "happenings," or free contingencies.

116. Note the similarity between the Noble Consciousness' Heroism of Service and Heroism of Flattery in the preceding section with the believing consciousness' service and praise of the Absolute here. For the Noble who wanted to avoid the sacrifices and risk of life that were considered "heroic", and/or heroic but degrading flattery, the service and praise of God might provide a fittingly sublimated calling. And *de facto*, the upper echelons of the influential Catholic religious orders and ecclesiastical hierarchy in the seventeenth and eighteenth centuries were heavily populated with those of noble blood.

takes in "emptying itself out" (since sensuous actuality is *ipso facto* uncomprehended). In the form of universal self-consciousness (the "religious community"),[117] however, it will eventually approximate this unity it desires.

[*1 (c) Faith in relation to the attitude of Insight.*] Faith becomes an object to be mediated by the attitude of Insight—as does everything else—since explicit conceptual thought (as manifested by Insight) is the absolute mediating force.

[*2 (a) Insight in itself*] is the effort of consciousness to reduce everything not to the immediacy of essence, but to a mediated and objectified form of the *self*, which is absolute for it. Thus it tends to cancel every form of independence—whether this is found in the "objective world" or in the immanence of consciousness—and bring it within the scope of the self. Likewise, it tends to dissolve all distinctions—whether these are real express determinations in the world, or subjective qualities like "genius" and "talents"—and bring them into the unity of absolute self-knowledge in the world of culture, as the universal achievement, and universal possession of all. "*Individuality*," according to this aspect of consciousness, is a mere quantitative determination, which like everything else, is brought into the self-identity of the absolute realized notion of self, where all otherness, including the otherness of quantitative difference, has already been transformed into qualitative distinctions (with the advent of the Distraught Consciousness), and now is being systematically canceled (with the advent of Insight).[118] If we were to sum up the essence of this strictly immanent and self-conscious standpoint in a summary dictum, it would go something like this: "be for yourself that which you are already are intrinsically: namely, rational."[119] This very subjective maxim is the *universal* intention (*Absicht*) which now comes to the forefront in Insight (*Einsicht*), as Insight endeavors to bring the essence of

---

117. See below, p. 154, the section on "Revealed Religion."

118. The important thing now is not individuality as a set of natural endowments, even though this admittedly produces quantitative differences in degree between people, but what self-realizing Insight can do with itself in a world where Culture or education is everything.

119. We have seen a preliminary formulation of this dictum earlier in the stage of Subjective/Objective Individuality (*die Sache selbst*: see K126 ff.), and will see it again later especially as a theme in the section on "conscientousness" (*infra*, pp. 111 ff.). Taylor (*Hegel*, p. 14ff. and *passim*) calls this basic idea, which is a kind of moral maxim, "expressivism," an orientation which was characteristic of Hegel's intellectual milieu and is a presupposition throughout the *Phenomenology*.

Culture into existence as the common possession of, and achievement of, *all*. Insight has become pure and universal Insight (Enlightenment).

II. Enlightenment.
[The Pyrrhic Victory of Insight over Faith]

Introductory Remarks:

We are about to witness the victory of Insight over Faith; but, as was the case earlier with the victory of the Weltlauf *over the Knight of Faith (see K124–5), and more recently with the victories of Human Law over Divine Law (supra, pp. 27 ff.), the "victory" is an ironical and dialectical one, because the victor is in a sense vanquished.*

The victory of Insight is attained essentially by means of the process of "Enlightenment," i.e., by the universal diffusion of Insight. (Note that Hegel gives a special technical meaning to "Enlightenment"—pure, universal Insight—as he has also given a special technical meaning to "Insight"—the ability to mediate contradictions conceptually). The "universal diffusion" of Insight is accomplished not by anything so overt as an advertising campaign or a campaign of propaganda, but by a subtle and almost imperceptible movement of, and to, Self-Consciousness throughout the entirety of Culture. The realization that the individual himself is the power behind good and evil, nobility and ignobility, state power and economic progress becomes not just the privileged "insight" of a few astute consciousnesses, but, like an infection or contagion, encompasses all, even the champions of Faith who were so opposed to Insight. Like the proverbial "idea whose time has come," there is no resisting Insight as it becomes potentiated into the awesome enthusiasm of the Enlightenment. This discovery of man, which will reach its culmination in a disclosure of the modern concept of freedom, is like the discovery of a New World, a discovery in which all the masses participate and for which they are willing to take the responsibility.

However, as was mentioned above, the Enlightenment, while victorious, is also conquered, in the sense that in order to achieve the acceptability and universality required for victory, it finds it necessary to incorporate many of the ideas that were formerly the province of Faith: the notion of a Supreme Being, now stripped of anthropomorphic or mythic trappings; the eschatological idea of a future heaven, now transformed into earthly eudaemonism and utopianism; and the perception of sensory objects as invested with sacred significance, now suitably metamorphosed into a new utilitarian version of object-worship.

In his History of Philosophy *III, p. 387, Hegel says that the German* Aufklärung *is a continuation of the Enlightenment begun in France by Voltaire, Montesquieu, Rousseau, D'Alembert and Diderot. In lumping together so many figures with such different viewpoints, Hegel is emphasizing one of the few things on which all these figures would find enthusiastic agreement:* Superstition is the greatest antagonist of cultural progress, and must be vanquished at all costs, because as superstition is vanquished all other evils (tyranny, social injustice, provincialism) will fall by the wayside.

[2 *(b)* Insight in relation to the world] is of three types:[120] (i) A tranquil but only implicit union[121] of insight (*Einsicht*) *and* intention (*Absicht*), attained by means of a retreat from the actual world into pure consciousness; also (ii) the restless, scattered (*zerstreut*) type of Insight,[122] which is unable to extricate its contingent (*zufällig*), single consciousness from the sphere of isolated "special" (*besondere*) insights, where it finds all to be vanity, broken pieces, worthy only of caustic, witty criticism (as an expression of the true situation). The successor to this antithesis is (iii) universal Insight (Enlightenment), a third type of consciousness[123] which is finally enabled to realize its still unrealized *universal* intention (*Absicht*). This type of Insight wants, like Faith, to rise above the contra-

---

120. Hegel continues here the tripartite division of Insight that he began in the previous section (see M§535, H381). The relation of Insight to the "vain consciousness" of the actual world begins in M§538, H383; the relation of Insight to Faith begins in M§541, H385.

121. The brief and cryptic reference to a "tranquil consciousness" in M§529 (H383) presupposes a long train of developments: A simple, honest, *ruhiges Bewusstsein* emerges in M§§521–524 (H372–374), rises above the contradictions of Culture and attains implicit self-identity in M§526 (H376), attains to "unreal actuality" in M§527 (H377), takes on the temporarily alienated form of Faith without any special insight in M§529 (H379), but comes to the vestibule of an explicit universal self towards the end of M§537 (H383).

122. Cf. the "vain consciousness," M§526 (H375).

123. Hyppolite (*Genesis and Structure*, p. 428) points out that this third, "enlightened" type of consciousness is especially exemplified in the Voltaire of the *Philosophical Dictionary* (1764) (a work which through the medium of dictionary definitions outlines many of the positions which will be ascribed to the Enlightenment in the present section, e.g., deism, anticlericalism, social utilitarianism).

When Hegel speaks here of a "compilation" or "collection" (*Sammlung*) as a product of the more sophisticated universal Insight now emerging, one thinks also of Diderot's *Dictionnaire encyclopédique*, a massive undertaking which was able to include even the eclecticism of Diderot's predecessors and contemporaries (proponents of "scattered" Insight) within its scope. (There is a long and laudatory article on *"Eclectisme"* in Diderot's Encyclopedia.)

dictions and confusion (*Verwirrung*) of the actual world, and also to exist as *Pure* Consciousness, like Faith; but *not* at the expense of self-consciousness. In order to accomplish this goal, it becomes a second-order Insight, an Insight about Insight, which is not content in simply reflecting the alienations of the world in a haphazard manner, and is not satisfied with mere spontaneous and extemporaneous expressions of "judging wittily" and "knowing better," but wishes to go beyond all such "special Insights" to a comprehension of the totality of special Insights possessed by the Cultural Consciousness, and strives to perpetuate both this comprehension and its peculiar cultural mode of expression in suitably comprehensive ways, especially through the device of literary compilation (*Die Sammlung*).

The survival of the attitude of Insight thus takes place by the resolution of both the former types of Insight into the third kind—*universal Insight* (Enlightenment), the universal Insight of all—which superimposes the unified view of the placid Insight over the specialized focus of the perturbed Insight. And the peculiar nature of this sublimated form of Insight will become evident as it begins to deal with Faith, which still stands forth as a knowledge of essential content.

a. The Struggle of Enlightenment with Superstition

[*2 (c) Insight in relation to Faith:*] Faith, in its essential nature, holds onto thought-content as Absolute Being, and allows every moment in this content to attain its unperturbed subsistence. However, as a *self-deceiving* insight subsisting in the cultural world, it perceives its content as an *object* (that which negates the self), and indeed is actively productive of an *objective* religious organization; and likewise, in putting its trust in the Absolute Being, and holding fast to this latter as another self whose disparate parts are gathered together in an existence-for-self, it is attaining something of self-consciousness, but by a rational *projection* of self. Thus it is not completely divorced from the proper characteristics of Insight: negativity, productivity, thought-activity, self-consciousness, and the attempt to overcome alienation.

Insight, on its own side, is properly engaged in the constant explicit negation of all distinctions of content—and now stands outside all content.[124] It is joined with Faith at its roots, i.e., as a co-aspect of cultural

---

124. Bonsiepen (*Der Begriff der Negativität*, p. 167) compares Insight to the abstractness of the Understanding, Faith to the concreteness of Perception: "In the battle of the

consciousness; but it accurately perceives Faith as a naive, false perversion of Insight[125]—which makes into an object what is not an object, etc. This "perverted insight" is further seen as having triplex form:

i. the bad, naive insight of the *multitude*;

ii. the conceit of the *priesthood*, which adds to this bad insight its own bad intention (*Absicht*) and becomes its self-conscious protector and perpetuator;[126]

iii. the craftiness of *despotism*, which at first allies itself with the priesthood, and takes on the aspect of a synthetic, crude unity of the aspirations of the multitude and the self-serving machinations of the priests, and then begins to despise them both (multitude and priesthood) for their stupidity, naiveté, and error.[127]

The combat of Insight with Faith now takes on a double form.

[2 (c)-1.] . . . *Insight as inherently one with Faith* (as springing from the identical pure consciousness) is able to affect it immediately by an interpenetration of sorts. Being itself now raised to the universality of *Enlightenment,* however, it does not direct itself to the particularity of the priesthood or of the despot, but rather to the bad insight of the naive multitude, which alone has that *universality* which renders it the true diametrical opposite of Enlightened Insight.[128] It affects this naive, grass-roots

pure Insight of the Enlightenment with Faith, it becomes evident that Faith has not extracted itself from the standpoint of Perception and pure Insight remains obdurately fixed in the conceit of the Understanding."

125. Randall (*Making of the Modern Mind,* p. 292) quotes from a letter of Diderot to Damilaville which illustrated the sort of animosity to Faith that pervaded the Enlightenment: "The Christian religion is to my mind the most absurd and atrocious in its dogmas . . . , the most flat, the most dreary, the most Gothic, and the most gloomy in its ceremonies . . . Lutheranism, freed from some absurdities, is preferable to Catholicism, Protestantism (Calvinism) to Lutheranism, Socinianism to Protestantism, Deism, with temples and ceremonies, to Socinianism. . . . "

126. Cf. Voltaire, *Philosophical Dictionary* I, p. 552: "God keep us from an abominable priest who should hew a king in pieces with his sacrificing knife, as also from him who, with a helmet on his head and a cuirass on his back, at the age of seventy, should dare to sign with his three bloody fingers the excommunication of a king of France! and from . . . and from . . . [*sic*]."

127. Cf. *ibid.*: "But also, may God preserve us from a choleric and barbarous despot, who, not believing in a God, should be his own God, who should render himself unworthy of his sacred trust by trampling on the duties which that trust imposes, who should remorselessly sacrifice to his passions, his friends, his relatives, his servants, and his people. These two tigers, the priest and the despot, the one shorn, the other crowned are equally to be feared. By what means shall we muzzle them? . . . "

128. The idea that only the masses have prerequisite universality to receive the message of Enlightenment is curiously paralleled by Marx's theory that only the proletariat, be-

insight much like a new scent begins to pervade a room: there can be no defenses put up against it, and those present suddenly find themselves inhaling it.[129] Thus the naive, bad insight is slowly, inconspicuously affected by the tendency of simple, self-reflective negativity which it shares in common with true Insight. When the believers finally perceive their condition, it is too late to do anything about it. Overnight, the "old idols" are overthrown:

> The Enlightenment as an invisible and imperceptible spirit infiltrates stealthily throughout the vital parts of the believing consciousness and before you know it is in absolute control of all the organs and innards of the unconscious idols of that consciousness. And then *"on one fine morning* [the new proprietor] gives its companion the elbow, and crash! bam! the old idol is lying on the ground." —"On *one fine morning,"* whose noon is unbloody, simply because the infection has so thoroughly penetrated all the organs of the life of Spirit. And now only memory still preserves the dead form of the previous stage [*Gestalt*] of Spirit, like a history that, somehow or other, has run its course. And the new serpent of divine wisdom which is elevated for worship has thus, when you come down to it, merely painlessly shed its wrinkled old skin.[130]

[2 (c)-2.]Insight as the antithesis of the world of Faith, however, takes up a different tactic. It examines the attitude of Faith towards Absolute Being, and (*i*) shows this up as being a mere production of self-consciousness, a self-distinction autonomously produced by consciousness. At

---

ing the focal point at which all the alienations converge, has the universality necessary to be the class that is to conduct the revolution. In "A Contribution to the Critique of Hegel's 'Philosophy of Right, '" Marx concludes: "Our answer [is] in the formation of a class with radical chains, a class in civil society that is not of civil society, a class that is the dissolution of all classes, a sphere of society having a universal character because of its universal suffering . . . " (See the Appendix to Marx's *Critique of Hegel's 'Philosophy of Right',* O'Malley tr. (Cambridge, 1970).

129. In this regard Hegel may have in mind, among other things, the immense popularity and universal dissemination of Voltaire's writings.

130. *B*295–296, H388: . . . *nun ein unsichtbarer und unbemerkter Geist, durchschleicht sie die edeln Teile durch und durch, und hat sich bald aller Eingeweide und Glieder des bewusstlosen Götzen gründlich bemächtigt, und* "an einem schönen Morgen *gibt sie mit dem Ellbogen dem Kameraden einen Schub, und bauz! baradauz! der Götze liegt am Boden.''* —An einem schönen Morgen, *dessen Mittag nicht blutig ist, wenn die Ansteckung alle Organe des geistigen Lebens durchdrungen hat; nur das Gedächtnis bewahrt dann noch als eine, man weiss nicht wie, vergangene Geschichte die tote Weise der vorigen Gestalt des Geistes auf; und die neue für die Anbetung erhöhte Schlange der Weisheit hat auf diese Weise nur eine welke Haut schmerzlos abgestreift.*

This passage is a variation on the following passage from Diderot's *Rameau's Nephew:* "The foreign god takes his place humbly next to the native idol, little by little asserts itself and one fine day elbows his fellow—before you can say Jack Robinson, there's the idol flat on its back.''

the same time, it (*ii*) sees the contents of Faith as a bit of hocus-pocus foisted on the believing multitude by a conjuring priesthood. But here it gets into *internal self-contradiction*. For (*i*) the attitude of Enlightenment is *supposed* to represent explicit averment of the *category*—the fact that *everything* is the product of consciousness.[131] In essential alliance with this category, Faith denies that this "reduction of the Absolute to consciousness" is something inherently hostile to, and the negative of, its attitude (since its highest aspiration is to find itself in this Absolute). Insight, on the other hand, in contravention of the category, now finds itself deriding one of its most essential procedures—the knowledge of oneself in and through the object. Also (*ii*) the assertion that the multitude of believers has an *alien* essence imposed on it by the priesthood obviously contradicts the contention that Faith is just producing "Absolute Being" out of its *own* essence. Thus Enlightenment, the would-be harbinger of truth to the world, shows itself up in this manner as a conscious lie, through such self-contradictions. And growing awareness of such self-contradictions will bring with it a concomitant awareness of the negativity of the self which is producing such contradictions. Insight will see that, in refusing to recognize its own inner nature, it is negating itself, i.e., becoming unreasonableness instead of insight, insincerity instead of pure intention (*Absicht*). The attempt to negate this unwelcome negation will eventually result in renewed self-possession.[132] But we must now pass from these general considerations to a more specific consideration of the interpenetration of Faith and Enlightenment in the three moments essential to Faith.

With regard to the three "moments" of Faith (*Absolute Being, Knowledge of Absolute Being, and Service*), Enlightenment takes on some initial manifestations of critical negativity, all based on misunderstanding:

(*i*) *With regard to Absolute Being itself*: The attitude of Faith *rightly* sees

---

131. Cf. *B*296, H389: "What is not rational [i.e. a manifestation of the unity of thought and being], has no *truth*; what has not been [rationally] conceptualized does not exist." [*Was nicht vernünftig ist, hat keine* Wahrheit, *oder was nicht begriffen ist,* ist *nicht: . . .*] This statement is a forerunner of Hegel's later statement in the Preface to his *Philosophy of Right* that "the rational is real, and the real is the rational." As here applied, the implication is that if Faith is, indeed, uniting thought with being, even by means of "projections" (to use current psychoanalytic terminology), it is proving itself to be eminently "rational" (in the Hegelian sense of reason), and thus should not be criticized by Insight, the purported champion of Reason.

132. This moment of negative self-possession is Absolute Freedom, treated in the next section.

thought itself as the only essential Reality, but overly objectifies this Reality, giving to it the form of an object which is merely "found" in the world, or even depicted in the imagination, without being an adequate object for the mind (a concept). Enlightened Insight, however, which prides itself on its high degree of self-consciousness and uses sense objects to enhance that self-consciousness by contrast, mistakenly thinks the believing consciousness is doing the same thing as Insight itself is used to doing. Thus it misinterprets the attitude, and thinks that the believing consciousness has for its object a stone,[133] or a host of bread,[134] or wood.[135] But on the contrary, these things do not even exist in themselves for the true believer, into whose internal attitude it is so hard for the man of "Insight" to place himself.[136]

(*ii*) *With regard to the knowledge of Absolute Being*: The attitude of Faith, *qua* thinking consciousness, has its quasi-object ("mediating" thought itself) *immediately* present to it as Being. And in regards to this immediate presence, it is impossible for Faith to be deceived.

> It is impossible to deceive the people in a matter like this. Brass may be passed off as gold, counterfeit money may occasionally be passed off as the real thing, a lost battle may be construed for the multitude as a victory, and other sundry lies about sense objects and particular happenings may be taken for the truth for a considerable period of time. But when it comes to the question of this knowledge of Being in which the believing consciousness attains a direct *certainty of itself*, all conjectures about the possibility of deception fall by the wayside.[137]

But the immediate certainty that thus ensues must be developed into *truth*, into an adequately and explicitly mediated form.[138] In other

---

133. Statues, altar stones.

134. The consecrated host in the Catholic Mass.

135. For example, large wooden crucifixes commonly affixed above altars or smaller ones kissed as objects of devotion.

136. On the "force field" that comes to pervade objects of worship for believers, cf. Aldous Huxley, the *Perennial Philosophy* (N.Y.: Harper & Row, 1970), p. 59 f.

137. B299, H392: . . . *es unmöglich ist, hierin ein Volk zu täuschen. —Messing statt Golds, nachgemachte Wechsel statt echter mögen wohl einzeln verkauft, eine verlorne Schlacht als eine gewonnene Mehrern aufgeheftet, und sonstige Lugen über sinnliche Dinge und einzelne Begebenheiten auf eine Zeitlang glaubhaft gemacht werden; aber in dem Wissen von dem Wesen, worin das Bewusstsein die unmittelbare Gewissheit seiner selbst hat, fällt der Gedanke der Täuschung ganz hinweg.*

138. Faith, in holding on to "divine" *thought* in an external, "projected" form, already preeminently possesses the power of mediation, since thinking is mediation. But Faith's "mediation" through imagination is of an imperfect sort, an ambiguous, "immediate" form of mediation *via* tokens and symbols. Faith must be elevated to explicit (i.e. *conceptual*) mediation.

words, the valid internal *ground* for Faith must become *explicit*. Enlightenment, on its side, failing to recognize this counterpart of its own certainty, interprets Faith's explication of grounds as a purely external process, as an "other"—and thus naturally tends to ascribe Faith to some external, contingent historical event (e.g., the coming of the Messiah), concerning which we would be dependent on the accuracy of interpretation of, and transcription and translation of, original texts. Such things, of course, could never constitute true grounds for Faith.

> Faith in its certainty is an ingenuous relationship to its absolute object, a pure knowledge of this object which does not interpolate [considerations about] written characters, documents and transcribers into its consciousness of Absolute Being, and does not mediate itself with the Absolute by dint of things like that. For Faith is Spirit itself, which gives its own testimony about itself, just as forcefully in the inwardness of the individual consciousness as through the universal presence of the Faith of the whole religious community in this Spirit.[139]

In other words, the grounds for Faith are constantly to be sought in the inner experience of the believing consciousness and in the shared experience of the community of believers. But the believers, unfortunately, sometimes show how infected they themselves are by the spirit of Enlightenment, and try to provide "historical proofs" for the validity of their religious commitment.[140]

---

139. *B*301, H394-5: . . . *er ist in seiner Gewissheit unbefangenes Verhältnis zu seinem absoluten Gegenstande, ein reines Wissen desselben, welches nicht Buchstaben, Papier und Abschreiber in sein Bewusstsein des absoluten Wesens einmischt und nicht durch solcherlei Dinge sich damit vermittelt. Sondern dies Bewusstsein ist der sich selbst vermittelnde Grund seines Wissens; es ist der Geist selbst, der das Zeugnis von sich ist, ebenso im* Innern *des* einzelnen *Bewusstseins als durch die* allgemeine Gegenwart *des Glaubens Aller an ihn.*

Hegel's defense of the inwardness of Faith here is so similar to Kierkegaard's emphasis on the inwardness of faith (cf. e.g. *Fear and Trembling* [Lowrie tr., Princeton, 1974] p. 79), that one is astonished to hear Kierkegaard say (*ibid*): "In the Hegelian philosophy *das Äussere (die Entäusserung)* [(the outer,) (the external)] is higher than *das Innere* ["the inner"] . . . Faith, on the contrary, is the paradox that inwardness is higher than outwardness." However, though there is a definite (Protestant) homology of thought in both Kierkegaard and Hegel in this matter, there is also a difference which becomes apparent in the last clause of the quotation from Hegel. In Hegel, here and elsewhere, there is insistence on the fact that the inwardness of Faith is not just a personal matter but should be expressed in the Religious community, i.e., a community of love. However, this is not to *subordinate* the "outer" to the "inner."

140. Some would-be champions of Faith, like the "Knight of Virtue" earlier (see K124) are reduced to the ignoble expedient of having to borrow weapons from their enemy. The only sort of "weapons" which the Enlightenment provides is the use of human ingenuity to compile impressive natural, empirical, nonsupernatural data. And, of course, those who ground their Faith in such explanations fall right into the hands of

(iii) With regard to the service of Absolute Being: The believing consciousness simply unites its own purposiveness (intention, *Absicht*) with its own
insight regarding means: It desires to experience independence from en-
tanglement with enjoyment and pleasure; therefore it fasts and denies
itself pleasure.[141] It desires to affirm the essential unity of itself with all
others; therefore it gives up private possessions,[142] and thus belittles the

---

their enlightened enemies, since all such explanations or proofs are beside the point
when it comes to the essential inner experience of Faith.

The inadmissibility of historical proofs for Faith is reiterated even more strongly and
clearly by Hegel in later works, e.g. *Philosophy of History,* pp. 325–6, 331. Hegel seemed
to have in mind not only Jesuits and others who used this approach in Christian apolo-
getics, but contemporary (German) theologians who were still infected with the spirit of
the Enlightenment. Pascal, whom we referred to earlier as an example of the position of
Faith, is also an early precursor for the sort of infection mentioned here. For example,
Pascal devotes Section XI of his *Pensées* to a minute and tedious analysis of Old Testament prophecies to establish the truth of the Christian religion, and looks to evidence of
miracles as a kind of necessary grounding for faith: "How I hate those who make men
doubt of miracles. . . . The church is without proofs if they are right. . . . But it is not possible to have a reasonable belief against miracles" (*Pensées* 813, 815); "Jesus Christ
performed miracles, and the Apostles also, who converted all the heathen; and all the
prophecies being thereby fulfilled, the Messiah is forever proved" (*Pensée* 616).

Reardon (*Hegel's Philosophy of Religion*, p. 111) points out the basic reason why the historical approach, however laudable in other contexts, is considered by Hegel to be compromising to the Christian apologist: " 'History occupies itself with truths that *were*
truths' [says Hegel in the *Philosophy of Religion*]; but with the real content of dogma (i.e.
the knowledge of God) the historian of theology has no concern." Similar sentiments are
echoed recurrently in the writings of the putative defender of Christianity against
Hegelian speculation, Kierkegaard, who for example, says in his *Philosophical Fragments*
(Swenson tr., Princeton, 1962), pp. 73–5: "Though a contemporary learner readily becomes an historical eye-witness, the difficulty is that the knowledge of some historical
circumstance, or indeed a knowledge of all the circumstances with the reliability of an
eye-witness, does not make such an eye-witness a disciple; which is apparent from the
fact that this knowledge has merely historical significance for him. We see at once that
the historical in the more concrete sense is a matter of indifference; we may suppose a degree of ignorance with respect to it, and permit this ignorance as if to annihilate one detail after the other, historically annihilating the historical; if only the Moment [of Faith]
remains, as point of departure for the Eternal, the Paradox will be there . . . As long as
the Eternal and the historical are external to one another, the historical is merely an occasion."

141. As in the fasts of the Lenten season or Advent, or in the prescribed fasts and pen-
ances of Catholic religious orders. Cf. also Pascal, *Pensée* 286: "Those who believe
without having read the Testaments . . . desire only to love God; they desire to hate
themselves." Or as in celibacy, whose extreme exemplification was the self-castration
of Origen (see M§570).

142. As in the vow or practice of poverty in the community life of the Franciscans, Do-
minicans, and Jesuits.

necessity of isolation and individual exclusiveness in human life. Enlightenment, on its side, as the champion of self-consciousness, harbors the "pure intention" of rising above natural existence—but criticizes Faith for actually trying to put this intention into effect. Thus it shows itself stupid in criticizing Faith's simple adaptation of means to end, and in addition gravitates towards "pure intentions" which are quite impure (since it *de facto* ascribes the ultimate value to finite enjoyment and possessions).

If it is demanded of Enlightenment that it go beyond its mere criticism of the three essential moments of Faith to state its own positive tenets, the following three countertheses emerge:

(*i*) It reacts to the tendency of Faith to ascribe *specific attributes* to the Absolute, by relegating all particularity and determinations to the universality of its own self-purposes and self-consciousness. Having thus despoiled the Absolute of its attributes, it naturally begins to view the Absolute of the believing consciousness as an *empty, self-less void*, married to empty universal predicates.[143] It proclaims the universe of particularities and limitations (the determinations that used to be ascribed to God) as its own proper domain.[144] And thus it hopes to prevent any future con-

---

143. Cf. Pascal, *Pensée* 556: "The worship of a God considered as great, powerful, and eternal [i.e., purely in terms of abstract attributes] . . . is strictly deism, almost as far removed from the Christian religion as atheism, which is the exact opposite." As deism developed it became associated not only with a very abstract idea of a Supreme Being (*Être suprême*), but also with the notion that this Supreme Being runs the world in a very business-like way through natural laws, absolutely avoids any kind of miracles, would not think of accepting sacrifices or human praise, but furthers morality by rewarding good deeds and punishing evil. Voltaire (who preferred to be called a "theist" rather than a deist) sums up some of the basic tenets of deism in his article on "God" in the *Philosophical Dictionary*: "My reason alone proves to me a being who has arranged the matter of this world; but my reason is unable to prove to me that he made this matter— that he brought it out of nothing. All the stages of antiquity, without exception, believed matter to be eternal, and existing by itself. All then that I can do, without the aid of superior light, is to believe that the God of the world is also eternal, and existing by Himself . . . . We feel that we are under the hand of an invisible being; this is all; we cannot advance one step further. It is mad temerity to seek to define what this being is—whether he is extended or not, whether he is in one place or not, how he exists, how he operates . . . . I say to you: Continue to cultivate virtue, to be beneficent, to regard all superstition with horror, or with pity; but adore, with me, the design which is manifested in all nature [the basis for the teleological proof for the existence of God], and consequently the Author of that design—the primordial and final cause of all; hope with me that our monad [the thinking part of man], which reasons on the great eternal being, may be happy through that same great Being."
144. It was Feuerbach who, as if trying to act out perfectly the role of the man of Enlight-

f the particular and the Absolute—the sort of confusion that is
:ding ground of superstition.

(*ii*) Enlightenment has traveled a full circle and comes back to *sense-perception* as a kind of Absolute. For sense-perception is the epitome of
that singleness or particularity which is now considered the proper ob-
ject of the enlightened self-consciousness.[145] So there is a certain similarity of this stage to the initial stage in the phenomenology of individual
consciousness, "Sense-Certainty" (Chap. I of the *Phenomenology*). But
whereas in that initial stage the sense object was immediately present,
here it is accepted through mediation; and whereas formerly it gave rise
to opinion, here it gives rise to consciousness of truth. For here we have
otherness in its primordial form—seen as an absolute fulcrum or pivot
for all the cognitive development of self-consciousness, which also itself
becomes absolute precisely in its primordial sensuous existence.

(*iii*) The previous two aspects (*i* and *ii*) are now synthesized: Sense-
facts as otherness-in-general are the Janus-faced boundaries of reality,
the limits of the world, leading naturally at *their* outer limits into the contentless void of the "Beyond." But the *form* of their relationship to *this*
Beyond takes on a dialectical character: Enlightenment begins to deal
with this "Beyond," not now by means of the pristine principles of good
vs. evil, but (at least implicitly) by means of the more abstract and fin-
ished dialectical notions of existence in-self and existence for-another.
Thus at one time sense-facts are taken as an in-itself participating posi-

---

enment described here by Hegel, used this idea as the basic instrument for criticizing
Hegel himself, in his *Essence of Christianity* (1840), whose basic thesis was that the attributes and perfections Christians ascribe to God (or to Hegel's "Absolute Spirit") are
really just projections of basic human qualities, and should be reappropriated consciously by man. This thesis in turn provided the foundation for Marx's own critique of
Hegel, which involved the extension of Feuerbach's demythologization to the secular
sphere (the capitalistic state authority on whom man's productive powers have been
projected) as well as in the religious sphere (see Marx's *1844 Manuscripts* and *Theses on
Feuerbach* [1845]). Thus Marx comes to carry the characteristics of the "enlightened
consciousness" described by Hegel to an extreme, jettisoning the idea of God altogether
instead of just despoiling it in the fashion of the deists, and denying any necessity for the
"State" in the traditional sense of the word.

145. This is the "other side of the coin" with reference to the deistic conception of God.
Having stripped the Absolute of all finite determinations, the deist cannot help but view
real sensory finite things as absolutes themselves, as altogether independent from any
connection with the infinite or spiritual. In the "nonphilosophical" realm, this sort of
emphasis on the finite and the sensory leads to "all the hustle and bustle of contemporary civilization" (*Faith and Knowledge*, p. 63).

tively in the Absolute as the ultimate in-itself which guarantees their permanence and reality; at another time the same sensible reality as a content subject to conscious determinations takes on the aspect of a vanishing and expendable for-itself-which-is-for-another (in imitation of consciousness itself), and becomes related to the Absolute in a negative way, i.e., as its own non-being. But enlightened self-consciousness, through its power of manipulating these two moments, in a sense holds the now bifurcated Absolute in its power.

(iv) This very capability of seeing the intimate dialectical relationship between the in-itself and the for-itself is leading to a "philosophy of utility,"[146] which is the peremptory realization that:

Both perspectives, i.e., the positive as well as the negative relationship of the finite to the Absolute in-itself, are, after all, equally necessary; and in the light of this realization everything becomes in-itself just to the extent that it is for-another. In other words, everything is "useful."—[147] Everything surrenders itself to others, allows itself to be used by others, and is for-these-others. And yet everything also rears itself back, as it were, on its hind legs, hardens its countenance towards these others, is for-itself and uses the other in turn.[148]

The following corollaries will result[149] from this philosophical perspective:

---

146. The "philosophy of utility" is a dialectical development which is the subject of the next section. But Hegel in the next section will concentrate on the way that the philosophy of utility amounts to a final synthesis of Faith and Insight.

147. This is fundamentally an insight about value: Under a philosophy of utility, objects become valuable intrinsically (in-themselves) just precisely insofar as they are useful (for-another).

148. B304, H399: *Beide Betrachtungsweisen, der positiven wie der negativen Beziehung des Endlichen auf das Ansich, sind aber in der Tat gleich notwendig, und alles ist also so sehr an sich, als es für ein anderes ist, oder alles ist nützlich.—Alles gibt sich andern preis, lässt sich jetzt von andern gebrauchen und ist für sie: und jetzt stellt es sich, es so zu sagen, wieder auf die Hinterbeine, tut spröde gegen anderes, ist für sich und gebraucht das andere seinerseits.*

149. Hegel in this section on Enlightenment's struggle with superstition gets ahead of himself. He summarily describes both present and future aspects of Enlightenment's critical stance, and then returns to the present to show in greater detail how the future results actually come about. (We are using the terms "present" and "future" here not in a chronological sense but with regard to the "before" and "after" of phenomenological developments discussed. Chronologically, the philosophy of utility may be developing at the same time as, or even prior to, the split into materialism and idealism that will provide the *final* full-blown emergence of a philosophy of utility in this chapter; but phenomenologically speaking, the philosophy of utility is more "mature" than that split, since it synthesizes them. Concerning the relative independence of the *Phenomenology* from chronology in an ordinary sense, see K10, 24 f.)

(*a*) Everything exists to be used by (to be "for-another" in regard to) other things, and in turn uses these other things.

(*b*) Man, walking in his paradise of pleasure,[150] plucks the fruit of the "tree of knowledge of good and evil." For man in his natural being is good, but the singleness and particularity of his drive for pleasure, after the manner of a natural, contingent entity, stands out, and informs him of his potentiality of distinguishing himself from everything else—even to his own destruction. Thus he develops the "principle of the mean"—which is in reality the principle of immoderation, since its objective is to keep pleasure steady and continuous, and prevent individual persons from "breaking off" from the mainstream of conscious delight by their variety or duration.[151]

(*c*) Men themselves become useful to one another—and cleave to one another as a herd,[152] with the realization that in serving others they are fostering their own interests, and *vice versa*.

(*d*) Finally, as an ultimate conclusion, *Absolute Being* would be the "most profitable of all things,"[153] for it is the source of the absolute value of something as an in-and-for-itself (as having a being all its own), as well as its absolute power to exist for-another (as being enabled continually to throw off the isolation or incommunicability which attaches to the moment of existence-in-self).

---

150. I.e., the eudaemonistic world of utilitarian philosophy.

151. Cf. La Mettrie, *Anti-Seneque, ou discours sur le bonheur*: "Away with all superfluity! The wise man knows only how to despise such superfluity. Oh, a thousand times unhappy is one who adds on to the necessities of nature (which are already overwhelmingly numerous), the superfluous "necessities" of pomp and vanity! To be happy, . . . it suffices to be able to say: 'I love life, because I am satisfied with a few things'. . . . Let us accustom ourselves gradually to being less attached to that which it would be very troublesome for us to have taken away from us; as a result, we will regret it less, when we actually have the misfortune to be deprived of it." See J. O. de la Mettrie, *Oevres Philosophiques*, I/II (Hildesheim: Georg Olms Verlag, 1970), II, p. 144.

152. Cf. Helvétius, *De L'Esprit*, II, 6: "A man is just, when all his actions contribute to the public welfare . . . 'Doing good' is by no means sufficient to earn for a man the title of 'virtuous'. . . . It is exclusively by his talents that a private person can render himself useful and commendable to his country. . . . Posterity does not particularly care if Juvenal was malicious, Ovid dissolute, Hannibal cruel, Lucretius impious, and Caesar the lover of married men: it is solely their talents that posterity judges."

Just as Hegel sees the herd mentality as an offshoot of the doctrine of social utility, Nietzsche, almost a century later, in *Will to Power* and other writings, sees it as a result of egalitarian democratic and socialist ideologies.

153. In conjunction with the philosophy of utility, the deistic God becomes the absolute source of value, hence absolutely "profitable."

Faith, on its side, is utterly appalled at the present and future "positive" implications which it perceives in Enlightenment. It is unwilling to find the epitome of reality in the enjoyment of sense objects, to despoil the Absolute of all concrete determinations to enrich itself, or to look upon Absolute Being as something "profitable" (or on religion as something "useful").[154]

Enlightenment, however, has the upper hand, since as the embodiment of self-conscious negativity it is engaged in producing the *Concept*—whose characteristic is the mediation of opposites:

> Enlightenment in its opposition to Faith shows its colors as pure Insight when, in encountering some determinate moment it catches sight of the totality, and thus brings forth another moment related as an opposite to the former—an activity which brings to the fore the *Concept*, that negative essence of both of the opposing moments which transforms the one into the other.[155]

---

154. The following quote from Diderot exemplifies the utilitarian position opposed by religion: "Supposing one to be initiated in all the mysteries of transubstantiation, consubstantiation, the Trinity, hypostatical union, predestination, incarnation and the rest, *will he be any the better citizen?*" (cited in Randall, *Making of the Modern Mind*, p. 283). The author of the article on *"Christianisme"* in Diderot's *Dictionaire Encyclopédique*, though far from sympathetic to Christianity, takes the same pragmatic position: "Jesus Christ, in proposing his religion to the world, had a nobler intent [than present-day sectarians]—namely, to educate men and make them better. It is this same viewpoint that motivates legislators in enacting laws, when, in order to make them more useful, they prop them up with the dogma of rewards and punishment in the next life. . . . The best religion for a state is the one that best preserves morality: and, since *Christianity* is more advantageous in this respect than other religions, it would be a travesty of sound politics not to employ every expediency that human prudence suggests to foster the progress of Christianity." In contemporary colloquial usage, we would call this a purely "pragmatic" position—especially in view of the fact that Diderot himself was certainly no believer. On the application of the criterion of "utility" to religion, see also Rousseau's *Social Contract* IV, 8.

One might take Pascal's famous "wager" to be a paradigmatic example of religion-as-utility, but Voltaire opts for something more useful in the strict Enlightenment sense (which emphasizes social welfare): "In the state of doubt in which we both are, I do not say to you with Pascal, 'choose the safest.' There is no safety in uncertainty. . . . You yourself [M. Spallanzoni, a translator of the ancient Roman anti-religious philosopher Lucretius] own, in some passages of your work [commentary] that the belief in a God has withheld some men on the brink of crime; for me, *this acknowledgement is enough.* If this opinion [belief in God] had prevented but ten assassinations, but ten calumnies, but ten iniquitious judgements on the earth, I hold that the whole earth ought to embrace it" [italics added]. This basic standpoint did not die an early death and is still prevalent in post-Hegelian philosophies, e.g., in J. S. Mill's "On the Utility of Religion" (1858), which recommends a "religion of humanity" as eminently useful.

155. B306, H401: *Sie erweist sich eben dadurch gegen es als reine Einsicht, dass sie bei einem* bestimmten *Momente das Ganze sieht, also das auf jenes Moment sich beziehende* Entgegengesetzte

Even though the Enlightenment because of its excessive subjectivity does not *comprehend* the Concept, it is continually and spontaneously producing the oppositions which are the hallmark of the (authentic) Concept. And Enlightenment is nondiscriminatory as regards the oppositions it generates. In opposing this or that determination, it will even generate an opposing moment characteristic of Faith, which leads to an implicit indictment of *itself* and an indication that it shares the same roots (cultural consciousness) with Faith. But in the last analysis, this ingenuous broadness of its compass will give it its decisive advantage over Faith. For in the pronouncements of Insight, Faith will be able to see itself (the opposite of Insight) regularly *included*.[156] Faith itself, as rooted in imagination, is implicitly the Concept which is always yet-to-be-revealed. Insight, however, as the instigator in bringing about this revelation, will at first take on a foreign and external attitude; and then only later will come to realize that it is actually producing its direct opposite, the objectionable aspects which it exposes in faith, in order to reveal *itself*.

The series of criticisms that Enlightenment directs at the contradictions and errors of Faith (we have discussed some of these criticisms already) thus tend to *boomerang continually on Enlightenment itself*. This ironical result pertains to all three of the moments of Faith discussed above, and we are now in a position to exhibit the ironical developments in some detail:

(*i*) *With regard to Absolute Being itself*: (*a*) Faith is subject to criticism in striving to *produce* the Absolute by the devout actions of its consciousness: i.e., by finite, contingent, single acts—which are obviously disproportionate to their objective; and by singular, contingent *imaginative*

---

herbeibringt und eines im andern verkehrend das negative Wesen beider Gedanken, den Begriff, *hervortreibt.*

It is obvious from this passage that Hegel considered the holistic views and "eclecticism" of Diderot and Voltaire, and the intellectual mediations which they performed for their alienated culture, to presage his own comprehensive, systematic, dialectical, philosophical mediation. However, theirs is only an imperfect form of dialectic, since it overemphasizes the production of negative (antithetical) moments, and cannot hold on to the opposites together, as the Concept (*Begriff*) requires. This final faculty comes only in the post-Enlightenment stage of "Absolute Knowledge" at the end of the *Phenomenology*.

156. In like manner, Hegel considered it a distinct advantage of his own philosophy, which synthesized opposites, that in the broader compass it both included and surpassed its opposite (the "philosophy of Understanding"). See e.g. Hegel's *Logic*, §82.

representations. And at the same time, Faith incongruously keeps referring to the Absolute as completely unattainable, "unsearchable in all its ways." (b) But Enlightenment itself, as it reflects on its own case, must realize that it similarly *both* states that Faith's God is purely a product (projection) of consciousness *and* nevertheless portrays the Absolute as a Beyond completely and unbridgeably separate from the world.

Likewise, (a) Faith is criticized for ineptly mediating the determinations of the Trinity, i.e., of failing to see them in their unity as an *Être suprème*. But (b) Enlightenment in its own domain does the same thing. It gets involved in finite this-worldly determinations, each of which stands isolated in its particularity from others and from the *Être suprème*.

(ii) *With regard to the Knowledge of Absolute Being*: (a) Faith is criticized for its emphasis on imagination and pictorial representations of the Absolute, although it uses such things to rise to an immediate spiritual knowledge of the Absolute. (b) But Enlightenment is even more culpable in this regard. It emphasizes contingent being to such a degree that it forgets about Being itself, and relegates the Absolute to the status of a mere "void."

(iii) *With regard to the service of Absolute Being*: (a) In its sacrifices, Faith looks for universality, but attains the opposite. It produces a particular act of self-abnegation, which gives it a transitory feeling of freedom from desire, but then still remains importuned by desire,[157] which remains in consciousness as a *universal*, and must be satisfied in one way or another. Or, in the matter of private property, Faith seeks to throw off isolated individuality and to attain a sense of community by sacrificing private property; but in the wake of this other-worldly act, it comes to be even more exclusive with what property remains in this world. And it justifies *this* exclusivity by pointing to the altruistic merit of the largely symbolic sacrifice which it made. (b) But Enlightenment, if it is only honest with itself, finds itself in a similar inconsistency. For it puts all *its* emphasis on the universal, the "intention" or "purpose" of maintaining the *freedom* of self-consciousness from what is "merely" natural; but in actual practice, unlike Faith, it rests in this abstract intention and makes hardly any effort to concretize this intention in particular acts which might make such freedom from Nature a *fait accompli*.

---

157. This is reminiscent of Hegel's critique of asceticism found earlier in the section on the "Unhappy Consciousness" (see K97).

The net effect of this set of ironies is felt profoundly by both Faith and enlightened Insight:

i) Faith, unable to mediate the contradictions now exposed in itself, gives up its "divine right" of remaining secure and satisfied in its immediate attachment to the Absolute. It joins the ranks of Enlightenment[158] in admitting that the Absolute is without real content, and accordingly becomes a restless, *dis*satisfied yearning for an Absolute now conceived as an empty void.

ii) The Self-Consciousness which gave rise to Enlightenment, on its own side, strives staunchly to maintain its "human right" to content itself with mediating and overcoming every contradiction that rears its head. But as it begins to confront the consequences of its own contest with Faith—the empty *Être suprême*, the usually inconsequential aspirations to be free of mere (unconscious) nature, the compromise with selfhood that is involved in the growing tendency to invest the "useful" thing with a kind of personhood of its own—it becomes an unsatisfied yearning to transcend such impasses.

Thus while Faith has converged with Enlightenment and become a dissatisfied yearning, Enlightenment, in failing to maintain its pretense of contentment and satisfaction, has likewise converged with Faith. The two join forces as complementary aspects of the selfsame movement of Enlightenment.

b. The Truth of Enlightenment
   [Utilitarianism]

Insight, the Concept, which emerged out of the vanities of Culture and eventually became the "universal individual" of the Enlightenment, has now returned to itself, and at the present moment has transcended Faith, as the aspect of pure immediacy of consciousness. It wins the victory over Faith precisely by internalizing the conflict that had previously obtained *between* Insight and Faith, i.e., by splitting *itself* up into two

---

158. Examples of Faith joining the ranks of the Enlightenment might be: the reliance of the Jesuits on a theory of a common natural law (a deistic tenet) as the basis for their worldwide missionary activity; Jesuit casuistry which rivaled the dialectical astuteness of the "Distraught Consciousness" in juggling opposites (see *Philosophy of History*, pp. 438, 440); and the general orientation of Christian theologians towards rational proofs for the existence of God (God's essence now being of less concern), a purely abstract God to replace former "anthropomorphic" versions, and towards rational justification for belief in Christian tenets.

parties, which emphasize the negative and positive aspects, respectively, of Insight's own self-distinction (a distinction which is, and has, no
abiding distinction since Insight is that distinction of essence and object
which is also the combination between the two—just as the copula
unites subject with predicate in the very act of dividing them).

Insight is essentially self-consciousness, a distinction (of self reflecting on self) which is no distinction (i.e., is one self). Insight, as we have
seen, exemplified its own internal character by creating in its environs
distinctions which are no distinctions—especially the incessant oppositions of its own positions to the positions of Faith, oppositions which
turn out to be no oppositions at all but rather areas of convergence. Now
Insight manifests its absolute mastery of this art of creating distinctions
which are self-nullifying (and also its mastery over Faith) by separating
into two camps, the Deist and the Materialist camps, which seem to be
saying different things, but are really just expressing the same insight in
two different ways. Both varieties of enlightened Insight are concerned
with showing Self-Consciousness' power of nullifying mundane distinctions by creating or projecting a distinctionless thought-thing.

For the *Deist* camp, [159] this thought-thing is conceived as a negative
Beyond, transcending the movements of the totality—pure unity
wrenched unnaturally from the distinctions it should be unifying.

For the *Materialist* camp,[160] on the other hand, the thought-thing is
conceived as a positive *presence* pervading all thought-determinations in
the sensuous world, but removed from them and transcending them all

---

159. Hyppolite (*Genesis and Structure*, pp. 448–9) suggests that this position is typified by
Robinet (1723–1820), the advocate of an ''Unknown God'' who oversees but cannot
overrule the natural equilibrium of good and evil in the world.
160. This would have to be a reference to the philosophy of Holbach (1723–1789), the
unique example of a systematic and uncompromising defender of atheistic materialism
during the eighteenth-century French Enlightenment. Hegel in *The Difference between
Fichte's and Schelling's System*, p. 177, sees this sort of pure materialism as a symbol of ''the
authentic philosophical need to suspend the dichotomy that takes the form of spirit and
matter,'' i.e., as an imperfect and inauthentic way of meeting this authentic need. More
authentic ways will be utilitarianism, Kantian moral philosophy, romanticism, and of
course, finally Hegel's own philosophy. The fact that the materialism that Hegel considered to be an inauthentic compromise is still ''alive and well'' becomes evident if we
consider Randall's twentieth-century defense of Holbach: ''Is it not more natural and
intelligible to derive everything which exists from the bosom of matter, whose existence
is demonstrated by every one of our senses, whose effects we each instant experience,
which we see acting, moving, communicating motion and generating ceaselessly, than
to attribute the formation of things to an unknown force, to a spiritual being which cannot develop from its nature what it is not itself, and which, by the spiritual essence attrib-

as a substratum—i.e., pure matter as a kind of in-itself or essence "left-over" after we abstract from all these finite determinations.

The universal[161] *common to both these camps* is a pure quivering within self—a circular holding-together of center and circumference—being and thought. But neither has come to *see* that the opposing camp expresses its own meaning, that the "negative" Being of the Deist camp is conceived as a self-identical entity and hence something positive, and that the "positive" presence of Matter extolled by the other camp is really the result of abstraction from all particular sense-determinations, and hence something negative. The notion of the unity of thinghood and thought is at this point only represented in the fact that these two kindred camps are existing side by side. Descartes' abstract, subjective, metaphysical insight into the union of being and thought is still not a *fait accompli* in the realm of Culture.

A *practical* synthesis of both these camps, however, occurs with the advent (already adumbrated) of the philosophy of *utility*, where the *in-itself* and the *for-another* and the *for-self* are effectively united. For in the useful object, the process of differentiation which already existed in a purely formal way in the oscillation between "negative" Deism and "positive" Materialism, finally focuses on the same content; and this content becomes the focus for a *mediated* differentation, in which some sensuous, thinglike in-itself becomes totally for-another as it is perfused with the *existence-for-self* of self-consciousness—i.e., a union of intrinsic value and extrinsic value is made by the mediation of self-conscious-

---

uted to it is incapable of doing anything and of setting anything in motion?'' (Randall, *Making of the Modern Mind*, pp. 302–3). Hegel would object that Holbach's ''matter'' is just as invisible, inexperienceable, inactive and impotent as the deistic ''unknown God.''

161. Note that the ''universal'' here is, as also in the earlier section on the Subjective/Objective Individuality (see K126, 158n.), a second-order universal—i.e., not just the abstract universal which unifies particulars, but a ''concrete'' dialectical synthesis of being and thought.

162. A further clarification of the relationship of utility especially to the ''materialistic'' camp is found in Hegel's later recapitulation in M§791. There Hegel shows that the materialist who has alienated *himself* completely into a thing by reducing everything to ''matter,'' can manage to reappropriate his ''self'' somewhat in the philosophy of utility, which makes inert material objects significant only insofar as they have relevance to the self. In this way the materialist thus reinvests material objects with the selfhood of which he had stripped them in his moments of extremism.

Modern utilitarianism is usually traced back to the philosophy of Jeremy Bentham (1748–1832). Although Bentham's *Introduction to the Principles of Morals and Legislation*

ness.[162] We should note, however, that the mediation of self-consciousness in this case takes on a special character insofar as it is thoroughly *object*-oriented:

(1789) appeared prior to the *Phenomenology*, it is unlikely that Hegel had that work in mind in his analysis of the "philosophy of utility." It is also unlikely that Hegel was thinking specifically of Hume, who in both his *Treatise of Human Nature* and *Enquiry Concerning the Principles of Morals* had proffered a theory of moral relations and justice based on considerations of utility. It is possible that, as Königson (*Hegel, Adam Smith et Diderot*, p. 63) suggests, Hegel was thinking here of classical political economics, especially Adam Smith's. But in the present context, heavily oriented towards French models, it is more likely that Hegel had in mind Diderot, Voltaire, and Helvétius, in whose writings a nonsystematic but nevertheless quite consistent and predictable philosophy of utility emerges. We have already noted (*supra*, n. 154) Diderot's effort to justify religion on utilitarian grounds. In Diderot's *Dictionaire encyclopédique*, a summary statement of social utilitarianism is given in the article on *"Société"*: "The whole dynamic of human *society* is grounded in the following simple and general principle: I want to be happy; but I live among men who, like me, equally from their own side want to be happy; let us search out the means by which we may assure our own happiness while also procuring theirs, or at least avoid endangering it" (Diderot, XVII, 133). This principle obviously is akin to "the greatest happiness of the greatest number" principle that gradually emerged in England in the philosophies of Jeremy Bentham and J. S. Mill. However, in the context of the French Enlightenment probably the most highly developed utilitarian ethic is to be found in the philosophy of Claude-Adrien Helvétius (1715–1771), whose theory that "public utility" must be furthered by maintaining a maximum of pleasure with a minimum of pain in society influenced Bentham. In *De L'Esprit, or Essays on the Mind and Its Several Faculties*, Helvétius states that moral value is determined by considerations of utility and "interest"; "It would, indeed, be very strange, that the general interest should fix a value on the different actions of men, and give the appellations of 'vicious' or 'lawful' as they were useful, detrimental, or indifferent, to the public, [if this same interest were not] the sole dispenser of the esteem or contempt annexed to the ideas of men" (Helvétius, II, 1). Helvétius proceeds to define more explicitly what he means by interest: "I apply [the term 'interest'] in general to whatever may procure us pleasure, or exempt us from pain" (*ibid*). One finds in Helvétius almost a metaethical reductionism of moral statements to statements about utility: "Each individual calls 'Probity' in another only the habitude of actions which are useful to him. . . . Different interests metamorphose objects: we consider a lion as a cruel animal, whereas, among the insects, it is the sheep."

Although among some English utilitarians (e.g. Shaftsbury) the emphasis was on the pursuit of private utility, in French utilitarianism the emphasis is on social utility, and this strain of utilitarianism was certainly reflected in, although not explicitly espoused by, later French socialists such as Saint-Simon and Fourier, and ultimately, one might say, in the communism of Karl Marx. Note that Hegel uses the term *Trupp* ("flock" or "herd") in M§560 as a description of mankind pervaded by a philosophy of utility, as if to emphasize (as Nietzsche was to do more stringently later) the leveling effect which a philosophy of social utility can have.

French utilitarianism, in consonance with the tendency of *enlightened* Insight to be diffused universally, was paralleled not only, as was already indicated, in England, but

Utility . . . is the means by which Insight [i.e., universal Insight or Enlightenment] achieves its realization and becomes object to itself. . . . For pure Insight is . . . the simple, pure self-consciousness which is in-itself to the same degree as it is for-itself in immediate unity. And so its existence-in-self is not a mere peaceful rest in being . . . but is intrinsically outer-oriented (for-another). . . . But this second aspect which contradicts the first, also disappears as spontaneously as does the first. In other words, Insight as existing just for-another is in a very real way this very process of *disappearance* [of the in-itself into the for-another] *itself*, and [thus we can say that] it is posited as that which continually returns to itself, i.e., as existence for-self. . . . Now, "the useful" is not Insight as such, but Insight as projected, or objectified. . . . And thus, while it is true that the moment of existence-for-another is "in" Utility, this does not imply that the moment of the for-itself holds together and actively sublates the other two moments (the in-itself and the for-another) in this case; for then the useful object would be a *self*![163] Thus [it should be emphasized that] when pure Insight holds on to the pure [oscillating] moments of its own [as yet incomplete] Concept in and through "the Useful"—it is doing so as in and through an *object*.[164]

These qualifications being made, we must reiterate the fact that in the philosophy of utility the "heaven" of the Deist and "earth" of the Materialist factions are finally synthesized; "heaven becomes transplanted to the earth below"[165] in this new compromise standpoint which is, of

---

also in Germany and other countries. In Germany, Friedrich Schiller (1759–1805), whose poetry is quoted by Hegel at the very end of the last chapter of the *Phenomenology*, observed in the 1790s that "Utility is the great idol of the age, to which all powers must do service and all talents swear allegiance."

163. Utility is not concerned *per se* with the self, but only with the self-as-*object*. The ironical extreme to which this philosophy can lead will become evident in the next section, which treats of the state of consciousness exemplified by the French Revolution, in which the treatment of men as objects by the ruling revolutionaries was rampant.

164. B314–315, H411-12: . . . *ist sie es, worin reine Einsicht ihre Realisierung vollendet und sich selbst ihr* Gegenstand *ist . . . Denn die reine Einsicht ist, . . . einfaches reines Selbstbewusstsein, welches ebensowohl* für sich *als* an sich *in einer unmittelbaren Einheit ist. Sein* Ansichsein *ist daher nicht bleibendes Sein . . . sondern wesentlich* für ein anderes. . . . *Aber dies zweite dem ersten, dem* Ansich*sein, entgegengesetzte Moment verschwindet ebenso unmittelbar als das erste; oder als Sein nur für anderes ist es vielmehr das* Verschwinden *selbst, und es ist das in sich* Zurückgekehrt-, *das* Fürsichsein *gesetzt . . . Das Nützliche . . . ist [sie] jedoch nicht als solche, sondern sie als* Vorstellung *oder als ihr* Gegenstand: . . . *das Moment des* Fürsichseins *ist wohl an dem Nützlichen, aber nicht so, das es über die andern Momente, das* Ansich *und das* Sein für anderes, *übergreift, und somit das* Selbst *wäre. Die reine Einsicht hat also an dem Nützlichen ihren eigenen Begriff in seinen reinen Momenten zum* Gegenstande. . . . .

165. "The *real* world (the world of culture) and the *ideal* world (the world of faith) have found their truth in the actual world of utility" (Hyppolite, *Genesis and Structure*, p. 451). The man of Faith finds in the doctrine of social utility a suitably concrete or positive secular eschatology, the hope of salvation for man here and now; while the man of Enlightenment finds in this doctrine the promise of a safe and sane world no longer dependent upon supernatural intervention for its perfection, a world and a social order which is ex-

course, viewed with suspicion by those who are still clinging to some form or other of an abstract in-itself: the sentimentalists, the proponents of abstract speculation, and the still extant remnants of the believing consciousness. But these latter die-hards of conservatism are merely trailing behind the spirit of the Enlightenment, without being able to check in any substantial fashion its progress towards its inevitable culmination, absolute *Freedom*.

III. *Absolute Freedom and Terror*
[Revolutionary Consciousness]

Introductory Remarks:
As we saw in the preceding section, the great rift between Faith and Insight finally was bridged by the Enlightenment's philosophy of social utility, in which Faith found eschatological-utopian inspiration and enlightened Insight found the means to show effectively man's complete mastery over the world. This new utilitarian philosophy infiltrates everywhere, and even begins to obliterate class differences. At the time of the French Revolution (the general period that is used as the model for the present section), the philosophy of social utility has infiltrated all three classes of the Estates-General: the Third Estate, the clergy, and even an influential minority of the aristocracy. Robespierre, the eventual architect of the Revolution who was dedicated to the social welfare of all, began his public career as a representative of the underprivileged Third Estate; from the ranks of the clergy, Père Jacques Roux, the impassioned leader of the Enragés, fought for equal distribution of food and money, and Abbé Sieyès wrote a highly influential pamphlet which identified the interests of the French Nation with the interests of the Third Estate; and Lafayette represented the minority of the nobility who were interested in replacing the old feudal class system with a new system in which rank would be determined by social utility. But the fact that some bedrock of utilitarian agreement could now be found in all strata of French society did not mean that the alienation which was endemic in Culture was once and for all superseded. For, as was indicated towards the end of the last section, one aspect of severe alienation still remained: the fact that the purported utilitarian "synthesis" was still object-oriented, i.e., still dependent on an external in-itself, still suffering spiritually from its love–hate relationship to a cultural

---

plicitly and indubitably under the control of man himself, who prides himself on having reached the zenith of self-conscious individuality. Enlightenment is victorious over Faith by joining the ranks of Faith; Faith salvages its existence, if not its honor, by accepting the new worldly faith excogitated by the Enlightenment.

world that is supposed to be both its source and its product, but in fact remains both independent and resistant to change. This independence and resistance to change shows up particularly in two areas of cultural life, corresponding to the two types of "useful" objects: (a) the main obstacle to the bourgeois-oriented wish to attach value to objects *in proportion to their utility is the system of feudal property rights which has taken root stubbornly and inhibits transactions patterned after the new capitalist economic philosophy; and* (b) *the main obstacle to the new social ideal that* men *should make themselves valuable by being useful to one another was an archaic and arbitrary monarchical system of power which constantly interfered with attempts to initiate social and political reform. The former problem is a problem of social inequality, the latter a problem of the lack of political liberty.*

If we keep in mind the evolution of utilitarianism through its long series of successive alienations, its reaction to this last bastion of alienation (inequality coupled with lack of liberty) is almost predictable. There is no place to proceed now except to a simple, decisive affirmation and reaffirmation of the self, of the pure ego, of the will. The Copernican revolution of Culture has been completed. It is no longer possible, or even desirable, to return to the old types of immersion in the external world or external social relations. The final retreat now must be to the power that has been trying to assert its absolute mastery all throughout the vicissitudes of Culture: the power of self-consciousness itself, conceived now as the will *to assert itself as the absolute, the standard to which everything else must conform. Thus a revolution in consciousness takes place. All the precious negations of Culture are themselves negated and man returns now full-circle to himself as the only important, the only essential thing. This revolution in consciousness does not* necessarily *entail an actual revolution in the socio-political world, but it does entail such a revolution in the sort of alienated situation described here. When there is a widespread consensus that the self-affirmation and freedom of the ego is the only important thing, and when the economic and political structures adamantly contradict or give the lie to that consensus, it seems to the Revolutionary Consciousness that there is no choice but to tear down these structures and rebuild them in such a fashion that they will favor the new consciousness of freedom which has been attained.*

A "return to the ego" for some other type of consciousness in some other existential situation might imply merely an intensification of willfulness, selfishness and impulsive activity. But not here; for here we are dealing with the enlightened consciousness whose basic "impulse," if we can call it that, is the self-conscious, mediated thinking which supervenes every mere impulse. And as self-consciousness rises above impulse, it becomes not just a single will, but universal will; for the particular individual who rises above his own empirical, impulsive will, negates its par-

ticularity, and orients himself simultaneously to the universal. The revolutionary consciousness, which makes the human will the most essential thing, must affirm the will as essential, as universal; otherwise he must waste his energy on mere transient impulses to which he cannot seriously ascribe any essentiality or stability. And so the mediated, thoughtful emphasis on will necessarily brings the revolutionary consciousness into a perpetual oscillation between particular and universal will, the universal will being now as it were the "immediate" and proper "environment" for the particular will, and more important than external objects or commodities or abstract theological or social ideals even though these latter may still be operative. At one moment, the universal will be immediately *subordinated to the particular, producing a spirit of factionalism in leaders and subjects alike. At the next moment, the particular will be* immediately *subordinated to the universal, producing a totalitarianism which strikes fear even in those who are administering it. The key to the peculiarity of revolutionary freedom is this aspect of* immediateness *(Hyppolite,* Genesis and Structure, *p. 453). It is the lack of mediation that accounts for this constant transition of particular into universal, and vice versa, producing the oscillation between factionalism and totalitarianism. Hegel's discussion of the dialectic between "particular and universal will" here is reminiscent of Sieyès' political philosophy, and also of Jean Jacques Rousseau's distinction between the "will of all" and the "general will." It will be recalled that Hegel referred obliquely to Rousseau earlier (see above, p. 54) as an example of the "honest" type of Insight which wanted to make sense out of present contradictions by harking back to ancient models of harmony. Rousseau, disgusted with the restriction on freedom found in modern civilization, characterized modern political life as slavery and extolled man's "state of nature" prior to complex political entanglements as the state of freedom. In the modern political world, according to Rousseau, there was an inevitable and incessant antinomy between the universal will (the "general will") and the particular wills (the "will of all"), but it is only when there are clear differences among wills that the possibility of a common will is perceived: "The agreement of all interests [the general will] is formed by opposition to that of each. If there were no different interests, the common interest would be barely felt"* (The Social Contract *II, 3). Just how does one determine what the "general will" is amid the mutual conflicts found in the "will of all"? Rousseau ended in the following passage offering a peculiar, quasi-mathematical formula for making the determination: "The [general will] considers only the common interest, while the [will of all] takes private interest into account, and is no more than a sum of particular wills: but take away from these same wills the pluses and minuses that cancel one another, and the general will remains the sum of the differences"* (ibid). *In the*

*two paragraphs which follow the one from which this quotation was excerpted,
Rousseau made it clear that he was using "sum" here in the sense of "average":
where there are a lot of differences which can be averaged up, the general will becomes
clear and thrives; when through partisan pleading and oppression the real differences become muted or obliterated, the general will disappears from sight. Although
Rousseau spoke much of liberty, he showed no special preference for a democratic or
republican government, and in fact in determining the comparative worth of gov-
ernments resorts to a purely mathematical criterion: "What is the end of political
association? The preservation and prosperity of its members. . . . The rest being
equal, the* government under which, *without external aids, without natural-
ization or colonies,* the citizens increase and multiply most, is beyond
question the best[!] The government under which a people wanes and
diminishes is the worst. Calculators, it is left for you to count, to measure, to compare" (ibid. *III, 9) (emphasis added). In truth, Rousseau was no
"champion of liberty" in the usual sense of the expression. He was not against ty-
rants but against the tyranny of civilization in general, and in particular of govern-
ments which did not foster and conform to the "general will," whatever this might
happen to be. Naturally, anarchists found these sentiments, and still find them, at-
tractive; but Rousseau was no anarchist. He favored a government on the Spartan
model (contrast this with Hegel's predilection for the Athenian model)—a government of absolute economic and social equality, in which with a minimum of inter-
ference from civic or economic or even familial associations each man could be counted as "one," and the differences between individuals could be clearly seen and calcu-
lated, determined and applied. In a word, Rousseau's emphasis is on equality,
rather than on liberty* per se.

*Although Hegel the dialectician was naturally attracted to the idea of a dialectic
between universal and particular will in Rousseau's thought, nothing was more
objectionable to Hegel in political philosophy than the one-sided emphasis on equality that resulted from Rousseau's theoretical orientations. Both here and elsewhere
(e.g.,* Philosophy of Right, *§49, Remark, and §200, Remark) Hegel
shows himself a resolute foe of the unthinking adherence to philosophers of equality
in the modern world. In the present instance, his main objection will be that the idea
of equality as a Spartan (we might say "totalitarian") leveling of wills is the result of an overly abstract conceptualization of the will and freedom which leads to a
purely* subjective *and* a priori *attempt to draw all particular wills into the unity
of a new "universal" revolutionary regime. Hegel will show that extreme emphasis on such a concept of freedom will recoil into a "state of nature" such as Rousseau never contemplated or wrote about, a state not of archetypal freedom but closer*

to that other "state of nature" that Hobbes had characterized more than a century earlier as the "war of all against all."

The philosophy of utility is deficient insofar as its basis is partly an intention, partly an object—i.e., utility is a predicate of an object, is not consciousness itself as immediately-possessed *subject*.

Consciousness gradually comes to *revoke* this empty semblance of objectivity which still remains in the world of "usefulness," and the mental withdrawal that subsequently takes place is not just an interesting psychological phenomenon, but is bound to have profound consequences in the actual world.

The *re*appropriation [by enlightened self-consciousness] of the "useful's" form of objectivity has now implicitly taken place, and out of this inner revolution there proceeds a real, matter-of-fact revolution, a new form of [social] consciousness—Absolute Freedom.[166]

Absolute Freedom is the attainment by consciousness of an abstract union of itself with it*self*—not self in the form of object, but as *ego*, the punctual starting point of all consciousness; and as *will*, the universal consciousness of all personalities as *equal* terminal points and starting points of ego. With this attainment, all "objective" forms of opposition vanish into the backdrop along with the empty "*Être suprême*" (the absolute negative Being fathered by the Enlightenment)—and opposition here becomes the pure abstract opposition of each subject with every subject; i.e., of the particular will with the universal (an opposition which is at the same time a merger, since the universal will is the proper element or medium for the particular will and the particular will wants to be taken as a universal will). Even the objective forms and structures of government collapse, and a host of wills has now no other interest but the assertion of itself. For its interest is now far removed from the production of objects; and also from the production of (objective, abiding) deeds, for these would have to be embodied in concrete individuals and universal will does not have it within its purposes to put any individual in the limelight; and again, also even from the creation of various "spheres" in the element of social universality, such as the judicial, executive and legislative branches of "representative" government, and

---

166. *B*316, H414:—*Diese Rücknahme der Form der Gegenständlichkeit des Nützlichen ist aber* an sich *schon geschehen, und aus dieser innern Umwälzung tritt die wirkliche Umwälzung der Wirklichkeit, die neue Gestalt des Bewusstseins, die* absolute Freiheit *hervor.*

social ranks or "estates" (for this would be to take personality in its moment of consciousness of freedom, and reduce it to *mere* existence, in some objective social category).[167] Consciousness at this stage, therefore, can produce nothing stable. Consequently there is mere chaos, conflict, abstract combat between particular will and universal will. For each will is concerned only with assertion of will-in-general. These assertions naturally become haphazardly focused and embodied in groups of particular individuals, or factions.[168] But every concrete action of these individuals is opposed to the *bare* universality of the universal will, and thus other factions arise, "convict" former factions of their error, and in turn are ousted in similar fashion—but with this difference: that the ruling factions as actually appropriating executive power are convicted for *actual* crimes, while the subordinate consciousnesses, excluded from actual power, can and are convicted for the mere "intentions" which the suspicious ruling faction imputes to them:

It is only the *victorious* faction that is called "the government," and the necessity for its overthrow lies simply in the fact that it is a faction; and the fact that it *is* the government *makes* it *ipso facto* into a faction and hence [in a context where only universal will is held in honor] guilty. If the universal will[169] can point to an actual deed of the government as a

167. In the French Revolution one of the leading ideals was to abolish all class differences so that all citizens, in effect, would be members of the "third Estate"; and during the dictatorship of Robespierre (whom Hegel in *Philosophy of History*, p. 264, compares to the Spartan ephors) any semblance that remained of a "balance of power" between executive and legislative branches of government was sacrificed to the ideal of a pure, direct forceable union of particular will and universal will. What actually results is a strange mixture of factional splintering and totalitarian conformism. For Hegel, it is the very lack of natural, "organic" articulation into spheres, classes, etc., that sounds the death knell for such a revolutionary "government." In Hegel's later (1821) *Philosophy of Right*, one of the most distinctive features of his political theory will be his insistence that the government and the "people" of a modern free state must be constantly and institutionally "mediated" by means of "corporations"—i.e., labor unions, professional organizations, lobbies—all of which would have an appropriate voice in, and direct influence on, the national legislature. In short, the solution lies not in a nostalgic return to "direct democracy," but in *representative* government.
168. For example, the Girondins, the Sansculottes, and the Jacobins in the French Revolution.
169. Although the government has official or "actual" universality, it continually shows itself to be at odds with the "essential" or "intentional" universality to which the equality-conscious citizenry subscribes. What is being described here is an "is-ought" dichotomy in the realm of politics, the sort of thing that the later Hegel explicitly set out to overcome in his *Philosophy of Right*, which depicts the idea of a nondichotomized free modern state in which the "real *is* the rational, and the rational *is* the real." But the political dichotomy here between the actual (real) will which is particular and the

crime perpetuated upon itself, the government in its turn can find nothing definite and publicly observable by reference to which it might [similarly] establish the guilt of the universal will aligned against it; since, when you come down to it, the only thing opposing itself to the actual universality of the government is the mere will, or "intention," which lacks actuality. Thus, "to be suspect" comes to count for the same thing as "to be guilty," and the official reaction against this other "actuality" that resides in the simple interiority of intention, consists in the tedious extermination of the existing suspect-self, from whom at this juncture there is really nothing left to take away except his existence itself.[170]

Conscious will, as pure abstract, self-distinguishing universality, comes naturally to focus its powers of negativity on the one subjective element which has the most semblance of objectivity or "content," namely, the punctual, abstract, self-identical ego still holding on to existence. This latter is thus destroyed relentlessly, in order to be subsumed into the abstract purposes of universal will as enforced by the faction in power. The proper effect, the proper production, therefore, of that absolute freedom which eschews all the usual forms of institutional mediation, and opts for direct control of the "universal" over the "particular," is terror and *death*.[171]

intentional (rational) will which is universal will not issue directly in a *political* synthesis; but in a moral synthesis which will break up in turn into the more cerebral, but also at least less overtly violent and destructive, dichotomy between moral behavior and moral intentions, in the following section on "morality," in which the alienations of Culture are sublimated into, and replaced by, certain internal self-contradictions in moral self-consciousness itself.

170. *B*320, H419: *Die* siegende *Faktion nur heisst Regierung, und eben darin, dass sie Faktion ist, liegt unmittelbar die Notwendigkeit ihres Untergangs, und dass sie Regierung ist, dies macht sie umgekehrt nur Faktion und schuldig. Wenn der allgemeine Wille sich an ihr wirkliches Handeln als an das Verbrechen hält, das sie gegen ihn begeht, so hat sie dagegen nichts Bestimmtes und Äusseres, wodurch die Schuld des ihr entgegengesetzten Willens sich darstellte; denn ihr als dem* wirklichen *allgemeinen Willen steht nur der unwirkliche reine Wille, die* Absicht, *gegenüber,* Verdächtig werden *tritt daher an die Stelle oder hat die Bedeutung und Wirkung des* Schuldig-seins, *und die äusserliche Reaktion gegen diese Wirklichkeit, die in dem einfachen Innern der Absicht liegt, besteht in dem trocknen Vertilgen dieses seienden Selbsts, an dem nichts sonst wegzunehmen ist als nur sein Sein selbst.*

171. Just as the "heroic" consciousness (see K88) just prior to the Master–Slave relationship risked its life and endangered the lives of others to gain recognition of its freedom, so also in the present case the Revolutionary Consciousness, in striving for an abstract, *immediate* fusion of universal and particular will, can neither wait for nature or history to take its course nor tolerate "mediating" public institutional arrangements to achieve that fusion eventually, but can only forge universal and particular together in violent, bloody fashion.

In the contemporary philosophical world, there was perhaps no more impassioned and persistent champion of radical freedom as an "absolute" and even a final sociopolitical criterion than Jean-Paul Sartre. And it is interesting to note that Sartre, in liter-

When consciousness finally comes to intuit its necessary dedication to death—that is, when it comes to the moment of the *terror of death*—it discovers in the negative quiet of the aftermath of destruction the positive necessity of substantial reality, if universal will is to function at all. Thus, under the tyranny of death (the new Lord and Master), the universal will begins to "build anew," creating spheres and estates once again.[172] But it does not merely return to the former phase of the "ethical substance" to begin all over again an endless triadic cycle of political consciousness (immediate harmony; alienation in culture; totalitarian terrorism as an attempt to restore the pristine unity and harmony), but moves into another sphere entirely, the sphere of *Morality*.[173] For absolutes merge at their extremes (self-conscious negativity, as a terror of terror, becomes extreme positivity). The "absolute negativity" found in the reign of terror is finally discovered for what it truly is: the product of the *thought* of *Freedom*. Now with the realization of this truth, on the one hand the purportedly "universal" will throws off the abstract and merely negative universality of terror and extermination, and on the

---

ary works such as the play *The Devil and the Good Lord* (1952) and in philosophical works, especially *The Critique of Dialectical Reason* (1960), has consistently been sympathetic to the revolutionary use of torture and terror. Returning to the eighteenth-century French Revolutionary model, we note that Robespierre, through the Committee of General Security and with the help of the various Jacobin clubs, created and administered in the name of absolute Freedom the terror of 1793–94, which was geared to eliminating all "counterrevolutionary" opposition both from the "left" and the "right."

172. In the early stages of Self-Consciousness (see K88) the stark realities of death led to the symbolic Master–Slave relationship, and in the earlier sections on Culture (see *supra*, pp. 45 ff.) similar realities led to a transition from Heroic Service to Heroic Language. In the present case the simple realization (which unfortunately only seems to emerge from practical and painful experience) that one must have *some* political and social institutions, if one is to experience revolutionary freedom at all, leads to a reconstruction of these new institutions on the ruins of the old ones. In the aftermath of the French Revolution, the "reconstruction" in the present context would be the period of stabilization which eventually followed upon the execution of Robespierre in 1794 and was marked by the ascendancy of Napoleon to power. In Hegel's view, Napoleon's claim to greatness resided largely in his ability to create effective "mediating" institutions and constitutional arrangements to achieve the revolutionary ideal of joining the universal with the particular will (*Philosophy of History*, p. 451). For a dialogic analysis of Hegel's concept of "mediated" revolution, see my *The Unbinding of Prometheus: Towards a Philosophy of Revolution* (Roslyn Heights, N.Y., 1976), III(D).

173. In the *moral* synthesis of universal and particular will that follows, the various customary and instinctive ethical relationships, the alienated cultural relationships and the concept of Absolute Freedom itself will be brought together in the basic moral idea that the particular person should do the universal.

other the particular, punctual subject-will throws off its "mere" particularity, that abstract particularity which had been artificially created by the very idea of "universal will"; and both sides actualize the Concept that had instigated all the previous negations and alienation—the thought of freedom—by interiorizing this concept as their own *positive* essence. Self-Consciousness, in its continuing devotion to Absolute Freedom, now concentrates its attention on determining the proper *form* in which the thought of this freedom must be construed within consciousness—an intellectual enterprise which, at least temporarily, mercifully delivers the inhabitants of the Earth from the stark terror of physical destruction. The element of objective reality, the being of the world, still remains, of course, for this consciousness. But this objective element takes on a new aspect, in accord with consciousness' new emphasis on *thought*: objectivity becomes "mere" natural being, that which is outside thought,[174] an extrinsic selfless form which stubbornly resists taking on the true form of Freedom which presumably can come only from thought. With this new development, Spirit enters into another "land," the land of Self-Consciousness:

Just as the realm of the actual world [of Culture] becomes metamorphosed into the realm of Faith and Insight, so here does Absolute Freedom emigrate to another land,[175] the ["unreal"] land of self-conscious spirit, wherein in this unreality it now falls exclusively under the rubric of "truth." It now revivifies itself with the thought of this truth, precisely insofar as the truth is and remains a *thought*; and it acknowledges *this* "being," locked within self-consciousness, as the perfect and consummate essence. We have arrived at this point at a new form [the form of ethical *self*-consciousness], the "spirit of Morality."[176]

---

174. Morality will locate the essence and existence of Freedom within Self-Consciousness itself, but in doing so will inadvertently despoil external reality of its richness, just as the Enlightenment despoiled the concept of God of *its* determination with the empty concept of an "*Être suprême.*"

175. The torch of Spirit now passes from alienated Catholic France to Germany, the land of integral, synthesizing Protestant Spirit (see *Philosophy of History*, p. 421), which gave rise to the inward revolution of Kantian morality. This inward revolution will now become the most important thing, the essential thing, happening in the world of Spirit.

176. *B*323, H422: *Wie das Reich der wirklichen Welt in das Reich des Glaubens und der Einsicht übergeht, so geht die absolute Freiheit aus ihrer sich selbst zerstörenden Wirklichkeit in ein anderes Land des selbstbewussten Geistes über, worin sie in dieser Unwirklichkeit als das Wahre gilt, an dessen Gedanken er sich labt, insofern* er Gedanke ist *und bleibt, und dieses in das Selbstbewusstsein eingeschlossene Sein als das vollkommne und vollständige Wesen weiss. Es ist die neue Gestalt des* moralischen *Geistes entstanden.*

C. SPIRIT THAT IS CERTAIN OF ITSELF. MORALITY
[MORAL CONSCIOUSNESS]

Introductory Remarks:

*Morality, or the moral consciousness, is (as Hegel indicates in M§442-3)
(H315-16, B460-61, B240) the stage in which Spirit arrives at "Self-
Consciousness." There are some difficulties in this statement, since Hegel is also
going to describe Religion as the attainment of "Self-Consciousness" (see* infra, *p.
129); but in the present context this means that Spirit, which began as intersubjective truth (i.e., the true immediate communality which characterized the Ethical
Substance), now becomes intersubjective certainty (i.e., the state of consciousness
in which each individual, by plumbing his own subjective depths, finds there the
roots of essential or necessary relationships to others, and in fact tries to deduce these
relationships from his subjectivity).*

*Among Hegel commentators there is some confusion as to what, if any specific,
school of philosophy Hegel is using as his model here. For example, Shklar (*Freedom and Independence, *pp. 182-3) thinks that Hegel's present critique ignores*
Kant's Fundamental Principles of the Metaphysics of Morals *and is based
on* Kant's Religion within the Limits of Reason Alone; *Robinson (*Duty
and Hypocrisy, *p. 53) thinks that Hegel wrote this critique with the last part (the
"Dialectic") of* Kant's Critique of Practical Reason *in mind, and perhaps
even with the text of the "Dialectic" in that book in front of him while he was writing; Loewenberg (*Hegel's Phenomenology, *p. 26) sees allusions in this section
to Fichte as well as Kant; Hirsch (in* Materialen, *p. 247) thinks that Hegel directed this critique at Fichte's* Attempt at a Critique of all Revelation, *as well
as* Kant's Critique of Practical Reason *and* Religion within . . .; *and both
Hyppolite (*Genesis and Structure, *pp. 470-1) and Lauer (*A Reading, *pp.
202, 217) seem to think that Hegel's criticisms against Kant are also directed
against the Pietist movement as a voluntaristic interpretation of Lutheran theology. Perhaps this confusion is due to the fact that the standpoint of "Morality" is
something larger than Kant, although Kant became its chief spokesman; in fact,
Hegel elsewhere even mentions (*Philosophy of History, *p. 269) that Socrates is
the "inventor of morality." But in this section Hegel is concerned with showing
how Morality develops out of, and offers a solution to, the alienations of Culture;
and, in particular, with showing how Morality (exemplified in the philosophy of
Kant et al.) is a continuation of the Revolutionary standpoint just considered, insofar as it internalizes the idea of the interrelationship between particular and univer-*

sal ego, and works out the theoretical ramifications in moral philosophy of Rousseau's basic insight in political philosophy about the absoluteness of Freedom (see History of Philosophy *III, pp. 425, 457); the analysis of Rousseau's "general will" is continued under the rubric of Kant's "pure will."*

Granted that Hegel was at least thinking about Kant in this critique, the reader familiar with the earlier sections of the Phenomenology *will not fail to notice a decided similarity between the present section and the earlier section on "reason as Lawgiver" (see K129), which* also *seems to be a critique of Kant's moral theory. However, there are two major differences between these two critiques: (1) As Hegel pointed out in the beginning of the sections on Reason in its practical aspects (M§347ff., H255ff., B374ff., B193ff., K118ff.), the stages of Reason can be considered either as leading into or emerging out of the spiritual substance. The earlier section on Reason as "testing laws" was concerned with a moral attitude as leading into immersion in the Ethical Substance; while the present section considers Morality precisely as a state of explicit self-conscious realization of the intersubjective associations that have been present from the origins of the Ethical Substance. (2) There is also a difference in content in the two sections: The earlier section concentrates on the Categorical Imperative, the manful attempts of consciousness to maintain consistency or non-self-contradiction, and the peculiar implications of a moral "ought"; while the present section concentrates on the Postulates of morality (including God as a Postulate), the dialectic resulting from these Postulates, and the Fichtean synthesis of Conscience that emerges from these dialectical antitheses.*

Pöggeler (Hegels Idee, *p. 81) observes that the relation between duty and inclination discussed here with reference to the "Second Postulate" is considered by Hegel as a kind of Master–Slave relationship. Corroboration of this can be found in* Early Theological Works, *p. 211, with reference to Kant, and in* Difference between Fichte's and Schelling's System, *pp. 138, 149, 150 with particular reference to Fichte. To call the moral stance a "Master–Slave" relationship would seem to imply that it is "alienated." However, towards the beginning of the sections on Culture (M§486), Hegel has already indicated that with the Moral Self the "alienations" of Culture will be transcended. And so one must emphasize that if we want to call the Moral stance "alienated," we are probably using the term in an existential sense that Hegel did not have in mind. The "alienations" of Culture were characterized by certain external and social contradictions that are not the case here, and that fact is important for Hegel: being a "slave" to one's (better) self at least bespeaks an internalization and assimilation of the alienations of Culture, whose contradictions posed obstacles to the progress of spiritual Self-Consciousness.*

In contemporary parlance there is a tendency to distinguish "morality" as customary behavior from "ethics" as a code of behavior. But the type of distinction Hegel makes between the two terms is quite different. In Natural Law, *p. 84, Hegel speaks of the "distinction of the Ethical* [des Sittlichen] *into Morality* [Moralität] *and Legality* [Legalität], *and explains that Morality involves an extreme of subjective emphasis while Legality involves an extreme of objective emphasis; the Ethical is a synthesis of the two extremes, i.e., a state of Spirit in which the individual sense of duty is in harmony with the laws and customs that make up his social environment, and the various laws and customs are also reflective of, and responsive to, the determinations of individuals. We find a somewhat similar scheme in the* Phenomenology: *the Ethical Substance was a kind of primordial and archetypal synthesis of duty and law; the "Legal Consciousness" which immediately followed upon it was an extreme emphasis on external, forceable predominance of law over the scattered remnants of the Ethical Substance; and the "Moral Consciousness" to be considered here will mark similarly extreme emphasis on the priority of internally excogitated duty as the primordial "substance" in which all ethical and legal relations, if they are not to become "heteronomous" (to use the relevant Kantian terminology), must be grounded.*

It is important to point out that Morality is a stage in the evolution of Spirit. We are not dealing here merely with an individual who is trying to determine what is best for himself or how he can maintain personal (psychological and intellectual) consistency, but with individuals who have a sense of being implicitly united with others through necessary laws, and want to trace the roots of these laws back to their own egos, to make the laws not only explicit but also explicitly grounded in individual legislating wills. In terms of Hegel's previous definition of Spirit as "the I which is a we, and the we which is an I" (H140, B108), we are now at the point where the I has thoroughly explored its identity with the we, and the universal we begins to manifest its roots in the individual self-conscious I.

Although Hegel, here and elsewhere (e.g., Philosophy of History, *p. 269), emphasizes the fact that Morality is an important manifestation of the profound levels which subjectivity can attain, he also, here and elsewhere (e.g.,* ibid., *p. 67 and* Philosophy of Right, *§150, 152,* Remarks) *goes out of his way to show that morality, because of its abstraction from Nature (both society as a second "nature" and the natural, sensuous aspects of consciousness) is not only one-sided and imperfect but also self-defeating, spiritually disastrous and even "immoral."*

In all the previous stages of Spirit, the *individual* self-conscious *spirit* has gradually been taking on form and acquiring substance. Beginning as the lifeless venerable shade emerging from the family during the stage of the Ethical Substance, acquiring some independence from external exigencies at the stage of Legal Status, then learning to internalize the contradictions of the world during the processes of Culture, self-consciousness finally came to erect itself upon its own foundation (the general will) during the stages of Freedom and Terror. Now in its extreme revulsion from the reign of Terror—a negation of negation[177]—it refuses to consider anything outside of individual self-consciousness (even a "general will") as its essence or substance. It takes itself as its own substance, looks upon its own ethical certainty as its appropriate "object," substitutes its own "pure will" for the "general will," and thus arrives at the stage of "Morality," which is characterized by (1) a transcendence through *thought* of the antitheses generated by Culture and revolutionary Freedom, and (2) a synthesis of the *immediacy* of duty which characterized individual consciousness still immersed in the being of the Ethical Substance, with that *mediation* of universalizing knowledge which came to the fore during the stages of Culture and Freedom.

a. The Moral View of the World

The Moral Consciousness, although it does not have an explicit object, nevertheless, insofar as it is consciousness, must be oriented to *some* "otherness."[178] The otherness which its concept contains implicitly here may be called, in the first instance, *"Nature in General."*[179]

The Postulates of Morality:[180]

---

177. Just as the "fear of fear" became tantamount to the attainment of reflection, mastery and self-consciousness for the Slave, and marked his transition to Stoicism (see K89), so also here the "terror of terror" as a double negation becomes equivalent to commitment to a positive and no longer nihilistic concept of freedom, the idea that one can remake himself (and indirectly possibly the world) by Morality.

178. This is a familiar and important theme in Sartre's phenomenology (cf. *Being and Nothingness*, Introduction, III and V).

179. The proper object of a fully self-sufficient and self-contained subjectivity is an equally independent "Nature" equally closed in upon itself. In this connection one also thinks of the "opacity" of the "in-itself" in Sartre's phenomenology.

180. As has been indicated above, Hegel seems to be thinking especially of Kant's moral philosophy in the present critique. However, it should be noted that when one speaks of "Postulates" in a Kantian context, the three postulates of God, freedom and immortality are usually meant (see *Kant's Critique of Practical Reason*, pp. 134 ff.). Hegel does not focus precisely on these three postulates, but on the following three dialectical postulates which are found in Kant's Critique (in Part I, and in Kant's *Religion within the Limits of Reason Alone*, Book II) but are restructured and reinterpreted by Hegel: the har-

(1) *The Postulate of a harmony between happiness and morality* arises from the fact that "nature in general" takes on an ambiguous relationship to the moral consciousness. For the moral consciousness, in taking a stand for absolute freedom of self-consciousness, simultaneously withdraws absolutely from nature as from something amoral, [181] and thus, to this extent, endows nature with an absolute independence from morality, another kind of "freedom," in the sense of unpredictability, capriciousness, and only contingent conformity to the exigencies of moral consciousness. And therefore nature is in this sense something that stands over against consciousness as *independent*, and yet something *for*-consciousness. Consciousness, however, as a purpose or intention, naturally desires its own actualization, or existence—which consists in the union of itself with its other. And it sees its opponent, the nonmoral consciousness, very often seemingly gaining such a realization of its union with reality in a haphazard, accidental way. Nevertheless, holding unwaveringly to its pure purpose, the moral consciousness adheres to pure duty as its essential objective, although (because it is a manifestation of Reason with consequently at least an implicit commitment to the harmonious unity of self and other) it cannot renounce happiness[182]

---

monies of (*a*) morality with happiness, (*b*) morality with the Holy Will, (*c*) God as sanctifying Legislator and God as executive Sovereign taking responsibility for the myriad sundry details of the moral order. In restructuring these postulates, Hegel seems to be saying, in effect, that he considers these to be *the basic* postulates in the moral point of view, although not all of them are represented explicitly as "postulates" by Kant. As might be surmised, the restructuring is a microcosm of the triadic dialectic found throughout the *Phenomenology*: the First Postulate is concerned with Morality-as-an-in-itself oriented towards Nature (the natural moral order, which involves the attainment of happiness); the Second Postulate, with Morality-as-a-for-itself oriented towards psychic Nature in the form of bodily inclinations or unconscious drives; the Third Postulate, with Morality-as-an-in-and-for-itself, i.e., God as a representation or symbol of both perfect objective happiness and perfect subjective holiness.
181. Cf. Kant, *Religion within* . . ., p. 16: "The expression *nature* [usually means] the opposite of freedom as a basis of action."
182. Kant in his *Fundamental Principles of the Metaphysic of Morals*, p. 17, defines happiness as the conception of the sum of satisfaction of all one's inclinations. As Hyppolite remarks (*Genesis and Structure*, p. 476) Kant's conception of happiness is a vulgar eudaemonism, which highlights, and perhaps is meant to highlight, the nobility of Kant's concept of morality by contrast. Hegel, on the other hand, like Aristotle in the *Nicomachean Ethics* (X, 7, 1177a, 11), construes happiness as essentially an active and spiritual state: "When happiness is conceived as Idea, it ceases to be something empirical and contingent, and it ceases to be something sensuous. In the highest being (*Dasein*) rational action and highest enjoyment are one" (*Faith and Knowledge*, p. 59). But in the present Kantian context, happiness (*Gluckseligkeit*) connotes the attainment of *naturally*

(its actualized content), just as it cannot renounce the desire for existence (its actualized form, the form of union with reality). Therefore it
must "*postulate*" the *necessity* of the *existence* of the ideal of happiness—a
postulate which, as referring to the attainment of an existence, is not
here based on the necessity of a conception *qua* conception (the necessity
of the concept of happiness), but rather upon the necessity of reason itself to form such a concept.[183]

(2) *The Second Postulate (of a Holy Will)*[184] arises from another aspect of
nature, which accrues to Morality as a for-itself, i.e., as a self-consciousness. For self-consciousness, considered as "merely" existing, is *sensibility* (inclinations, etc.)—and this latter constitutes another "otherness" or "*inner* nature" which stands over against consciousness, in its
other moment of existence-for-self; i.e., personal sensible desires and
inclinations are the immediate "being" with which a *self*-consciousness
must deal. The resolution of such opposition can only come about when
the opposition itself is something completely transcended and projected
in its transcended condition as a "for-consciousness"—a state which
would constitute actual morality *par excellence* (the holy will, in which
there is no longer left any discrepancy between natural inclinations and
duty). And therefore morality must postulate such an ideal. But as a
necessary corollary it postulates the attainment of a holy will in some
indefinite infinity,[185] since if it definitely attained it at some particular

---

good (amoral) consequences of one's purposes or intentions, i.e., worldly fulfillment
or lack of frustration—the specific sort of "nature" that the moral consciousness seems
to be interested in.

183. Kant formulates this rational necessity in the form of the antinomy of the *summum
bonum*: "The desire for happiness *must be* the motive to maxims of virtue, or the maxim
of virtue *must be* the efficient cause of happiness. The first is absolutely impossible because . . . maxims which put the determining ground of the will in the desire for one's
happiness are not moral. . . . The second is, however, also impossible, since every practical connection of causes and effects in the world, as a result of the determination of the
will, is dependent not on the moral intentions of the will but on knowledge of natural
laws and the physical capacity of using them to its purposes" (*Critique of Practical Reason*,
pp. 117 f.). Hegel takes this basic dilemma and reformulates it as the first dialectical
moral postulate.

184. See Kant's *Critique of Practical Reason*, pp. 126 f.: "Complete fitness of the will to the
moral law is holiness, which is a perfection of which no rational being in the world of
sense is at any time capable. But since it is required as practically necessary, it can be
found only in an endless progress" [and hence is unattainable]. Kant used this as a
premise for a proof for the immortality of the soul, but Hegel will simply focus on the
premise itself as the second dialectical postulate of morality.

185. "In order for the synthetic activity [of moral freedom] to be pure and infinite still,

time, morality itself as an essential mode of being would vanish (i.e. as a basically negative force of consciousness, morality would no longer find the requisite "otherness" necessary for its self-definition). But it still must definitely *postulate* the attainment of unity-in-opposition with sensibility. Therefore the actualization of morality contains an inherent contradiction (it should be, but yet can never be); but at the same time consciousness as a manifestation of Reason is convinced of the possibility of a holy will, and this sacred conviction leads it to view its own postulate as noncontradictory.

(3) *The Postulate of a God* emerges from the very process of moral activity itself, and functions as a kind of synthesis of the two former postulates.[186] On the one hand, (*a*) when moral consciousness as an in-itself (i.e., as a consciousness rather than as a self-consciousness) strives in its multifarious activities to attain some proportionality between morality and happiness-as-a-consequence-of-morality, it is continually frustrated by the very multiplicity of objective duties (the special type of objectivity it must deal with), and seems to meet with failure just as often as with success. Thus it postulates a masterful and provident God as the

---

it must be thought as an objective activity whose final purpose is absolute freedom, absolute independence from all of nature. This final purpose can never be achieved; [it turns into] an infinite series through whose continuation the Ego would become absolutely equal to Ego" (Hegel quoting Fichte in *Difference between Fichte's and Schelling's Systems*, p. 138).

186. Hegel later (M§676) refers to the development of this Third Postulate as the "religion of Morality." The God that is represented in this Postulate is, on the one hand, an advance over the impersonal deistic *Être suprême* of the Enlightenment, but on the other hand, as we shall see, is still affected with some of the ambivalences of the Enlightenment.

The passages here (M§606–608) are rather difficult, but Hegel, perhaps suffering from a guilty conscience from these obfuscations, later goes out of his way to recapitulate and clarify the dialectic taking place here (see especially M§630, §636, §676). Basically the dialectic here is between (*a*) God considered as an ingenious Ruler who can handle all the detail in connecting virtue and happiness, while moral consciousness simply holds fast to the pure form of duty; and (*b*) God as a transcendent Legislator who sanctifies the multiplicity of man's imperfect moral acts by his Grace. This formulation of the dialectic seems to be based on Kant's own distinction of God as (1) Benevolent Ruler, (2) Holy Legislator, and (3) Righteous Judge, in *Religion within the Limits of Reason Alone*, p. 131; the idea of God as Judge seems to be a synthesis of the two other aspects of God. (Hegel in showing how a satisfactory synthesis is impossible at this level, is implicitly also denying the validity of the synthetic concept of God as Judge.) The dialectical developments here can be clarified by a comparison to parallel developments in the chapter on Perception (K67 ff.) and the final parts of the chapters on the Enlightenment (*supra*, pp. 72 f.): Just as in Perception consciousness oscillates between perceiving the

only one who can fully accomplish such a union of the universal (morality) with the particular content presenting itself in the world as a "duty to be done." In other words, God is perceived as the great Sovereign Consciousness who is alone capable of handling all the complex connections to be made between duty as a universal law and its practical applications and consequences.[187] And since the objectivity of "nature" is now replaced by, and symbolized by, the objectivity of the multiplicity of duties, a kind of synthesis between the objective (which here = the *multiplicity* of *determinate* duties) and the subjective (which here = the indeterminate thought of duty-in-general) results. Thus God as so conceived is synthesis of nature (the manifold of duties) and pure duty and stands as the guarantor of "happiness."

On the other hand, (b) when moral consciousness as a for-itself (i.e., as a self-consciousness rather than as a consciousness) strives to attain the postulated harmonization of its pure moral will with its own empirical will or sensibility, a somewhat different state of affairs results: it finds it must now postulate God as the Divine Legislator who maintains morality in its purity and universality, in contrast to the finite self-consciousness which must continually deal with particular manifestations of sensibility (the in-itself *within* the for-itself) which seem to depart from this universality.[188]

By combining *per impossibile* these two opposite notions of (a) the provident Sovereign and (b) the divine Legislator, moral consciousness ar-

---

object as (a) a multifaceted "also" which it unifies and (b) a unifying one which it distinguishes into parts or aspects, so also moral consciousness here oscillates between representing God (a) as a Master of multiplicity contrasted with the simple devotion to duty in the moral consciousness and (b) as a transcendent unity standing above our multiple human transactions and giving them universal merit. And just as the Enlightenment oscillates between (a) a concentration on the finite as absolute and (b) an infinite God absolutely empty of determinations, so also morality oscillates with somewhat less extreme schizophrenia between (a) God as even more involved in the determinate world than moral consciousness and (b) God as aloof and transcendent.

187. "Therefore . . . the existence is postulated of a cause of the whole of nature, itself distinct from nature, which contains the ground of the exact coincidence of happiness with morality" (Kant, *Critique of Practical Reason*, p. 129).

188. "The moral law leads to religion. Religion is the recognition of all duties as divine commands . . . , as essential laws of any free will as such. . . . They must be regarded as commands of the Supreme Being because we can hope for the highest good . . . only from a morally perfect (holy and beneficent) and omnipotent will" (*Critique of Practical Reason*, p. 134). Similarly Kant also says in *Religion within . . .* , p. 142, "Religion is (subjectively regarded) the recognition of all duties as divine commands."

rives at the syncretic, imaginative representation[189] of a provident Sovereign who takes it upon Himself to keep the order of the *world* in its bewildering multiplicity essentially a *moral* order (and thus essentially happy), and who is also a Lawgiver existing as an in-*and*-for-itself "beyond" the imperfections of the empirical state of existence of the moral consciousness, and *making* the imperfect actions of moral consciousness perfect and moral by guaranteeing the sacredness of duty-in-general, and by imputing "grace" or justification to mortals who fall short of morality.

Although this syncretic representation is not a completely successful synthesis, we definitely achieve through it an insight into the Concept,[190] and we also become aware of some of the limitations and *ambivalences* present in this incipient Concept in this form:

> In the Concept of the moral self-consciousness the two sides—pure Duty and Actuality—are established in a unity . . . [*a*] Pure Duty is posited as an essence other than the moral consciousness, i.e., it is posited partly as a bona fide representation, but partly as something which does not really count as a being in-and-for-itself (so that in this latter sense it becomes inferior to the amoral stuff of existence). Likewise [*b*] the actuality of moral consciousness is posited as something which, not being commensurate with duty, is transcended and, only as transcended, (i.e., as the representation of Absolute Being) transcends its contradiction with Morality.[191]

In other words, the "synthesis" thus produced is ambivalent because it tries to combine (*a*) valid use of imagination with consciousness of the

---

189. Continuing with the comparison to Perception and Enlightenment suggested above (n. 186), this final synthetic representation of God, *if* it were possible, would be analogous to (*a*) the simultaneous conception of the perceptual object as both a manifold and a "one" in Perception; and (*b*) the doctrine of social Utility, which synthesized the mastery over worldly details by the Enlightenment with the devotion of Faith to eschatological singleness of purpose. But the true synthesis of all these present dichotomies is to come only in the section after the next, "Conscience."

190. I.e., the paradigmatic *Hegelian* Concept, which is a dialectical union of the in-itself and the for-itself, of Being and Thought, and (at this juncture) is an imperfect union of the abstract thought of pure duty with the concrete reality of multifarious concrete duties, or of the sensuous facticity of human inclinations with the ideal universality of moral law.

191. *B*330, H431–2: *in dem Begriffe des moralischen Selbstbewusstseins sind die beiden Seiten, reine Pflicht und Wirklichkeit, in Einer Einheit gesetzt . . . ; die reine Pflicht nämlich setzt es in ein andres Wesen, als es selbst ist, d.h. es setzt sie teils als ein* Vorgestelltes, *teils als ein solches, das nicht das ist, was an und für sich gilt, sondern das Nichtmoralische gilt vielmehr als vollkommen. Ebenso sich selbst setzt es als ein solches, dessen Wirklichkeit, die der Pflicht unangemessen ist, aufgehoben [ist] und, als* aufgehobne *oder in der* Vorstellung *des absoluten Wesens, der Moralität nicht mehr widerspricht.*

unreality of mere imaginative "projections"; and (*b*) the grounding of the idea of a God in the notion of morality with the consciousness that morality in turn must be grounded in a God to remain non-self-contradictory.

It should be mentioned here that there is also an alternative way of demonstrating how moral consciousness arrives at its present state of imaginative projection. This alternative manner of demonstration emphasizes the progression of the *Concept* of the harmony of duty and actuality from (*a*) unity to (*b*) difference to (*c*) unity in difference. In the first stage (*a*) moral consciousness concentrates only on the fact that aspects of actuality can be *thought* of as in conformity with duty, and thus brings about an "actual" unity *in thought* of duty and actuality. Next (*b*) moral consciousness contrasts the harmony produced in thought with the actual *disharmony* in the world as a whole, and formulates the tentative and despairing proposition: "There is *no* morally perfect self-consciousness [acting in the objective world]." But finally (*c*) as a manifestation of Reason (which feels confident of being able eventually to unite the extremes of duty and actual existence), it now projects the ideal of a harmony of morality and reality as a transcendent "beyond," i.e., as a state of affairs that "ought to be" and actually "is," but only as an imaginative representation.

b. Dissemblance or Duplicity
    [*Verstellung*[192]]

The moral viewpoint in all three of the dialectical stages just considered contains one outstanding and one fundamental equivocation or duplicity, which can be summarized as follows:

---

192. Robinson (*Duty and Hypocrisy*, pp. 73,74) observes that Baillie's translation of *Verstellung* as "dissemblance" would not make much sense if "dissemblance" is used in its ordinary denotation of "feigning," but would be meaningful in a Shakespearean sense of "role-playing." Taylor (*Hegel*, p. 193) thinks that *Verstellung* is best translated as a "shift," i.e., an evasion that consciousness goes through to avoid perceiving its own contradictions. Miller, to play safe, translates *Verstellung* as "dissemblance *or* duplicity."—In truth, it would seem that all the above senses of *Verstellung* are operative in the present section: The moral consciousness feigns or pretends to certain characteristics, as if to conceal other characteristics from itself; plays now one role, and then the opposite role; shifts skillfully just when it is about to perceive its own contradictions; and is a personification of a duplicity that contradicts its aspirations to moral purity and singleness of purpose.

Moral Consciousness knows [the objective essence, i.e. duty] as its very self, since it knows itself to be the *agent* who produces this essence. Thus it *seems* in this case to attain to peace and satisfaction—the attainment of which is only possible where consciousness no longer needs to transcend its object (because the object no longer transcends *consciousness*). From another perspective, moral consciousness itself is *projecting* its object outside itself, as a "Beyond." But this "Beyond" which is supposed to exist in-and-for-itself is thus presented in this case as something that is not free from self-consciousness, but exists only on behalf of, and by means of, self-consciousness.

Thence, the "moral point of view" is in fact nothing more than the further unfolding of this initial basic contradiction according to its various facets; and the moral viewpoint which is thus explicated turns out to be—to use a Kantian expression in its most appropriate application—"a whole nest" of contradictions[193] bereft of thought.[194]

Contradiction infects all the bones and sinews of the three postulates of morality we have just differentiated in the preceding section. Let us begin with the first postulate, to point out some of the salient symptoms of this infection:

(1.) *The Postulate of Happiness*

(*a*) There is no doubt about it: with every moral *action*, consciousness produces a concrete union of morality with reality or "nature." Yet in spite of this, moral consciousness holds that morality must remain separated from nature, unfulfilled and incomplete, i.e., nonexistent, unreal.

(*b*) The moral consciousness complains that happiness is only contingently and thus unpredictably connected with morality; but yet it is continually striving to attain moral satisfaction (which is certainly a species of happiness) in and through every moral action.

(*c*) Instead of using the postulate of the harmony of moral purpose and actuality (as it could conceivably be used) to affirm the positive possibil-

---

193. Kant uses the phrase "whole nest of dialectical contradictions" (*ein ganzes Nest von dialektischen Anmassungen*) in the *Critique of Pure Reason* (A609, B637) to describe the questionable nature of the "cosmological proof" for the existence of God. Here Hegel turns the tables on Kant, asserting that the postulate of the harmony of morality and actuality is also a "nest of contradictions."

194. B332, H434: . . . *es weiss dasselbe also als sich selbst, denn es weiss sich als das tätige, das es erzeugt. Es scheint somit hier zu seiner Ruhe und Befriedigung zu kommen, denn diese kann es nur da finden, wo es über seines Gegenstand nicht mehr hinauszugehen braucht, weil dieser nicht mehr über es hinausgeht. Auf der andern Seite aber setzt es selbst ihn viel mehr ausser sich hinaus, als ein Jenseits seiner. Aber dies Anundfürsichseiende ist ebenso als ein solches gesetzt, das nicht frei vom Selbstbewusstsein, sondern zum Behuf des letztern und durch dasselbe sei.*

Die moralische Weltanschauung ist daher in der Tat nichts anderes als die Ausbildung dieses zum Grunde liegenden Widerspruchs nach seinen verschiedenen Seiten; sie ist, um einen Kantischen Ausdruck hier, wo er am passendsten ist, zu gebrauchen, ein ganzes Nest gedankenloser Widersprüche.

ity of effective moral action, moral consciousness, remaining in its strictly negative stance, relegates such postulated harmony to the status of a merely remote, negative possibility, i.e., a "beyond" having no intrinsic connection with action at all.

(d) Moral consciousness disparages concrete, determinate acts as being "contingent." It is so enamoured of the "universal best" that it actually becomes paralyzed when it comes to performing concrete, particular moral actions.

(e) Moral consciousness would like to say that it is concerned with the *fulfillment* of duty and the making of moral law into a law of nature[195]; but it is even more interested in maintaining that the one and only important thing is the moral "intention," i.e., morality as a pure product of *consciousness*, and hence completely independent of, and indifferent to, reality or nature, and its actualization therein.[196]

(f) Moral consciousness posits as its "ideal" a fusion of morality and reality (the *bonum supremum*); but it must, at least covertly, try to keep such an ideal from coming about, since morality, to exist as a specific attitude of thought, must have something negative to deal with (i.e., to attack).[197]

One fact stands out starkly from all the preceding contradictions: Moral consciousness definitely has a problem maintaining a commitment to moral *action*, in view of its overriding commitment to the first postulate. It then tries to solve this problem by turning to the second postulate, which concentrates only on the harmonization of morality and *inner* nature, i.e., sensible inclinations and impulse. It seems that if we just concentrate on this second type of harmony, we may be able to maintain a commitment to action, and at the same time keep the first postulate basically unscathed. But this "solution" turns out to be superficial and, as we shall see, equally replete with contradictions. For instance:

---

195. Kant argues in *Fundamental Principles* that the Categorical Imperative as universal (first formulation) functions as "natural law."

196. "Man's moral growth of necessity begins not in the improvement of his practices but rather in the transforming of his cast of mind and in the grounding of a character" (Kant, *Religion within. . .*, p. 43).

197. Fichte carries this moralistic dependence upon attacking evil even further than Kant, leading Hegel to remark in *Faith and Knowledge*, p. 181, "If the badness [in the world] were not absolute [in Fichte's moral philosophy], then the other Absolute would fall away, the realm of freedom, this pure will that needs a world in which Reason is still to be realized."

(2.) *The Postulate of a Holy Will*

(*a*) Moral consciousness according to the second postulate has to distinguish itself clearly from its sensibility, and to negate the latter as something that "ought" to be in conformity with duty or morality, but actually is not. But moral consciousness itself is a form of consciousness erected, like every other form of consciousness, on the bedrock of the immediacy of sensibility and sensible impulses.

(*b*) In accordance with the second postulate, moral consciousness seems to be sincere in its expectation of a synthesis of sensibility and morality. But moral consciousness *knows* that it cannot maintain the purity of moral will if it allows the moral will to be "contaminated" by determinate sensible inclinations. And so it relegates this postulate, like the first, to the status of a remote "beyond"—in this case, the purely hypothetical, actually unrealizable "Holy Will."

(*c*) Moral consciousness glibly praises "advancement or progression in morality"[198] as something meritorious. But such progression, if it came about, would actually spell a decrease in morality as a pure, autonomous attitude which thrives on immorality as something to be overcome. And besides, it is shallow to talk of morality in terms of "progression" (which implies increase and the existence of degrees, i.e. *quantitative* determination), for morality in its essential nature is concerned only with pure universal form (i.e., when you come down to it, there is only *one* selfsame "pure duty" to be imposed serenely on all disparate moral contents).

(*d*) Thus realizing that all "advance in morality" would really be a falling away from *pure* morality, moral consciousness can no longer consistently hold that there is a necessary relationship between "moral" progress (now shown to be essentially imperfect and hence immoral) and happiness. In its desire to maintain credibility, consciousness

---

198. "[Moral change] must be regarded as nothing but an ever-enduring struggle toward the better, hence as a gradual reformation of the propensity to evil, the perverted cast of mind" (Kant, *Religion within...*, p. 43). In *Faith and Knowledge* p. 84, Hegel remarks that it is a gross inconsistency for Kant to challenge the possibility of infinite regress in his cosmological "Antinomies" (in the *Critique of Pure Reason* and the *Prolegomena to Any Future Metaphysics*), and then to allow infinite progress to stand unchallenged in his moral philosophy. Kant also saw the idea of infinite progress as a ground for postulating a corollary immortality of the soul, but Hegel, in *Faith and Knowledge* p. 94) portrays Kant's defense of immortality as unoriginal and unphilosophical, and in the *Phenomenology* does not refer to it even in connection with the notion of "infinite progress."

consequently takes on the explicit posture of the immoral consciousness [the sinner] for whom happiness is no longer claimed to be merited or deserved, but is a "grace," i.e., something given only contingently, given only by chance, although each individual should strive to be worthy of happiness.

(*e*) In light of the first postulate, moral consciousness had been disgruntled at observing that evil people often unmeritedly find happiness.[199] But now, in view of the immediately preceding reflection (*d*), it realizes the *essentially* imperfect (i.e., immoral) character of all "moral" activity, and so must re-examine that initial discontent: *now* it decides that, since morality in general is so imperfect, one cannot say with any precision which action is moral enough to merit happiness; and in fact if one made a complaint about "evildoers" becoming happy, he himself would definitely be under suspicion of a specific form of immorality (i.e., *envy*).[200]

At this juncture, resigned to the awareness that actual (practical) morality must always be imperfect, consciousness proceeds to champion the third postulate, the existence of a God who will embody morality in its perfect and essential form.

(*3.*) *The Postulate of God*

(*a*) This third postulate, conveniently, seems to alleviate the present impasse, by offering absolute and perfect "grounding" for all determinate and imperfect moral duties, thus rescuing them from wholesale and absolute imperfection. But consciousness must realize that the ideal of a "Divine Legislator" as a "sacred guarantee" of pure morality is also a sham, for the whole idea behind morality from the very start is that it is essentially a product of our own free conscious intentions. *Nothing* can be "sacred" to *moral* consciousness unless it is *immanent in* consciousness itself. But God as Divine Legislator is patently transcendent.

(*b*) Since the "imperfection" of morality is here the big problem that (it seems) just won't go away, and since this imperfection seems to stem radically from the dependency of temporally progressing moral activ-

---

199. "The sight of a being who is not adorned with a single feature of a pure and good will, enjoying unbroken prosperity, can never give pleasure to an impartial rational spectator" (Kant, *Fundamental Principles of the Metaphysics of Morals*, p. 11).

200. "There arises in many, if they are candid enough to confess it, a certain degree of *misology*, that is, hatred of reason . . . . They end by envying rather than despising the more common stamp of men who keep closer to the guidance of mere instinct, and do not allow their reason much influence on their conduct" (*ibid.*, p. 13).

ity on sensible impulses or inclinations, consciousness tries another tack: it portrays God now not as the Lawgiver who guarantees the sacredness of otherwise imperfect instances of duty, but as the provident Sovereign who alone possesses and dispenses at will throughout the bewildering vastness of specific moral activities that simple positive harmony of natural achievement and moral intention that moral consciousness lacks. But if pure morality is God's prerogative, not only the administration of specific cases, but also the form of pure duty would have to be relegated to Him, leaving human consciousness, bound up in the contingencies of nature, with no morality at all. On the other hand, if God is extolled as having a positive relation to nature, this is a "left-handed compliment," because such a relation is precisely the source of man's moral imperfection. And finally, if morality unfulfilled in nature is worthless, but nature itself is "morally nothing," why should God's postulated ability to *unite* morality with *nature* be considered *morally* significant at all? $(0 + 0 = 0)$ On all these counts this latter concept of God must be judged as basically unsatisfactory and certainly not conducive to morality.

When the moral consciousness tries to formulate a syncretic representation of God now as Legislator and now as provident Sovereign, it is advantaged by the fact that all of the various contradictions are brought "closer" to each other, so to speak, in this syncretic idea; but it is also frustrated and dismayed by the fact that the various contradictions and oppositions must be considered one after the other, and cannot really be considered together, in a true synthesis such as can be found in the Concept.

Moral consciousness thus ultimately becomes aware that its various positions and postulates are forms of hypocrisy, and that its attempts to camouflage or "correct" these hypocritical positions merely leads to further compounded hypocrisy.[201] It now summarily turns its back on the abstract "moral idea of the world" which has been demonstrated to generate such endless contradictions. It returns to repossess itself, and this very act of repossession constitutes the ultimate state of self-

---

201. He who has become aware of the contradictory nature and untenability of abstract and negative moral norms would concur with Nietzsche's observation in *Twilight of the Idols*, p. 46: "Insofar as morality *condemns* as morality and not with regard to the aims and objects of life, it is a specific error with which one should show no sympathy, an idiosyncracy of the degenerate which has caused an unspeakable amount of harm!"

consciousness attainable in the progress of the world-spirit: the state of *Conscience*, a stage in which the rational self-consciousness "is in its own self the simple Spirit that, certain of itself, acts conscientiously regardless of such ideas, and in this immediacy possesses its truth."

c. Conscience. The "Beautiful Soul". Evil and its Forgiveness.

Introductory Remarks:

The present subsection of the section on Morality describes the achievement of the synthesis that Morality proper had been unable to achieve. Morality's attempted synthesis reached its culmination in the ego's self-mediated union of universal and particular will by means of its spontaneously produced concept of duty (e.g. Kant's "Categorical Imperative" as the formal statement of how the particular individual brings his will in line with the universal). But try as it might, Morality could not overcome the embarrassing resistance of external and internal "nature" to the excessively subjective "synthesis" it had made. Its most noble and notable attempt to overcome this last obstacle was in the elaboration of God as the harmonizer of (a) pure moral intention with its "natural" expressions, and of (b) the rebellious human will with the universal will. But this attempt failed because of the element of unreality which attached to God-as-projection. But now, discovering God as its own projected "synthesis," moral consciousness takes the next dialectical step: very simply, it brings about in its own self the desired harmony between self-conscious freedom and nature. For Moral Consciousness, as the source of all the antitheses between nature and moral freedom we have discussed, is also the sole agent that can bring about their reconciliation, once their opposition has been fully understood. The moral consciousness which brings about this reconciliation is called Conscience.

"Conscience" in Hegel's usage means a type of moral consciousness whose natural "inclination" or instinct is to do one's duty, but whose most serious "duty" is to express one's most fundamental feelings or passions. In other words, we have here a kind of conscious, mediated return to the ancient Greek idea of the emergence of virtue (acquired virtue) out of temperament (natural virtue), a unique fusion of the "is" and the "ought" since the man of Conscience interprets Conscience as a self-perpetuating circle of certitude which starts from self-certainty, expresses itself naturally in one's existential situation, and returns to augment the self-certainty with which it began. With the ascendancy of this attitude, we have the epitome of what

Taylor (Hegel, pp. 14 ff.) calls "expressivism"—the ideal of a perfect correspondence and harmony between the outer and the inner. There is also a hint of what in contemporary ethics is called "situation ethics," since one of the distinguishing features of the man of Conscience is that, like the situationist, he has no patience with abstract, universal moral norms and is intent only on bringing full consciousness to bear on his present concrete situation.

At the very beginning of the sections on Religion which are to follow, Hegel (M§677) briefly recapitulates the developments in Morality and refers to Conscience as the stage in which Spirit finally attains "self-consciousness." This causes some confusion, and perhaps betokens some ambivalence in Hegel, since he has already at the beginning of "Culture" (M§442 f.) referred to Morality proper as a stage of "Self-Consciousness," as contrasted with all the sections of Spirit covered so far in this book as "Consciousness." This problem will be taken up again at the end of this chapter (p. 123) but suffice it to say for now that Spirit, as opposed to the monadic individual, comes to "self-consciousness" only when "the I that is a We, and the We that is an I" fully and concretely realize their interrelationship. Morality is a step in that direction since it involves the alignment of the individual with the universal will; Conscience is a further step, since it preserves the advantages of Morality without the disadvantage of disequilibrium with nature; and the final stage of Conscience in which (as we shall see) mutual understanding of Consciences leads to mutual forgiveness and reconciliation is the first full and explicit emergence of a stable, controlled and mediated realization by the spiritual community that it is essentially a *spiritual* community, *a "Universal Individual" in a transcendent or cosmic sense.*

"Conscience" as a type of consciousness is typified in a number of eighteenth-century literary and philosophical works. Imanuel Hirsch (in Materialen, *p. 253) observes that the expression "moral genius"* (moralische Genialität, *M§655) seems to be borrowed from Friedrich Jacobi's novel* Woldemar *(1796). For Woldemar, the "science of the good . . . falls under the province of taste," and moral action is something similar to artistic creativity. One might also discern in the "Acting Consciousness" towards the end of this present section a similarity to Woldemar's confession about having disregarded social conventions towards the end of that novel. But those who would like to find parallels to all the various stages of the present section in Jacobi's unremarkable novel come up with an interpretation that appears overly forced. Hegel does seem to be using the term "Conscience," however, in a sense at least kindred to Jacobi's usage, as Hirsch maintains (ibid.): "For Jacobi, conscience is a primordial feeling in each individual for what is right, and as*

such can be measured by no standard or conventional measuring tape.''

However, as Hirsch (ibid., p. 254) points out, the clearest homology is with Fichte's *doctrine of conscience: "Fichte, in a sharp, clear, and comprehensive exposition of the judgement of conscience, had distinguished the 'conviction'* [Überzeugung, *see e.g.* M§637, B648, H449, B343] *of the individual conscience concerning its specific duty from the question about the validity of the universal moral law, and derived this 'conviction' of conscience from a state of inner certitude; and insofar as for Fichte 'action according to conscience' is practically the last word in ethics . . . , Hegel's statement that the conviction of Conscience must be expressed or declared [see* M§653, B661, H459, B351] *corresponds (for example) to the Duty of Publicizing one's Maxim, on which Fichte had expatiated in his 1798 ethics* [Das System der Sittenlehre. (*Title in English:* Science of Ethics)]. *''*

In Fichte's system of ethics the first two sections are concerned with the deduction of morality, while the last section is concerned with the application of the principle of morality. Fichte summarizes the results of his theoretical deductions at the very end of the second section, as the principle of conscience: "1) I am to act, in general, *with considerateness and consciousness, not blindly and in obedience to mere impulses, and,* in particular, *with the consciousness of duty . . . 2) I am never to act against my conviction* [Überzeugung]. *To do so is completest perversity and wickedness. . . . Both these results gathered into one might be expressed: Act always in accordance to your conscience* [Gewissen]*''* (Science of Ethics, *p. 164). And in an even more emphatic way Fichte, in the role of the disciple of Spirit in the dialogue in Book II of* The Vocation of Man *(p. 90), asserts that "Conscience alone is the root of all truth. Whatever is opposed to conscience or stands in the way of the fulfillment of her behests in assuredly false; I could never become convinced [of an opposed duty], even if I should be unable to discover the fallacies by which it is produced.''*

The "self," or the Person, (1) as the culmination of the *Ethical Order,*[202] was merely the terminal point at which universality ended. (2) As the culmination of the sphere of Culture,[203] it took the form of absolute Free-

---

*Hirsch also mentions (*ibid.*, p. 255) that ''the last pages of [Novalis'] *Heinrich von Ofterdingen* develop a concept of 'conscience' which is completely consonant with Hegel's concept of Conscience.'' And Hyppolite in his French translation of this section notes that the initial stages of Conscience are reminiscent of Schiller's *On Grace and Merit* (1793).

202. See *supra*, pp. 32 ff.
203. See *supra*, pp. 83 ff.

dom, and took the universal[204] into itself as content, *without* giving it an autonomous form of existence.

In the sphere of morality there was an attempt to give the universal[205] an "autonomous" claim to existence, but this attempt resulted merely in the development of *nature* as an element indifferent to morality. Now (3) with Conscience, the Person takes on a new, eminently *concrete* form. Faced with the self-contradictory idea of morality,[206] consciousness realizes that the "beyond" is within the ambit of *consciousness,* and "duty" is nothing but the existence of the *self.*[207] Thus the abstract moments of duty are incorporated into life, and this incorporation takes place directly in and through one's (finer, aesthetic) sensuous nature[208]—i.e., as an immediate conscious certainty. Thus we have the *"conscientious self"* which does not become bewildered over the crisscrossing multiplicity of duties, or become thwarted in action on their account; but in the course of its practical judgments goes beyond that stage where knowledge of duties is an accidental abstract exercise of thought, and explicitly adheres to the *self* as the absolute. In the simple negative unity of this self the abstract moments of duty are transcended, lose their mutual contradictions, and become realized as existent reality, i.e., something *produced,* a true Subjective-Objective Individuality (*Sache*

---

204. I.e., the "General Will."

205. I.e., duty initially abstractly conceived as the pure universal form of duty.

206. Cf. Goethe's *Wilhelm Meister* (p.396): "From systems of morality I could obtain no comfort. Neither their severity, by which they try to bend our inclinations, nor their attractiveness, by which they try to place our inclinations on the side of virtue, gave me any satisfaction."

207. Cf. Kierkegaard, *Either/Or* II, p. 275: "So soon as in despair a person has found himself, has absolutely chosen himself, has repented himself, he has himself as a task under an eternal reponsibility, and thus duty is posited in its absoluteness . . . . His duty is in no case something abstract . . . . "

208. The ultimate result of this aspect of Conscience is reflected in the advice of the uncle to the "Beautiful Soul" in Goethe's *Wilhelm Meister* (p. 410): "Those do not act well, who, in a solitary exclusive manner, follow moral cultivation by itself. On the contrary, it will be found that he whose spirit strives for a development of that kind, has likewise every reason, at the same time, to improve his finer sentient powers; that so he may not run the risk of sinking from his moral height, by giving way to the enticements of a lawless fancy, and degrading his moral nature by allowing it to take delight in tasteless baubles, if not in something worse." Friedrich Schiller expresses similar sentiments in his *Aesthetic Education of Man,* 25th letter: "We must . . . be no longer at a loss to find a passage from sensuous dependence to moral freedom, after we have seen, in the case of Beauty that the two can perfectly well subsist together, and that in order to show himself spirit Man does not need to eschew matter."

selbst) which is here no longer a predicate (as it was in the stage of the
"Honest" consciousness[209]), nor substantiality in general (as it was in
the "Ethical Order") nor an external existence like power or wealth (as
it was in the Realm of Culture), nor an unwieldly thought-synthesis (as
it was in "Morality"), but is *subject*. That is, the subject himself, as
immediate moral self-certainty, is the "truth", the essential "fact"
(*Sache*) produced. And the self at this stage does not jealously try to despoil universality (i.e. Wealth and Power) of autonomous existence, as
the Distraught Consciousness did in the sphere of Culture, but liberally
gives it existence-in-self as well as existence-for-self—as two distinct
moments drawn and held together through the dynamism of the self—
such that the fact or deed which gains subjective truth in the unity of the
self is *at the same time* something objective, or "for-another," a publicly
recognized fact in which intention *and* accomplishment, form *and* content, thought *and* nature, moral idealism *and* the "happiness" of sensuous existence—are identical.[210]

This is not to say that duty is no longer present as an in-itself. But duty
as an in-itself is now a moment directly and explicitly created by, and
controlled by, the self,[211] rather than an unmediated universal or a projection into an unreal "beyond." More specifically, duty now is the objective, public manifestation of one's certitude as something factual and
existent; and it becomes for-another, and is recognized by others for
whom such certitude is counted as conscientiousness; it "falls off from"
the self, so to speak, becomes disengaged from the milieu of self-conscious Reason that had generated it, and is, for all practical purposes a
very special kind of in-itself, a new (moral) kind of objective existent.
And for those who have risen beyond Morality to this present stage,

---

209. See K126 ff.

210. It will be recalled that the motto of Insight was "be for yourselves what you all
are in-yourselves—Rational [i.e., syntheses of thought and being]" (H383, B292). The
present stage of Conscience shows the specifically moral implications of that motto.

211. Cf. Goethe's *Wilhelm Meister*, pp. 383–4: "I drew off the mask, and on all occasions acted as my heart directed . . . . I explained to [my family] . . . that I required full
freedom in my conduct, that my doings and avoidings must depend upon my own conviction; that indeed I would never bigotedly cleave to my own opinion, but on the other
hand would willingly be reasoned with; yet, as it concerned my own happiness, the deci-
sion must proceed from myself, and be liable to no manner of constraint. The greatest
physician could not move me by his reasonings to take an article of food . . . . so soon as
my experience has shown that on all occasions it was noxious to me . . . , and just as little, nay still less, would I have any sort of conduct which misled me, preached up and
demonstrated upon me as morally profitable."

There is no more complaining about good intentions not being fulfilled or about the good man who does not actually attain happiness; rather, what is known as "duty" at this stage is fulfilled and actualized by the very fact that the "dutiful" here is something *recognized*[212] as universal by all these self-consciousnesses, and [through this very act of recognition] becomes something existent.[213]

Qua knowledge, the self-certainty of dutiful Conscience is related to a many-faceted reality which "divides endlessly and breaks up backwards into the conditions [of the conscientious deeds], sideways into their corollaries, and forwards into their consequences."[214] The self absolutely unites these various factors, because it has absolute self-certainty. It is, however, an *incomplete* knowledge; i.e., it does not *encompass all* these factors absolutely. But rather, their totality is present only as a *moment*, standing in contrast to their determination by consciousness (cf. the "world-in-general" vs. "my world").

Qua content, this self-certainty is merely *sensibility* in general—a content which is not absolute in itself, but is the natural determinable element at this stage of consciousness. For just as "pure duty" in the stage of morality had to receive determinate duties as a content, so also pure conviction, here, producing *itself*, and expressing *itself*, must make use of the various impulses and inclinations[215]—i.e. "natural" consciousness.

---

212. "Happiness" or fulfillment for *Conscience* is simply to have its certitude recognized and respected by others.

213. H450–1, B345: *Es ist also da keine Rede mehr davon, das die gute Absicht nicht zustande komme, oder dass es dem Guten schlecht gehe: sondern das als Pflicht Gewusste vollführt sich und kommt zur Wirklichkeit, weil eben das Pflichtmässige das Allgemeine aller Selbstbewusstsein, das Anerkannte und also Seiende ist.*

214. B346, H452: " . . . *die sich rückwärts in ihre Bedingungen, seitwärts in ihrem Nebeneinander, vorwärts in ihren Folgen unendlich teilt und ausbreitet.*"

215. Fichte sees moral conscience and its certitude as a development out of impulse or feeling, rather than as contrary to it: "Whosoever is sure of himself, is so at the risk that he never *can* change the principles which govern his actions . . . . Whether I doubt, or am certain, is a matter which I become anxious of, not through argumentation . . . but through *immediate* feeling. It is only in this manner that subjective certainty, as a state of the mind, may be explained" (*Science of Ethics*, p. 179). In like manner, the "Beautiful Soul" in Goethe's *Wilhelm Meister* (p. 421) asserts: "I scarcely remember a commandment; to me there is nothing that assumes the aspect of law; it is an impulse that leads me, and guides me always aright. I freely follow my emotions, and know as little of constraint as of repentance."

The importance of passion in moral decision-making is a prominent theme in the philosophies of Kierkegaard and Nietzsche. Kierkegaard's Judge William in *Either/Or II*, p. 270, says: 'In the matter of ethics it is not a question of the multifariousness of duty but of its intensity. When with all his energy a person has felt the intensity of duty he is then ethically mature, and in him duty will emerge of itself." And Nietzsche proposes

The essential thing in the sphere of Conscience is the pure and empty certainty of self. This certainty is mediated by universal laws of right and wrong, but it is not constituted by them. Thus the self has absolute power to bind or loosen, and even to judge so-called "universal" laws. Thus what to one individual is "courage" and to another is "coward-ice" may *both* be possessed of the same essential attribute of self-certain-ty—i.e. *both* be conscientiously moral.[216] The universal laws are thus mere predicates for which *consciousness* supplies the subject. The *true universal*[217] at this point is the selfhood of all, which is affirmed in every such act of self-certainty; and the reality and meaning of an individual is thought to be so intertwined with the existence of other individuals, that in acting for the sake of his own self-certainty he is implicitly acting for the benefit of all.

A difficulty ensues here, however, insofar as the *content*, i.e., the actual effect, of a *deed* of conscience, is nonessential and arbitrary; it is the can-celled or transcended existence of pure empty self-certainty, which—as soon as it is accomplished—falls off from the spirit that gave birth to it, becoming detached, "displaced." Thus it takes on the aspect of a for-eign, inherent being to the conscience which posited it; and to other consciences, who do not even have the sense of being remotely responsi-ble for the deed, it seems suspiciously bereft of the only *publicly acknowl-edged* redeeming factor—conscientious self-certainty, and thus it takes on the aspect of mere *fulfillment of pleasure*, and even of *evil* (since it is

---

his own version of morality as the *inverse* of what Hegel above called the "First Postu-late" (i.e. that happiness should be a consequence of morality): "A well-constituted hu-man being, a happy one, *must* perform certain actions and instinctively shrinks from other actions . . . . His virtue is the *consequence* of his happiness . . . . Everything *good* is instinct—and consequently easy, necessary, free" (*Twilight of the Idols*, p. 48).

216. This Fichtean principle is the foundation for moral tolerance: "What exercise of freedom is in violation of the moral law, and who can be the universally valid judge thereof? If *the other* asserts that he has acted in accordance with his best conviction, whilst *I* act under the same circumstances differently, *he* is as convinced that I act immorally, as I am convinced that he acts immorally. Whose conviction is now to be the rule? Neither, so long as both are in dispute, for each is to act solely according to *his* conviction, and therein consists the *formal* condition of all morality" (*Science of Ethics*, p. 245). Fichte real-izes the potential of this principle in creating ethical disorder, but merely expresses opti-mism that if such consciences discuss things communally with each other they will be able to iron out their differences.

217. Note that the "universality" which emerges here is a peculiarly Hegelian univer-sality—not the universality created when thought unifies external content, but a sec-ond-order universality uniting the thoughtful Conscience with its special, moral, ex-ternal milieu.

something inorganic which may be analyzed and reduced to nothingness by these other consciences; for, after all, it is not the product of *their*
self-certainty).

Language here again (as in the realm of Culture) supplies the way out
of the difficulties:[218]

> Here again it is Language that gives existential instantiation to Spirit. Language is
> *self*-consciousness immediately present as such, and existing for-another; and although
> a "this," is also simultaneously universal. Language is the self-sundering [*sich abtren-*
> *nende*] self which as pure "ego=ego" objectifies itself, *but remains this* self throughout this
> objectification, in which it fuses directly with other selves and becomes their self-con-
> sciousness [also]. The self through language thus grasps itself in being grasped by
> others, and the very act of grasping is simultaneously a transmission of *existence* into self-
> hood.[219]

Language is an existent which is also at the same time thought: it is
"for consciousness," and simultaneously "for others"—thus uniting
individuality with universality, unity with multiplicity, self with others.
And so with the advent of language whose very essence is to unite particular and universal, there is no longer the problem of the particular
"detaching itself" from the universal. But it should be noted that the essential thing to be expressed by the language of Conscience is not the existence of this or that duty, or the relevance of a duty to this or that situation—but only one's *conviction* that one's act was a duty.[220] For we have
left behind that sphere where there was a dichotomy between the universal and the particular, and have come to the point where *self-certitude itself*
is acknowledged by one and all to be the absolute. And language gives us
direct access to, or a perfect mirror of, such self-certitude. Therefore,
when through language, a person expresses his immediate certainty of

---

218. Hyppolite (*Genesis and Structure*, p. 512, and in footnotes to his translation of this
section) notes that the emphasis on expressing one's conviction in language is found frequently in eighteenth-century literature, in Rousseau's *New Héloise* and *Confessions*,
and in Goethe's *Wilhelm Meister* and *The Sorrows of Young Werther*.

219. *B*351, H458: *Wir sehen hiemit wieder die* Sprache *als das Dasein des Geistes. Sie ist das*
für andre *seiende Selbstbewusstsein, welches unmittelbar* als solches vorhanden *und als*
dieses *allgemeines ist. Sie ist das sich von sich selbst abtrennende Selbst, das als reines Ich = Ich sich*
gegenständlich wird, in dieser Gegenständlichkeit sich ebenso als dieses *Selbst erhält,*
wie es unmittelbar mit den andern zusammenfliesst und ihr Selbstbewusstsein ist; es vernimmt eben-
so sich, als es von den Andern vernommen wird, und das Vernehmen ist eben das zum Selbst ge-
wordne Dasein.

220. "It is [man's] duty to communicate his convictions, and thus to make them of common use . . . . " (Fichte, *Science of Ethics*, p. 262).

conscience, no one of his hearers (who also consider such certitude to be the only important thing) can doubt him, or gainsay him[221]—but such an utterance is *ipso facto* an utterance of a publicly accepted "first principle,"—a truth. Thus Conscience takes on the aspect of a moral genius [*moralische Genialität*], creative through the very act of forming moral conceptions which are equivalent to a "divine voice" and constitute one's own private divinity[222]—to be served and worshipped.

This solitary worship and service of God, which are the marks of an acme of *self*-consciousness, also comes to take on the aspect of consciousness, pure and simple (i.e. a subject–object relationship). Thus, in a religious community of ethical fellowship,[223] self-consciousness finds objective

---

221. It is conceivable, of course, that a person might *say* he has certitude about his actions when he really does not, just to get public acceptance for what he is doing. But such a person does not really belong to this circle of *Consciences*, for whom the only "entrance requirement" is the acceptance of the principle that self-certitude is the only essential thing. Once this principle *is* accepted, there would be no point in pretending to have a certitude one doesn't have. For such a pretense would indicate that one doesn't actually hold to certitude as the essential thing. As far as his basic philosophy and values were concerned, he would be "speaking another language"; and presumably he would either become dissaffected with the others, and detach himself from them, or be discovered by them.

In a way the problematic here is analogous to that of determining "good faith" in Sartre's schema, or "authenticity" in Heidegger's. How could we tell if a person really had chosen to be free, accepted his/her facticity, etc. except on the basis of his/her own personal testimony?

The following example may help to illustrate the interesting effect of subjective presuppositions on the sort of situation envisaged here: If one accepted *tolerance* as his absolute value, then anything, even insincerity, might be *accepted* in others, provided only that these others give evidence of tolerance. If one accepted *sincerity* as absolute, then intolerance, for example, might be accepted, as long as it was sincere. If, as in the present situation with Conscience, the absolute value is the-forthright-expression-of-one's-innermost-sentiments, then even if a person were intolerant or insincere, he might be accepted if he insisted that this was the expression of his innermost self (i.e., his inner self is basically insincere and intolerant, so his only "duty" is to express *that*).

222. In Goethe's *Wilhelm Meister* (pp. 392–3), the "Beautiful Soul" writes: "When I sought God sincerely, he let himself be found of me, and did not reproach me about bygone things. On looking back, I saw well enough where I had been unworthy, where I still was so; but the confession of my faults was altogether without terror . . . . The thing, the wicked and inexplicable thing, which separates us from the Being to whom we owe our life, and in whom all that deserves the name of life must find its nourishment; the thing which we call Sin, I yet knew nothing of."

223. This conception of a kind of Church of Consciences is found in Fichte's *Science of Ethics*: "[The] reciprocity amongst all rational beings for the purpose of producing common practical convictions, is called a *Church*, an ethical commonwealth; and that about which they all agree is called their *symbol*. Each one ought to be a member of the

expression and confirmation of its own divine certitude. This religion, *qua* objective knowledge, becomes the utterance of the religious communion regarding its own spirit. But at the present stage of religion there is merely an *immediacy of* relationship to the Supreme Being and to the fellowship, which obviates any true and stable integration and mediation of the distinct moments of consciousness and self-consciousness. For self-consciousness, in spite of its accomplishment in making the divine (which had formerly been projected into a "beyond") into a present possession of its own soul, has therein merely become more firmly wedged into an extremely subjective intuition of the ego as ego, and this intuition of ego = ego provides a very fluid and unstable foundation for religious community. And thus the moments of existence-for-self, existence-in-self, and determinate existence collapse immediately into one another; the more stable aspect of consciousness that the religious community will eventually bring remains at present[224] still unattainable, and self-consciousness is magnified to such an extent that the absolute certainty which made it possible now begins to become manifest as absolute *untruth*.

For, considered in its "substance," or as knowledge of knowledge, self-consciousness at this stage flees from objective existence-in-self, and is so lost in consciousness of self (existence-for-self), that it refuses to endanger this abstract self-possession and externalize itself in grappling

---

church" (p. 248). "All, necessarily, as sure as their destination is dear to them, are desirous to infuse their convictions into all others, and the union of all for this purpose is called the Church" (p. 254).

224. The Fichtean religious fellowship described here is only an imperfect approximation to the idea of a true religious community, which will emerge especially in the later section on "Revealed Religion." Note that the religious orientation, whether here or later in Revealed Religion, is characterized as a moment of "Self-consciousness," but Hegel also gauges the relative maturity of the religious orientation by using the yardstick of Consciousness, i.e., the communal aspect of religion. This needs explanation. Religion in its various forms is a manifestation of Spirit, which in all its forms is a relationship of the individual to the community and vice versa. Religion accentuates the element of Self-Consciousness, but any augmentation of *Self*-Consciousness in Spirit must go hand-in-hand with a corresponding maturation in the communal or "conscious" aspect. We are a long way now from the religion of the abstract Unhappy Consciousness which could find no substantial reflection of its beliefs. Even the momentary reappearance of the Unhappy Consciousness later in the chapter on "Revealed Religion" must be taken in the context of "Spirit" (as defined above), which overrides and gives meaning to even the most abstract and subjective moments that make their appearance within its parameters.

with reality. Thus we have the unworldly purity of the so-called "Beautiful Soul,"[225] which

lacks the power to externalize itself, to make itself into a thing and to put up with existence; which lives in dread of sullying its inwardness by concrete being and action; and, in order to preserve the purity of its heart, flees from contact with reality[226] and remains

---

225. In *Early Theological Writings,* (p. 234), Hegel considers Jesus a paradigmatic example of "beauty of soul" because he was able to synthesize the opposites of courage and passivity in his personality. But as Niel (*De la Mediation*, pp. 173–4) and others have observed, the term "Beautiful Soul" as used in the *Phenomenology* has a more pejorative sense. Niel (*ibid.*) suggests that Hegel here has Novalis in mind as a "Beautiful Soul," and Hegel's very short section on "Novalis" in *History of Philosophy* III (p. 510) does bear a strong resemblance to the description of the "Beautiful Soul" given here. Hirsch (in *Materialen*, p. 256) notes the strong resemblance of the "Beautiful Soul" to Jacobi's character Woldemar, and Hölderlin's hero Hyperion. Hyppolite (*Genesis and Structure*, p. 513) sees the concept of the Beautiful Soul reflected in "Jacobi's characters, the Allwills and the Woldemars," while Gray (*Hegel and Greek Thought*, p. 35) traces the idea to Schiller's influence. Loewenberg (*Hegel's Phenomenology*) adds Goethe to the above roster, and indeed it would seem (see Appendix, #6) that the various developments in these passages that deal with the Beautiful Soul are similar in pattern to those in the long narrative paper entitled "Confessions of a Beautiful Soul" included in Goethe's *Wilhelm Meister*. And the description given by Wilhelm Meister of his impressions of the author of this narrative coincide very well with Hegel's descriptions of the general characteristic of the Beautiful Soul. Wilhelm Meister says (p. 515): "What most impressed me in this paper was, if I may term it so, the purity of being, not only of the writer herself, but of all that lay around her; that self-dependence of nature, that impossibility of admitting anything into her soul which would not harmonize with its own noble lovely tone."
In general, the Beautiful Soul is one final noble attempt to overcome the Kantian dichotomies of morality with that synthesis of duty and inclination that has characterized Conscience from the beginning. However, there is also something added here to the general characteristics of Conscience—and this is the attempt to produce the most perfect synthesis possible by withdrawing from hostile or troublesome worldly obstacles into a kind of aesthetic–moral hothouse of contemplative solitude. Thus the basic deficiency of this "solution" is its excessively abstract nature, its affirmation of the universality of Conscience at the expense of that practical engagement with particulars that can prove so inimical to the serenity of Conscience. As it turns out, the tragedy of the Beautiful Soul, as Bonsiepen (*Der Begriff der Negativität*, p. 170) observes, is that it lacks the power to make itself into a concrete thing, or being, thus giving the lie to the basic insight of Reason that emerged at the end of the chapter on "Observation" (see K115), expressed in the formula, "the mind is a thing."
226. Reminiscing about the very beginning of her "conversion" from her previous ordinary upper-class life, the Beautiful Soul writes in her Confessions: "What could it be which so changed my tastes and feelings, that, in my twenty-second year, nay earlier, I lost all relish for the recreations with which people of that age are harmlessly delighted?...I knew, from experiences which had reached me unsought, that there are loftier emotions, which afford us a contentment such as it is vain to seek in the amusements of

adamant in its stubborn powerlessness—powerlessness to renounce a self reduced now to the most rarified abstraction, powerlessness to give any substance to itself or to convert its thinking into existing, powerless to entrust itself to that which is so utterly "other."[227]

In view of this general orientation, it is not surprising that

the empty "object" which the Beautiful Soul produces fills it now with the consciousness of . . . emptiness[!]; and its "deed" is a passionate longing[228]which loses itself to become an object without substance, and only returns to itself from its forlornness to find that it is . . . lost[!].[229]

Thus the unhappy[230] Beautiful Soul

finally flickers in the transparent purity of its moments, then disappears as a formless vapor that loses itself in the air.[231]

In stark contrast to the Beautiful Soul as universal consciousness there appears another mode of Conscience, which speaks the same "language"—the language of simple self-certitude and simple self-expression—but engages in *action* and grapples with the hard realities of

---

the world. . . ." (Goethe's *Wilhelm Meister*, pp. 381-83). Then later, regarding the period in which she had become stabilized in her new way of life, she writes: "My most peculiar advantage lay in this, that love for quiet was my ruling passion, and that in the end I still drew back to it. I perceived, as in a kind of twilight, my weakness and my misery and tried to save myself by avoiding danger and exposure" (*ibid*, p. 393).

227. *B*354, H462-3: *Es fehlt ihm die Kraft der Entäusserung, die Kraft, sich zum Dinge zu machen und das Sein zu ertragen. Es lebt in der Angst, die Herrlichkeit seines Innern durch Handlung und Dasein zu beflecken; und um die Reinheit seines Herzens zu bewahren, flieht es die Berührung der Wirklichkeit und beharrt in der eigensinnigen Kraftlosigkeit, seinem zur letzten Abstraktion zugespitzten Selbst zu entsagen und sich Substantialität zu geben oder sein Denken in Sein zu verwandeln und sich dem absoluten Unterschiede anzuvertrauen.*

228. Loewenberg sees in this reference a reflection of the romantic creed, expressed in Schlegel's *Lucinde* as a "longing for longing" or everlasting longing.

229. *B*354-5, H463: *Der hohle Gegenstand, den es sich erzeugt, erfüllt es daher nun mit dem Bewusstsein der Leerheit; sein Tun ist das Sehnen, das in dem Werden seiner selbst zum wesenlosen Gegenstande sich nur verliert, und über diesen Verlust hinaus und zurück zu sich fallend, sich nur als verlornes findet.*

230. Unhappy, not because it can't objectify itself (the predicament of the Unhappy Consciousness), but because the objectification it produced (the expression of feeling and passion) is so unsubstantial. Hirsch (in *Materialen*, p. 256) sees this unhappiness exemplified in Novalis, who depicted "the unending development of feeling into a state of emptiness, and into a longing for death."

231. *B*355, H463: . . . *in dieser durchsichtigen Reinheit seiner Momente eine unglückliche sogenannte schöne Seele, verglimmt sie in sich und schwindet als ein gestaltloser Dunst, der sich in Luft auflöst.*

the world.[232] It is hardly to be wondered at if this latter consciousness, the Acting Conscience, finds itself intermittently in difficulties trying to subsume all its multifarious duties under the rubric of "conscientious self-certainty." Aside from the practical difficulties entailed in keeping the two sides (universal expression and inner certitude) together, there is a built-in limitation of language itself, which in joining subjective certitude with its many external predicates also at the same time keeps the subjective and objective apart and accentuates their separation. The failure of the particular to jibe with the universal (the good) counts, however, as *evil*. And the fact that the Acting Conscience, being a form of Conscience, still has to affirm the unity of its particular desires with the universality of its public expressions, while *de facto* this unity is not recog-

---

232. While the Beautiful Soul, in order to maintain the synthesis of Conscience between morality and reality, had gone to the extreme of withdrawing from reality, or at least restricting the compass of particular realities that it would have to deal with; the Acting Consciousness, on behalf of maintaining the same synthesis, goes to the other extreme and severely restricts the scope of moral principles he would like to realize in the world, and then *afterwards* is very conscientious about justifying what he has accomplished. As an exemplification of this type, one thinks of geniuses in the practical realm like Caesar or Napoleon who are impelled by highly idealistic visions even though, as Hegel observes in *Philosophy of History,* p. 67, they do not meet up to the strictest standards of morality.

Hyppolite (*Genesis and Structure,* p. 515) also suggests that the "Acting Consciousness" in the context of Goethe's *Wilhelm Meister* is typified by Natalie, the active and resourceful "Amazon" who rescued Wilhelm and later became his wife.

However we instantiate this type, the important thing to remember is that the Acting Conscience is not your stereotyped unprincipled "pragmatist," but the man whose only fault is that he is overoptimistic about uniting adaptability and flexibility with genuine seriousness of conscience.

The ensuing relationship between the Beautiful Soul and the Acting Consciousness is comparable to the previous dialectic between Master and Slave (K89 f.). The Beautiful Soul, like the Master, holds on to essential universality through the power of thought, but does so in an extremely abstract fashion and thus loses firsthand contact with reality. The Acting Consciousness, like the Slave, is preeminently in contact with reality in all its manifold particularity; but, as a reaction to his negative experiences (analogous to the Slave's "fear of fear"), attains to a vision of his essential human condition (and the concomitant conviction that he is hypocritical) and thus finds that he is identical with the Beautiful Soul (which will also more reluctantly and hesitantly become convinced of its own hypocrisy). The result will be dissolution of the difference between the opposites, but in the present case this dissolution will be much more highly mediated than in the case of the dissolution of the Master–Slave dichotomy. While Master and Slave were amalgamated into the single "Stoical" Self-Consciousness (K93), the Beautiful Soul and Acting Consciousness will maintain their identity while simultaneously contributing to the emergence of something greater than themselves: Spirit as *Self*-Conscious, i.e., religious consciousness.

by *the* universal consciousness, makes it not only evil but *hypocriti-*

The Beautiful Soul which manages to keep its personal impulses "universal" by withdrawing itself from all public expression—by refraining from action[233]—prides itself on the purity thus maintained, and considers itself the champion of universality. It naturally is quick to notice the less-than-successful attempts of the Acting Conscience to maintain its simple certainty amidst all its deeds, and it judges the Acting Conscience to be defective in universality, i.e., sullying its commitment to duties by allowing its own particular intentions to come to the fore, indulging in selfish motives, and seeking personal satisfaction. From this new development it becomes obvious (1) that the absolute moral certainty (of pure duty) that prevailed among consciousnesses in the initial stage of Conscience, can *only* be maintained in a state of relative withdrawal from the world, as epitomized by the Beautiful Soul; and (2) that in judging the Acting Conscience, the Beautiful Soul places itself spiritually *alongside* the latter, and must sooner or later come to notice its peculiar similarity to the latter as well as its difference. (Yes, the Beautiful Soul *is* different from the Acting Conscience because it champions the Universal, while the latter cannot, and desires not to, conceal the particularity of the sensible impulses that enter into his multiple activities. But there is also a very important *similarity,* in fact an identity: While the Acting Conscience is hypocritical for trying continually to justify any conceivable kind of deed by his conscientiousness, the Beautiful Soul is equally hypocritical for trying to pass off its personal conviction as a prevailing universal, and its mere stance of judgment and criticism, as its "adherence to duty," as its actual deed. Thus they are fundamentally kindred souls.)

The Acting Conscience is the first to notice this. Recognizing that he is similar to, and, indeed equal with, the Beautiful Soul, he decides to acknowledge the censorious judgments of the latter by Confession.[234] He confesses his failure to align himself with the Universal; i.e., he con-

---

233. In the chapter on the Ethical Substance, Hegel similarly equated innocence with a state of relative passivity: "Innocence is . . . mere inaction like the being of a stone; it is not even on the level of the being and activity of a child." (*Unschuldig ist . . . nur das Nichttun wie das Sein eines Steines, nicht einmal eines Kindes.* [*B*254, H334].

234. In Goethe's *Wilhelm Meister,* the Beautiful Soul, after years of a rather withdrawn existence as a canoness, meets a middle-aged man called "Philo," who keeps her informed about matters in the world, and, little by little, begins to reveal things about him-

fesses his condition as evil. By this spoken confession he purports to bring Spirit into real existence through the mutual recognition that he expects to result from this confession.

But this expectation is aborted. The Beautiful Soul hard-heartedly rejects the "mere words" of the Acting Conscience, stands fast in the mere words of its own judgment-without-action, and instead of responding with a similar confession, simply retreats further and further within itself, so as to avoid all possibilities of losing its certitude of pure universality in future encounters with reality and with the "evil" consciousness. But in doing this, the Beautiful Soul (1) shows that it is not truly superior, but is rather the proverbial "valet"[235] who, because of his expert knowledge of, and jaundiced concentration on, the insignificant particulars of his master's behavior, fails to perceive the universal or the "heroic" in the latter; (2) definitely proves itself to be in the wrong according to its very own principles: that everyone should give public utterance to the true condition of his inner soul; and (3) in failing to acknowledge any imperfection, does a grave injustice to Spirit itself, which "is lord and master over every deed and actuality, and can cast them off, and make them as if they never happened."

The Beautiful Soul, opposing its own unacknowledged judgments to the unacknowledged confession of the Acting Conscience, remains stubbornly hinged to its vaunted purity of conscience, but, because of its discomforting encounters with the latter, cannot help but become more conscious of its complete aloofness in the world. As a result, it "is disordered to the point of madness, wastes itself in yearning and pines away in consumption."[236]

This ultimate state of depression and abstraction, however, proves to be the necessary and sufficient impetus for Spirit's supersession of the present impasse. For this state of "madness" breaks up the hard and self-centered heart of the Beautiful Soul, and leaves it in a new state of uni-

---

self: "There were some confessions he had still kept back; and even at last he told me only what enabled me to guess the worst."

235. Hegel's allusion here is to Madame Cornuel's (and also Napoleon's) dictum: "No man is a hero to his *valet-de-chambre.*" Hegel refers again to the above comments from the *Phenomenology* later in *Philosophy of History*, p. 32.

236. Loewenberg (*Hegel's Phenomenology*, p. 285) remarks that this is an obvious and cruel allusion to the cause of Novalis' death—consumption. The cruelty of the remark, however, may be mitigated by the fact that Novalis himself strenuously insisted on the correspondence of outer conditions to inner states.

versality, a universality with the new awareness of the necessity for a living, conscious reciprocity with particularity. This state of universality, however, which is only possible through an awareness of the true condition of the Beautiful Soul, now makes possible for this ''universal consciousness'' the attainment of the goal which it had been implicitly pursuing throughout all these developments: *recognition*—not just recognition by a select coterie but recognition in the actual spiritual world by the contraposed Acting Conscience. Both consciences now perceive each other as consciousnesses that have, each in their own way, renounced an overly subjective, merely verbal assurance of the synthesis of thought and reality, and thus have risen to true universality. So now the Beautiful Soul, forced into a recognition of its own sin and hypocrisy, and of its identity with the Acting Conscience,[237] is finally able to reciprocate the Confession made by the latter, and extends the hand of forgiveness to the other. This forgiveness

is the Beautiful Soul's renunciation of itself, of its own *unreal* essence with which it [now] compares that other side that presented itself as *real* activity; and it [now] recognizes such activity as ''good'' (whereas formerly it had been designated as ''bad'' because of the determination that ''activity'' had connoted in its thinking); in other words it drops this [former] adjudication from such ''determinate'' thinking, and its own ''*self*-determined'' [*fürsichseiendes bestimmendes*] judgment; and the Acting Conscience reciprocates by dropping his claims about the ''self-determined'' character [*fürsichseiende Bestimmen*] of his own practical activity.[238]

This mutual forgiveness and recognition is the healing Word that not only reconciles two opposing spirits but also, in ''closing the circuit,'' so

---

237. After the Beautiful Soul mentions Philo's confession to her (see *supra*, n. 234), she says: ''What an effect had this upon my heart! I attained experiences which to me were altogether new.... After having long occupied myself with the temper of his mind, I at last turned round to contemplate my own. The thought, 'thou art no better than he,' rose like a little cloud before me, and gradually expanded till it darkened all my soul'' (*ibid.*). And she goes on to reflect (*ibid.*, p. 396): ''For ten years, I had already practised more than mere virtue; and the horrors now first discovered [upon the confessions of her friend, Philo] had all the while, lain hidden at the bottom of my soul. Might they not have broken out with me as they did with David when he looked on Bathsheba?''

238. *B*361, H471: *Die Verzeihung, die es dem ersten widerfahren lässt, ist die Verzichtleistung auf sich, auf sein unwirkliches Wesen, dem es jenes andere, das wirkliches Handeln war, gleichsetzt, und es, das von der Bestimmung, die das Handeln im Gedanken erhielt, Böses genannt wurde, als gut anerkennt, oder vielmehr diesen Unterschied des bestimmten Gedankens und sein fürsichseiendes bestimmendes Urteil fahren lässt, wie das Andre das fürsichseiende Bestimmen der Handlung.*

to speak, between these paradigmatic oppositions, simultaneously brings about the advent of the Concept in its completeness, i.e., explicit Spirit,[239] in the world as a whole:

> The Word of reconciliation [mutual Confession and forgiveness] is the coming into *existence* of Spirit, which is this intuition [of the unity-of-opposites, i.e.] of the pure knowledge of self as *universal* essence [typified by the Beautiful Soul], in its opposite, i.e. in the pure knowledge of self as absolute self-possessing *individuality* [typified by the Acting Conscience]—and this recognition as reciprocal and reciprocated is *Absolute* Spirit.[240]

In other words, Spirit, which is essentially the unity of opposites, is now created as an objective presence in the world (although, from another point of view, one might say that Spirit as implicit Concept has been "working behind the scenes" all the while to bring the present stage about). As the Beautiful Soul and the Acting Conscience become reconciled with *each other*, those formerly unmediated oppositions of essence and self-consciousness, duty and evil, universality and particularity, now become *concretely* mediated with one another in the world as a whole, producing the phenomenal presence of a spiritual totum. Absolute Spirit is explicitly present in the world, appearing necessarily in the midst of the mutually reconciled consciousnesses.

At this point it would be helpful to stop to consider the past and future dialectical movements which supply the context for the present developments: In Part I, Consciousness and Self-Consciousness became synthesized in Reason, and this synthesis culminated in Spirit as manifest intersubjectivity (self-consciousnesses who organize themselves into an Ethical Substance appearing objectively for Consciousness). This manifest intersubjectivity (Spirit, with which Part II began) then is treated as a kind of immediate "Consciousness" which gradually arrives at the *vestibule* of "Self-Consciousness" (i.e., the present point, where individual Consciousnesses of opposite persuasions—represented by the Beautiful Soul and the Acting Conscience—become explicitly aware that they are mediating their own intersubjective unity, which now appears

---

239. As in the message of the Gospel, man in attaining reconciliation (*Versöhnung*) with his fellow man is in that very act reconciled to God; and vice versa, reconciliation with God is impossible without reconciliation with one's fellow men. Cf. e.g., Matthew VI, 14; and John's First Epistle, IV, 20.

240. *B*361, H471: *Das Wort der Versöhnung ist der* daseiende *Geist, der das reine Wissen seiner selbst als* allgemeinen *Wesens in seinem Gegenteile, in dem reinen Wissen seiner als der absolut in sich seienden* Einzelheit *anschaut, —ein gegenseitiges Anerkennen, welches der* absolute *Geist ist.*

explicitly as Spirit). Thus the present point is analogous to the earlier stage of Understanding, at the conclusion of which Consciousness arrived at the vestibule of Self-Consciousness (see K81 f.). And now in the major section on "Religion" immediately following, the intersubjective experience of Spirit will be examined in its phase of Self-Consciousness.

We will see how in this stage the self-consciousness of Absolute Spirit progresses in its own right towards its culmination in the full revelation of truth. In this culmination, the reconciling "Yea" will bring about a final union between saint and sinner, contemplative and activist, in a fully reflective manifestation of Absolute Spirit, which will simultaneously amount to the actual, concrete revelation of God among men. Then in the final section, "Absolute Knowledge," the various strands of the Conscious and Self-Conscious stages of Spirit will be brought together in a synthesis.

VII.
Religion
[Spirit as Self-Conscious or Transcendent]

Introductory Remarks:

Here we enter into a completely new realm of Spirit. All the preceding stages of Spirit were stages of "Consciousness," in the sense that they emphasized the "horizontal" progress of Spirit through the dialectical development of stronger and stronger, more and more effective intersubjective ties, which from a phenomenological point of view are the external or objective aspects of Spirit's overarching and absolute unification of opposites. The outer limits of this horizontal process were reached in Morality, where the relation of the individual will to the universal will became internalized and conceptually mediated; and finally in Conscience, where the community of mutually respecting Consciences formed themselves into an ethico-religious fellowship and ultimately stabilized this fellowship by recognizing the necessity of, and even institutionalizing, mutual forgiveness. In these latter stages, concomitant with the "horizontal" process of unification, we can also begin to see glimmerings of a "vertical" process* by which each individual spirit is

---

*P.-J. Labarriere in his ingenious schema of the relation between Religion and prior chapters of the *Phenomenology,* uses "vertical" differently, to designate the various preceding phenomenological spheres (see *Structures et mouvement...,* p. 159). However, as Labarriere himself notes (*ibid.,* pp. 162, 167, 182), some problems develop in the application of his simile to the various substages of Religion.

not only drawn into a greater one-to-one relationship with other individual spirits but also is gravitating to a unity with Spirit itself, the *Spirit that animates all, as a unity and entity in its own right. Here we are reminded of the Christian idea that unity with fellow man and unity with God are inseparable coordinates (see n. 239* supra). *One can make only a mental distinction between these two aspects, since they are really "two sides of the same coin." At the present juncture in the* Phenomenology *we* are *making such a mental distinction. Having traced the "horizontal" progress of Spirit, we now begin to trace the "vertical" process, the process of unification with Spirit itself, perceived phenomenologically as a* self-conscious *entity moving through time and gradually manifesting its true countenance— which, as it turns out, is a synthesis of the human and the divine. From the point of view of the individual consciousnesses undergoing this "vertical" process, the experience is not to be described as "Self-Consciousness" in the ordinary sense, with emphasis on the monadic ego's ability to take itself as object and transcend itself, but in a special and restricted sense: as a gradually increasing awareness that something or someone greater than the self, greater than any individual ego, is emerging within the individual consciousness, especially in and through its interrelationships with the religious community. In contemporary parlance, we could call this latter experience the experience of "transcendence," as long as it is clearly understood that the transcendence experienced is a "second-order" transcendence—not just (1) the divine transcendence of the human, but (2) transcendence of the dichotomy between the divine and the human. Transcendence in this second-order sense is analogous to Hegel's use of "universal" in a second-order sense, to connote not just (1) the negative abstraction from particulars but (2) the positive synthesis of the negative universal unity with the discreteness of particulars; and also Hegel's second-order use of "supersession" (aufheben) to connote not just (1) the dialectical negation of a thesis but (2) the negation-of-the-negation, resulting in a new thesis.*

Hegel, in his emphasis on the transcendent, vertical unifying and integrating function of Religion, is in line with much contemporary thinking in theology, cultural anthropology and sociology, if we are to give credence to Hans Mol, who in his Identity and the Sacred *sifts current scientific opinion on religion-as-phenomenon and concludes that "there is a dialectic between [differential] adaptation and identity or between differentiation and [unitive] integration and . . . religious organization and orientations (but also art and play) are anything but impartial in this dialectic. My definition puts them squarely on the identity/integration side of the dialectic where, since Durkheim, empirical research has located them." (Op. cit., p. 3.)*

In view of the fact that Hegel in the Phenomenology *(in contrast with his later*

System in the final editions of the Encyclopedia*) does not treat art separately from religion but in conjunction, as "Art Religion," Mol's ascription of the unifying/ integrating function to "art and play," as well as religion, is significant. For Hegel, especially in the chapter on "Art Religion," presents the aesthetic and the religious as two almost indistinguishable orientations geared to bringing about the experience of second-order "transcendence," or the truth of Self-Consciousness.* **

Granted that the treatments of Art, Religion and "Absolute Knowledge" (a philosophical synthesis) in these last chapters of the Phenomenology *will differ somewhat and undergo some loosening of relationships in their evolution in equivalent concepts in Hegel's later System, Hegel throughout all of his works consistently considers them all as related to the self-consciousness of the Absolute, or what we have called here "transcendence." As early as 1801, Hegel includes art and philosophy in a category that we customarily reserve to religion: "Both art and speculation are in their essence divine service—both are a living intuition of the absolute life and hence a being at one with it"* (Difference between Fichte's and Schelling's System, *p. 172). And as late as 1830 Hegel portrays Art and Religion as closely related to, and indeed subsumed into, philosophy: "Philosophy not merely keeps [art and religion] together to make a totality, but even unifies them into the simple spiritual vision, and then in that raises them to self-conscious thought. Such consciousness is thus the intelligible unity (cognized by thought) of art and religion, in which the diverse elements in the content are cognized as necessary, and this 'necessary' as free"* (Philosophy of Mind, §572). *In reading statements like this, one is struck by the thought that, in view of such a conception of philosophy, it is hardly any wonder that Hegel's philosophy (even his logic and political philosophy) is so heavily laden from beginning to end with theology and theodicy, elements of Greek tragedy and the ironical twists of Greek comedy (tragedy and comedy will be presented as the two highest art forms in the section on "Art Religion"). In view of this (to us) strange and unique conception of philosophy, it is perhaps appropriate that Hegel will entitle the last chapter of the* Phenomenology *"Absolute Knowledge" instead of simply "Philosophy."*

The various phenomenological stages which we have considered so far—Consciousness, Self-Consciousness, Reason, and Immediate Spirit—have had a temporal, historical aspect, insofar as they have been represented in concrete forms (*Gestalten*) which are discrete from one another and can be related to one another in temporal succession.

**A similar synthesis of the two orientations is noteworthy in Harvey Cox's theory of "theology as play" (Ch. XIII in *The Seduction of the Spirit* [New York, 1973]).

But now with the stages of Absolute Freedom, Morality and Conscience the historically-related segments of the *Phenomenology* which describe the progress of Spirit in the *World* have come to their terminus. Now as we embark on the second major stage of Spirit—religious consciousness—we will be relating a quite different species of "history": the history of the self-conscious interiorization and supercession of the actual world, a narrative which must necessarily depart from the linear, chronological order that has characterized the phenomenology of Spirit so far.[1]

---

1. As was mentioned above, Spirit in the preceding section was considered in its "horizontal" progression, laying the foundations for an extensive intersubjective network, while in the present sections Spirit is considered in its "vertical" aspect, as an intensification and deepening of spiritual transcendence, which from the point of view of the finite consciousness appears as the experience of being united with some Entity greater than consciousness, and from the point of view of that entity (at least in the beginning, when the two points of view can be distinguished), means the attainment of Self-Consciousness in and through the historical progressions of mankind.

In the *Addition* to *Philosophy of Right*, §258, Hegel makes the statement that the existence of the State is attributable to the march of God through the world ("*Es ist der Gang Gottes in der Welt, dass der Staat ist*"). This statement has often been translated as if "dass" were "das," so that we end up with the unnecessarily totalitarian statement that "the state is the march of God in the world." Leaving aside such mistranslations, and also leaving aside the particular application to the State, I would like to emphasize here the fact that Hegel speaks there of *God marching or journeying through the world*, embodying Himself *(among other things)* in various State-forms. This metaphor is important for understanding the reason why Hegel says now that the section on Religion which is to follow is not subject to historical progressions in the way that all former stages were. He says this because he considers Spirit (in its "vertical" aspect, i.e., as an overarching Unity, as a self-conscious Entity gradually taking on person-like features) to be, yes, marching through the world, or more precisely through time and the progressions of human history (a point which he elaborates at the very end of the last chapter of the *Phenomenology*). The metaphor is clear enough if Spirit is not just some epiphenomenon concomitant to history, but some supreme Entity which remains essentially the same while making its way through world history and emerging in *human* consciousnesses, although it embodies itself in various concrete forms at this or that time or place, as it proceeds (Hegel would emphasize that Spirit *has* to so embody itself). Therefore Spirit supersedes time, and the religious community which unites itself with Spirit and manifests the self-consciousness of Spirit is a symbol of man's independence of time, a fortress against complete subjection to historical developments. This is perhaps one reason why religion is such an important element in Hegel's philosophy of history and philosophy of right, which are structured around the basic premise that man is teleologically ordered to freedom. (In *Philosophy of History*, p. 435, Hegel says that a free State is inconceivable without Christianity, specifically Protestantism.)

The fact that Spirit is perceived as a kind of dynamo of freedom working its way through the world and gradually gathering momentum does not mean that it does not have its own dialectical stages or *Gestalten*. Spirit will appear now as the worship of light,

Whereas up to now one Series [i.e., the preceding stages of phenomenological devel-
opment] as it progressed formed "knots" here and there to signify the moments of dialectical recoiling which were integral [to each development]; but then proceeded out of
these again as one Horizontal—now, in contrast, this linear series is broken up at each of
these universal "knots"[2] and thus falls apart into a plurality of lines, which, reorga-
nized into one Grouping [*Bund*], thereupon rearrange themselves symmetrically, in such
a way that similar distinctions which were formerly formulated as intrinsic to each particular line now [in Religious self-consciousness] become fused with one another [e.g.,
both Sense-Certainty and the Master–Slave dialectic will come together in Light-
Religion, as will be shown below].[3]

In other words, we will be concerned in what follows not so much with
that somewhat linear process through which consciousness and Spirit
have unfolded themselves, but more specifically with the way that religious consciousness in all the essential stages of this unfolding has managed to recapture and epitomize the intensity and distinctness of the
actual state of consciousness of the world that it emerged from. In describing this process, we will also establish the fact that there is a certain
unity and universality in the religious spirit generally, a unity and universality which enables it to incorporate discrete moments which seemed
to be essential to this or that "Spirit" at this or that stage of the consciousness of the world, and show that they are really mere "predicates," all of which can be traced to Religion itself as the selfsame "Subject" from which they have emerged.

Religion is essentially the *self*-consciousness of Spirit. The necessary
and sufficient impetus to Religion *for us* has been the stage of Morality,
which (as we have just seen) culminated in Conscience, a state which in
its ultimate developments became "religious" insofar as it brought all

---

now as the cult of Ceres and Bacchus, etc. But what has to be emphasized here is that in
the context of the present section we would have to say that Spirit "embodies" itself in
these sundry forms, not that Spirit is necessarily produced *by* these various forms, and
certainly not that Spirit is reducible to, or even subject to, these forms.

2. The "knots" here signify crowning moments of the intensification and deepening
of Spirit, e.g., the stages of the Supersensible World, the Unhappy Consciousness, and
Conscience. These "knots" are "universal," in the peculiar Hegelian sense, as higher
dialectical forms which conclude and synthesize earlier antithetical developments.

3. B367, H478: *Wenn also die bisherige Eine Reihe in ihrem Fortschreiten durch Knoten die
Rückgänge in ihr bezeichnete, aber aus ihnen sich wieder in Eine Länge fort-
setzte, so ist sie nunmehr gleichsam an diesen Knoten, den allgemeinen Momenten,
gebrochen und in viele Linien zerfallen, welche in Einen Bund zusammengefasst, sich
zugleich symmetrisch vereinen, so dass die gleichen Unterschiede, in welche jede be-
sondre innerhalb ihrer sich gestalten, zusammentreffen.*

the immediately preceding developments of the world of Spirit to the state of self-consciousness (the religious–moral community as a source and result of mutual forgiveness, mutual reconciliation and mutual recognition). Now we will proceed to analyze the phenomenon of religious self-consciousness in depth, according to its own essential moments.

But first it should be noted that in previous chapters we have already encountered some *precursors* of religious self-consciousness: the need of the Understanding to project the thing-in-itself as the suprasensible "Beyond" standing behind appearances; the agonized attempts of the Unhappy Consciousness to attain some kind of external, objective union with the "Unchangeable"; the dim belief of the Ethical Consciousness in individual "Shades" existing just beyond the clutches of the dark night of Fate; then the transformation of this belief into the more positive belief in "heaven" through the attitude of Faith (although this positive belief became subsequently modified through the influence of Enlightenment into an earthly paradise); and finally, with the appearance of the "moral view" of the world, consciousness' projection of a new, more personalized "Provident Legislator" as God— followed by the discovery that it had to contradict its own dearest principles to make this projection.

In all these preceding stages we find only approximations to Religion, not Religion in the strict sense. The reason for this is that they all are related to the Absolute as an object or projection of *Consciousness*, while Religion is precisely the *Self*-Consciousness *of* the Absolute[4] (or a relation of consciousness to the Absolute as to its own self—which is to say the same thing in different words).

As has already been indicated, Religion is the interiorization, the elevation to Self-Consciousness, of previously actualized forms we have considered in the *Phenomenology*; and our concern in the following sec-

---

4. The idea that the Absolute exists in, and becomes self-conscious through, the spiritual community is a familiar idea in Hinduism, Sufism, and in Christian mystics such as Meister Eckhart. The idea is very well summed up in a parable of mediaeval Islamic mysticism, Farid al-Din Attar's "Conference of the Birds": "The sun of majesty sent forth his rays, and in the reflection of each other's faces these thirsty birds of the outer world contemplated the face of the Simurgh [the Lord of creation] of the inner world. This so astonished them that they did not know if they were still themselves or if they had become the Simurgh. At last, in a state of contemplation, they realized that they *were* the Simurgh. . . ." (italics added) (quoted by W. T. Stace, *Teachings of the Mystics* [New York, 1960] p. 210).

tions will be simply to develop in its own right this process of interiorization, according to the moments of (*a*) Consciousness, (*b*) Self-Consciousness, and (*c*) rational synthesis, through which it will proceed. We will begin, then, (*a*) with Nature-Religion, the religion in which the self-consciousness of the Absolute is transmitted immediately through this or that aspect of nature (and the Absolute, correspondingly, assumes the aspect of this or that godlike "spirit" in nature); we will proceed thence (*b*) to the Religion of Art, in which the self-consciousness of the Absolute is derived precisely in and through the creative productions of self-consciousness; and finally we will come (*c*) to Revealed Religion, in which the self-consciousness of the Absolute comes to a true presentation of itself in that equipoise of being and thought, consciousness and self-consciousness, attained in and through the God-Man.[5]

In all of these stages, however, there is still the semblance of a dichotomy left: the division between the secular world and the religious (self-) consciousness which finds and gives absolute significance to that world.[6] It is not until a post-religious stage (Absolute Knowledge, Ch. VIII) that this *final* dichotomy will be bridged and, simultaneously, the true *Concept* of Religion will finally become explicit and intelligible.

A. NATURE-RELIGION
   [INTERSUBJECTIVE SELF-CONSCIOUSNESS THROUGH
   NATURE]

---

5. It is noteworthy that Hegel seems to find no place in his triadic schema for Taoism, Buddhism, and the deeper (Yogic) elements of Hinduism. Hegel did seem to have some familiarity with Oriental religions, although, as Michel Hulin points out (*Hegel et l'Orient*, pp. 28 ff.) this familiarity was largely second-hand and uneven. If we may assume the omissions were not caused by unfamiliarity, an obvious reason for them would seem to be that these are ambiguous examples of religion and could be considered philosophies as well as religions and also that these three religious forms emphasize solitude and thus stand outside the mainstream of communal religious orientation which Hegel thought to be essential. Another, and perhaps paramount, reason may be that Hegel here, as also in his *Philosophy of History*, focuses primarily on civilizations and philosophies that have contributed to the development of Western Germanic culture, and Far Eastern religions do not fit into this category. Hegel does include Indian religion under the rubric of "Nature-Religion," but only considers the more popular aspects of Hinduism.

6. This last dichotomy, which remains in spite of the wholesale integrative aspects of Religion, is due to the pictorial-symbolic nature of religious representation. Only the Concept (which is properly in the domain of philosophy) can so thoroughly mediate self-consciousness and the objective world that there is no semblance of dichotomy left.

Introductory Remarks:

Instead of "Intersubjective Self-Consciousness through Nature," one might speak of "Spiritual Self-Consciousness. . . ." But since "spiritual" in the English language as well as in non-Hegelian German usage is often used with an individual emphasis, I think it best to use the adjective "intersubjective" to bring out the essentially communal *connotation that "Spirit" has in Hegel's philosophy.*

There is a long-standing controversy in aesthetics as to whether "aesthetic experience" should be used broadly to encompass experiences of beauty in Nature, or should be restricted specifically to experience of art. Hegel himself (see Art, Religion and Philosophy, *pp. 22,23) thought that a* philosophy *of aesthetics was possible only regarding* art, *and was dubious as to just how "beauty" could be ascribed to natural objects, or at least as to how one could make aesthetic–philosophical categorizations in that domain. But regardless of whether Nature-induced aesthetic experiences are susceptible to philosophical categorization, there can be little doubt that the phenomenological religious forms that Hegel considers in the present subsection of "Religion" emerged originally from some such "aesthetic" (in the* wide *sense) experiences. In other words, the experience of the beauty of a sunrise, or of the sublimity of large natural formations, or of the delicate charm and fragrance of floral combinations, or of the awesome power of certain animals was certainly the catalyst which led men to band together to institutionalize and ritualize these experiences, which were at least dim reflections or portents of man's power to rise above his own limited existence to the self-consciousness of Spirit. At any rate, the important thing for Hegel is that men did band together in communal Nature-oriented celebration or worship, and that there is a certain logical or dialectical evolution in the forms of such celebration or worship—from worship of the rising sun, to ritual identification with plant and animal deities, to final extraordinary attempts to recapture the incommensurable awesomeness of natural spectacles by gargantuan architectural monuments such as pyramids or obelisks.*

*As has already been mentioned (*supra, *n. 5), Hegel considers here only religions that he thought to be "historical" from the viewpoint of the development of Western Culture. Thus we do not find any discussion of Chinese or Buddhist or African folk religions or Shintoism in Hegel's treatment of Nature-Religion.*

The various forms of religion are—all of them—Nature-contained-in-thought or thought-as-existent, such that consciousness is self-consciousness, and self-consciousness is a conscious presentation.

The form of Religion is not concerned with the *mere* existence of Spirit as Nature-divorced-from-thought, nor yet with Spirit as thought-divorced-from-existence; rather, the form taken by Religion is that of existence-imbued-with-thought, or (to put it another way) thought which is actually present to itself [*sich da ist*].[7]

Likewise, all of the imagery and conscious ideas which differentiate the various forms of religion from one another can be found implicitly in other forms.

> The series of disparate religions that is about to be given is just as much an exposition of multiple facets of one selfsame Religion as an exposition of each individual religion: and the characterizations which seem to make one religion stand out from another, actually can be found in all of them.[8]

But sometimes a specific form will be found to be *"essential"* to some particular religion, to be the *"truth"* (explication) of that religion. This happens when some form of the emergence of spiritual Self-Consciousness from Consciousness obtains in which the actual *concrete self* actively imbues certain objective forms of religious formulae with life, and the *actual concrete spirit* of a religion is consonant with its beliefs. Thus, for example, the Incarnation of God is held in Eastern religion, but God-as-incarnate is not imbued with the concrete self, and the spirit corresponding to this belief—the awareness of reconciliation with God—is not extant. Therefore incarnation is not "essential" to Eastern Religion, does not constitute its "truth"—but rather, if it is a "higher" form, has merely been made subsidiary to "lower" forms, and thus is found not in its significant spirit, but merely after the manner of an extrinsic presentation. [In the same vein it should be observed that while all religions are "Nature-Religions" in the broad sense adumbrated above, there is a certain form of religion which is essentially and distinctively a "Religion of Nature"—and it is with this form and its variations that we will be concerned in the immediately following sections.][9]

---

7. *B*369, H481: . . . *die Gestalt der Religion enthalt nicht das Dasein des Geistes, wie er vom Gedanken freie Natur, noch wie er vom Dasein freier Gedanke ist; sondern sie ist das im Denken e`-haltne Dasein, so wie ein Gedachtes, das sich da ist.*

8. Ibid: *Die Reihe der verschiednen Religionen, die sich ergeben werden, stellt ebensosehr wieder nur die verschiednen Seiten einer einzigen, und zwar jeder einzelnen dar, und die Vorstellungen, welche eine wirkliche Religion vor einer andern auszuzeichen scheinen, kommen in jeder vor.*

9. Hegel's remarks at the beginning of this section concerning the "essential" vs. the generic instantiation of religious forms would seem to be out of place *in this section* (he has just begun this subsection on Nature-Religion yet says nothing specifically about Nature-Religion in these introductory paragraphs) *unless* they were meant to imply that, while *all* religions are "Nature-Religions" (ways of attaining intersubjective Self-

a. The Religion of Light
    [*Lichtwesen*]

Nature-Religion is *essentially* oriented towards the unification of self-consciousness and Nature. In its primal stages it seizes upon *light itself* in Nature as a "formless form" which is the least determinate and ostensibly the most "spiritual" aspect of Nature-as-a-*totality*.[10] It is in and through the simple essence of light that Nature-Religion begins to find (and *create*) self-conscious transcendence in suitably objective form. Religious consciousness at this stage, therefore, is on the one hand analogous to the stage of Sense-Certainty, insofar as it is oriented immediately to sensory being, and derives spiritual sustenance from this orientation; but, on the other hand, it is also comparable to the stage of the Master–Slave dialectic, insofar as it is subjecting itself to a Being which is imbued with the sacred power of self-consciousness and is, indeed, taken to be Lord and Master.[11] And this sacred Being which is adored,

---

Consciousness through Nature), only the specific ones treated here in this subsection are distinctively and "essentially" "nature-Religions."

But Hegel doesn't actually come out and say this, doesn't actually make this application. If he didn't *mean* to say this, then these paragraphs would seem to be more appropriately included in the immediately preceding introductory subsection, which contains general remarks pertaining to all three stages of religion to be considered in the chapter on Religion.

10. In *Philosophy of History* (p. 178), Hegel ascribes this form of worship more specifically to the Zoroastrian religion which emerged among the Zend people in ancient Persia: "Among the Persians . . . Universal Being . . . is still [in the stage he is considering there] clothed with a form—that of Light. But Light is . . . sensuous Universality itself. . . . The Persian Religion is therefore no idol-worship."

11. In this reference to numinous light as "Master," Hegel would seem to have Judaism in mind, as Fackenheim (*The Religious Dimension*, p. 250) suggests. Hegel writes that this deity "is clothed with the manifold forces of existence and with the forms of reality as with a selfless adornment; and these selfless forms are mere messengers of his will without any will of their own, evidence of his majesty, voices in his praise." (H484: *Dieses ist mit den mannigfachen Kräften des Daseins und den Gestalten der Wirklichkeit als mit einem selbstlosen Schmucke angekleidet; sie sind nur eignen Willens entbehrende Boten seiner Herrlichkeit und Stimmen seines Preises.*) Hegel here seems to be paraphrasing Psalm 104 of the Jewish scriptures (New American Bible, verses 1–4): "Bless the Lord, O my Soul! O Lord, my God, you are great indeed! You are clothed with majesty and glory, robed in light as with a cloak. . . . You make the clouds your chariot; you travel on the wings of the wind. You make the winds your messengers, and flaming fire your ministers."

Hegel underwent some vicissitudes in regard to his later classification of religions, and the Jewish religion became reclassified accordingly. In the 1817 (Heidelberg) *Enzyklopädie der Philosophischen Wissenschaften*, Hegel replaces the threefold classification in the *Phenomenology* with a twofold division into "Art Religion" and "Revealed

because it itself is emerging from the darkness of the Concept's still implicit or unconscious form, is also taken to be in opposition to darkness, which here epitomizes simple negation. Nevertheless even this Numinous Light, which is simply imparted to all beings in a direct manner, fails to manifest the full and mediated negativity of self-consciousness. And, as if to make preliminary attempts to express that higher state of negativity, it favors, and fosters the development of, numinous plants and animals, which offer closer approximations to the perfection of self-consciousness.

b. Plant and Animal Deification

Religious consciousness as it transcends the mere immediacy of light-worship thus finds itself entering upon a new pantheistic unity of quasi-selves: the quiescent "selves" of plants, flowers and trees, as well as the more active and hostile "selves" of animals. Its relationship to these "selves" is a kind of spiritual "sense-perception," which finds its adequated object only in this lush and colorful chain of self-possessing (*fürsichseinde*) organic manifolds.[12]

The "quiescent" innocence and indifferent subsistence of the plant-deities is but an intermediate state of life that masks the full implications of being-for-*self*, i.e., independent existence. These latter implications become explicit only in the animal-deities, openly hostile and actively repelling folk-spirits symbolized by this or that animal and worshipped

---

Religion.'' Within the context of that new division, Hegel refers (§458) to the notion of God as an ''immediately determined figure'' in Art-Religion and subdivides this notion into God as an elementary ''Being-of-Nature'' and God as *Pure Thought*; and in his lecture notes on this paragraph (see Helmut Schneider [ed.], *Hegels Notizen . . .* , p. 20) indicates that the Jewish religion is to be included in the latter subcategory. In Hegel's lectures on the philosophy of religion, given at Berlin in the early 1820s and published posthumously in 1832, there is a new tripartite division of religion into Nature-Religion, Religion of Spiritual Individuality, and absolute Religion (Christianity). In this schema, Judaism is no longer alluded to (as in the *Phenomenology*) under the rubric of ''Nature-Religion,'' but is classified as a ''Religion of Spiritual Individuality'' because its deity is a personal God. This differing classification in Hegel's later work may be taken as an example partly of a change of opinion, but partly also of Hegel's quest for a new and more comprehensive schema for systematic-dialectical classification.

12. From the ''spiritual sense-certainty'' of light worship, we proceed now to the ''spiritual perception'' of plant worship. Under the heading of ''plant worship'' Hegel would probably include the worship of trees in Indian polytheism, the worship of a god of wine in the Indian and Egyptian religions, etc.

by this or that national faction. And so with the emergence of the ani-mal-deities, the innocence of plant-worship passes into the background, and the attention of the religious consciousness is overwhelmed by guilt and blood and the constant war of independent self-existences which in their wanton animal-like territoriality fall far short of universality in their action.[13]

But the all-consuming animal-spirits finally consume *themselves*, their destructiveness finally destroys *itself*; and the religious consciousness which is present at this ultimate consummation searches its spiritual environs for some surety of stability and permanence by which it may permanently transcend the incessant hostilities which were associated with animal religion. It finds this surety in and through the emergent genius of the master-builder (*Werkmeister*), who begins to establish the self in the form of great *objects* which might rival the magnificence of Nature.

c.   The Religious Artisan

The religious consciousness making a "thing" out of the self may be compared to *Understanding*, the attitude of consciousness which re-forms the native "incommensurability" of sensory givenness according to its own commensurate requirements. So also the artisans now, as if driven like a hive of bees by some instinctive force, begin to seek out ways of im-pressing the forms of spiritual Understanding upon raw materials. In the first instance they produce works such as *pyramids* and *obelisks*, which, being well beyond the "incommensurability" of roundness, possess the "immediate" abstractness of products of the Understand-ing—but are still a far cry from the *auto*commensuration of the spiritual self (the teleological objective, to produce which the artisans are being impelled by Spirit). And thus these relatively dead works (judged by the standard of autocommensuration) are fittingly used as sepulchres for

---

13. Cf. *History of Philosophy* III, p. 420: "The intuitive knowledge of the Egyptians told them that God was an ox or a cat, and the Indians still possess similar sorts of knowl-edge."

In M§700 Hegel speaks of a "caste-system" as being symptomatic of some forms of Nature-Religion, and he no doubt sees this as one major instance of the class rivalries connected with, and symbolized by, animal worship. Modern anthropologists would describe such connections in terms of totemic customs in primitive and ancient societies. In *Philosophy of History*, p. 204, Hegel speaks of the caste-system in Egyptian society.

departed spirits; or, if they are related to spirit in a more positive sense, it is still in a very external type of relationship (e.g., the built-in capability of the polished surfaces of some great monuments to reflect the "Orient Light"[14]).

But the master-builder himself is not deceived. In his own way, he perceives with dismay the constant sundering of the in-itself (the external material) from the for-itself (the self-consciousness which fashions it). And he thereupon addresses himself to the task of fusing these two polarities, i.e., of giving spiritual animation to bodily existence-in-self, and of clothing spiritual existence-for-self with embodied shape. This task is accomplished only by painstaking and gradual approximations.

First of all, the master-builder begins to employ plant forms for his architectural purposes. He skillfully cancels the singular and particularizing aspects of plant forms and weaves their universalized forms into his work, using them as instruments for imparting a new organic animation to his *architectural* creations—such that he now produces monuments which seem to be animated, the so-called "free architecture." Then he lays hold upon the more individualized forms of animals, and adapts these forms also to his purposes (which are *the* purposes of Spirit). Thus the animal shape becomes the hieroglyphic symbol (an embodiment of *thought*), or is given the head of a human being. (This amounts to a further approximation to the external production of the self *qua* self.) Finally, he produces human-like forms purified from explicit concomitance of animal forms (the colossal statues of Memnon[15] would be an example of this new form)—but still merely forms of the *outer* self, giving forth not speech but at most noise.[16] Seized by the awareness that the inner being of his creations is still in spiritual darkness, the religious artisan then, in a kind of artistic counterpoint, begins pointedly to de-

---

14. Egyptian pyramids used to be covered with slabs of polished stone which reflected the sun and thus contributed to their symbolic function. (See Jack Kaminsky, *Hegel on Art*, p. 53.)

15. Giant stone statues built to the memory of Amenhotep the Magnificent, who ruled Egypt from 1417 to 1379 B.C.

16. This is a reference to the moaning harp-like noise produced by the statues of Memnon at sunrise, a noise produced by the effect of rapid changes of temperature at sunrise on the porous stones.

17. Offhand this appears to be a reference to Moslem veneration of the Black Stone in the Ka'bah at the Great Mosque at Mecca. If so, this would be an apparent anachronism and dislocation comparable to Hegel's earlier reference to the "Penates" in the exclusively Greek-oriented context of the phenomenology of the Ethical Substance. How-

emphasize the explicit manifolds of externality and produces, for example, a formless black stone,[17] a fetish which accentuates the inner darkness of yet-to-be-uttered thought in religious consciousness, in contradistinction to the multiform clearness of expression which is attained in the objective nonconscious world.

At this point the religious artisan, beginning to apprehend the significance of the self from these imperfect foreshadowings, abandons these inferior modes of expression, and devotes himself with intensified effort to the task of *uniting* once and for all the interiority of the self with congruent external expression:

> The artificer thereupon unites both sides, fusing the forms of Nature with those of self-consciousness, and these new creations, ambiguous and enigmatic even to themselves (consciousness sparring with unconsciousness, simple interiority with variegated exteriority, the darkness of thought with the clarity of externality), break into the utterance of a wisdom which is as profound as it is difficult to comprehend.[18]

This utterance is the "language" of art, and the artisan at this point has become the *artist*.

B.   RELIGION IN THE FORM OF ART
[INTERSUBJECTIVE SELF-CONSCIOUSNESS THROUGH ART]

Introductory Remarks:

In regard to Nature-Religion, we observed above above (n. 9) that while all religions are "Nature-Religions" in the sense that they tend to enshrine certain Nature-oriented aesthetic experiences, only this or that religion is essentially and explicitly *a "Nature-Religion." A similar observation is appropriate in the case of Art-Religion: All religions to some extent are associated with some form of artistic creativity— music, literature, sculpture, architecture, choreography—and Hegel in his later*

---

ever, Hegel may have had in mind the Arabian tradition that God had given the Black Stone to Adam after his sin, as a sacramental of forgiveness, and that Ishmael, son of Abraham and founder of various Arabian tribes (see *Genesis* XXI, XXIV), had erected the original shrine at Mecca for the Black Stone. If this is meant, the reference would then be to ancient pre-Muslim Arabian religious tradition.

18. *B*375, H489: *Der Werkmeister vereint daher beides in der Vermischung der natürlichen und der selbstbewussten Gestalt, und diese zweideutigen sich selbst rätselhaften Wesen, das Bewusste ringend mit dem Bewusstlosen, das einfache Innre mit dem vielgestalteten Äussern, die Dunkelheit des Gedankens mit der Klarheit der Äusserung paarend, brechen in die Sprache tiefer schwerverständlicher Weisheit aus.*

aesthetics goes even further and insists also that the various forms of art are invariably related to some religious context; but only in this or that religion (in particular, Greek religion) is intersubjective self-consciousness derived essentially *and explicitly from various forms of artistic creativity.*

The distinctions we *now make between religion and art were, for the Greeks, purely academic: "The primary end of [Greek] sculpture was to make statues of the gods and heroes; the primary end of painting was to represent mythological scenes; and in either case the purely aesthetic pleasure was also a means to a religious experience" (Dickinson,* The Greek View, *p. 135). And although such a religion, like other religions, had its specialized priests and prophets, in a very real sense here it was* the artist *who was both priest and prophet. As Gray* (Hegel and Greek Thought, *p. 41) observes, "Hegel found primary significance in the sentence of Herodotus that Homer and Hesiod gave the Greeks their gods, their religion. What vould that mean except that poets and artists had been their very teachers and seers? Prophecy in Greece was poetry."*

*The religious art-forms that Hegel portrays and analyzes here are almost entirely Greek in inspiration and context: classical sculpture, Greek tragedy and comedy, etc. * But it should be noted that Hegel, almost as if to make up for his restriction of "aesthetics" in the strict sense to art forms (see* supra, *p. 132), here includes many things under that rubric that one would not ordinarily think of as "art," such as athletic competitions, festive celebrations, ecstatic Bacchanalia, and sacrificial rituals.*

The transition from the religious spirit which expressed itself in more or less instinctive artisanry to the religious spirit which expresses itself in art proper can only take place at a certain stage of ethical consciousness, namely, at the stage that we referred to earlier as the "Ethical Substance."[19] It will be recalled that this stage was characterized by the

---

*Schleiermacher in his *Reden über Religion* (1799, pp. 110 ff.) proposes a trifold schema for the consideration of religion: (*a*) the inner-oriented type; (*b*) the outer- or Nature-oriented type; and (*c*) an art-oriented type (art being considered a synthesis of inner and outer). He saw Eastern mysticism as an exemplification of the first type, Egyptian religion as an instance of the second, and Greek religion as an instance of the third type (although he denied that the Greek religion or any religion *originated* in art), and a possible model for the regeneration of Christianity. Hegel in the present section seems to be following up on this characteristic of the Greek religion, but tends to portray this religion as emerging *from* artistic experience and also as subordinate to a higher stage of religion (Revealed Religion) which is one step beyond art and closer to conceptual mediation.

19. See *supra*, pp. 20 ff. Hegel in the preceding sections mentioned that Nature-Religion wove together some of the strands from earlier sections in the development of natur-

immediate but free identification of individuals with their national communality, in such a way that they took this community to be not only their origin but also their production or proper work. Now it is precisely at the junctures where this immediate identification begins to weaken, when the communality begins to undergo unrest and division, that the self, suddenly loosened from its moorings and no longer enjoying the wonted illumination of fixed rights and duties and peaceful civic participation that it had formerly enjoyed, grapples about in this newly-induced spiritual night for some way to resurrect and objectify anew this former harmonious spirit that is now only a dim memory. This process of grappling towards renewed self-consciousness is centered in certain paradigmatic individuals whom Spirit chooses as the "vessels of its sorrow." These great individuals, as we shall see in the following sections, will deliver themselves over to the bleak and impersonal "pathos" which now confronts them, struggle with it, and finally subdue it by transforming it completely into self-consciousness. The result of these encounters and struggles with pathos is Absolute Art, the state of consciousness—and the only state of consciousness—in which the actual Spirit of the world is brought to self-consciousness (i.e., the religious standpoint) in and through *art*.

a. The Abstract Work of Art

First of all, it should be recalled that Art-Religion, like Nature-Religion, is concerned with producing a synthesis of Nature and self-consciousness. But here the emphasis is on *self-consciousness* rather than on Nature.[20]

---

al consciousness: Thus light worship was related to Sense-Certainty and the Master-Slave relationship, plant and animal deification to Perception, and the Werkmeister to Understanding. (One may also surmise that the eventual coordination of inner and outer by the Werkmeister is related to Reason, which was essentially concerned with that task.) In the present section Art-Religion is shown to be similarly bound up with the earlier phenomenological development of the "Ethical Substance" and its breakup with the advent of "Legal Status."

20. The focus of Greek Art-Religion is not Nature *per se* but Nature which has emerged into self-consciousness, i.e., human nature, i.e., man. As Dickinson (*The Greek View*, p. 134) observes, the emphasis on the human in Greek art becomes all the clearer if we reflect on the fact that "among all [Greek] pictures of which we have any record there is not one that answers to the description of a landscape; the subject is always mythological or historical, and the representation of nature merely a setting for the main theme. . . . The interpretation of 'nature' for its own sake (in the narrower sense in which 'nature' is

In its initial stages, Art-Religion produces an external work which offers an immediate and unmistakable reflection of self-consciousness. This work is on the one hand the temple, the architectural creation which as a habitation or environment of the gods symbolizes the universality which accrues to them, a universality which at this stage of development weaves together in an extraordinary manner the crystaline patterns of the massive geometrical determinations of the Understanding with "incommensurable," life-like organic patterns. But on the other hand, and most importantly, the primal production of Art-Religion is the *statue* of the god, the individuality housed in the temple. With the advent of the gods of Art-Religion, the supersession of animal worship (which began with the Black Stone [see *supra*, p. 138] as a symbol of the unknown divinity emerging in the shrines of Nature-Religion), and of the worship of the elements[21] which had characterized even the prehistory of Art-Religion itself, is now complete. The fully humanized statue of the god in one sweep elevates the contingencies of Nature and the unstable individuations of national existence[22] to one serene and stable representation of supreme individuality and self-consciousness.

But in contrast to the stability of this strictly *abstract* representation stands the absolute restlessness of the self-consciousness of the artist who produces this work and/or its complementing environment. In spite of the praise of those who admire his work, the artist knows in his deepest consciousness that an external work like this can never embody the creative spirit that he experiences in his subjectivity.

If [the admirers of his production] with their knowledge set themselves above that production, *he* knows how much more important his own deed is than their critical un-

---

opposed to man) is a modern and romantic development that would have been unintelligible to a Greek.'' The fact that Nature is de-emphasized and devalued by the Greeks is indicated, for example, by the fact that Narcissus' mythical metamorphosis into a *flower* (instead of some higher form) after death was construed by the Greeks as a humiliation (*Aesthetics* I, p. 303–4).

21. In Greek mythology, the progenitors of Zeus and the other Olympian and underworld gods were the Titans, including Cronus (time) and Oceanus (Ocean), and these in turn descended from Uranus (Heaven) and Ge (Earth).

22. The gods were often personifications of national existence. For example, the ideas of the city-state of Athens and the goddess Pallas Athena were inseparably connected in the mind of the Greek (see Hegel, *Philosophy of History*, p. 53). And in general, "sculpture and painting . . . to the Greeks . . . were ways of expressing and interpreting national life. . . . The cult of the gods was the center, not only of the religious but of the political consciousness of Greece'' (Dickinson, *The Greek View*, pp. 135 ff.).

derstanding and comments; if they set themselves beneath his work and acknowledge it as an essence which subjugates them, he knows that the master they are recognizing is really himself.[23]

The artist accordingly begins to turn towards a higher, less abstract[24] form of art—the *hymn*—which is capable of embodying and more aptly representing this powerful, creative subjectivity that he is becoming conscious of. The hymn is a higher form of art because it is embodied in a higher element:

> This higher element is *language*,—a determinate "being" [*Dasein*] which is also directly a (self-conscious) Existence [*Existenz*]. The individual self-consciousness is presented *here or there* in language, yet presented directly as an "infection" which is *universal*; and thus the very act of particularizing one's existence-for-self in language is simultaneously [the communication of] the fluidity and universally participated unity of many selves. In other words, language is the soul coming to *existence as soul*.[25]

The devotional outpourings of the religious hymn are intrinsically *ensouled* creations, which give expression to the universal truth of Spirit. The advance which is made in the development of this form of language can perhaps be best understood in contrast with its forerunner and antithesis, the *oracle*, that intermittent utterance of some particular god or spirit, both in Nature-Religion[26] and in the Religion of Art. The oracle *had* to come about because the Concept of Spirit had to express itself in some way, but takes on the aspect of something *foreign* and now also of

---

23. *B*380,H495: . . . *wenn sie sich mit ihrer Kenntnis darüber setzen, weiss er, wieviel mehr seine* Tat *als ihr Verstehen und Reden ist; wenn sie sich* darunter *setzen und ihr sie beherrschendes* Wesen *darin erkennen, weiss er sich als den Meister desselben.*

24. As is usual in Hegel, "abstract" here means "isolated from living thought," as contrasted with "concrete": "imbued with thought."

25. *B*380, H496: *Dies höhere Element ist die* Sprache,—*ein Dasein, das unmittelbar selbstbewusste Existenz ist. Wie das* einzelne *Selbstbewusstsein in ihr da ist, ist es ebenso unmittelbar als eine* allgemeine *Ansteckung; die vollkommne Besonderung des Fürsichseins ist zugleich die Flüssigkeit und die allgemein mitgeteilte Einheit der vielen Selbst; sie ist die als Seele existierende Seele.*

26. *Aufgang* is translated both by Miller (M§711, §712) and by Baillie (B718) as "Sunrise" or "Rising Sun," but the reference is meant to show how the artistic or Greek spirit is just beginning to forge beyond the external, oracular "universality" of the Zoroastrian numinous luminosity (*Lichtwesen*), and beyond its own unconscious, oracle-dominated past. Note that Hegel's references (M§712) to the "divine light" which withdraws into the "inner or nether world of being" is a reference to the evolution of light worship into the cult of the underworld gods. An evolution in the oracles also takes place: the oracles of the present stage of religious consciousness are more concerned with human affairs than the oracles of Nature-Religion.

something *contingent* because it is recognized as being, not the self-conscious creation of spirit, but something that one "meets up with" in some contingent way (similar to the way that the diviner strives to derive knowledge of contingent truths in an appropriately contingent way—from birds or trees or fermenting earth). Thus in its most "self-conscious" form, such as the divine inner voice that directed Socrates, the oracle is consulted only for the contingent, not for the universal. And, all in all, the oracle now takes on the appearance of something petty and trivial, a poor substitute for, and a poor parody of, the rational processes of deliberation and choice by which self-consciousness in more advanced form comes to specify itself.

But while the language of the hymn marks an advance in universality over the oracle, it is also beset by a constitutional defect: the extremely subjective "existence" which it attains, the essentially fleeting and transient nature of a work of art whose existence consists in its being *sung*.

It is through the development of ritual celebrations (*Kultus*) that this defect is overcome.[27] *Religious rituals* in the stage we are discussing are a new form of art which, like statuary, have a certain permanency, stability and predictableness, but also, like the hymn, are means by which the artist creates reflections of the divine explicitly and manifestly within self-consciousness, i.e., within the self-consciousnesses of the participants in the rituals.

We are speaking here primarily of the secret celebrations connected with religious "mysteries,"[28] which are "abstract" as long as they are still lacking in universal public expression.

---

27. Ritual or liturgical celebrations are a synthesis of the two previous extremes, the extreme of abstract exteriority manifested in sculpture, and the extreme of abstract interiority manifested in the religious hymn. Dickinson (*The Greek View*, p. 19) also testifies to the "synthetic" nature of the Greek *Kultus*: "The religion of the Greeks," he says, "one may almost say, consisted in ritual; and to attempt to divide the inner from the outer would be to falsify from the beginning its distinctive character."

28. Cf. *Aesthetics* I, pp. 468–9: "The Greek Mysteries were not secret in the sense that the Greek people were not generally familiar with their subject-matter. On the contrary, most Athenians and many strangers were amongst those initiated into the Eleusinian secrets [the rites of Ceres and Bacchus], only they might not speak of what they had learnt through the initiation. . . . The character of the undisclosed and the unspoken [i.e., the symbolic expressions which characterized the Mysteries] belongs also to the old gods, to what was telluric [e.g., Ceres], sidereal, and Titanic, for only the spirit is the revealed and the self-revealing [the Olympian gods were *not* celebrated in these mysteries, because they were more 'spiritual,' less elemental]."

First of all, we should note that such religious rites are very unlike the rituals or liturgies of Christianity in one important respect: they are not, for the most part, affected with the consciousness of evil, or of the need for reconciliation and "atonement" in the Christian sense[29]—notions which involve a process of mediation. The rituals we are discussing here are characterized by immediacy. The soul which participates in them

. . . is a self immersed in existence, a soul which purifies its outer nature by washing, dons its white vestments and guides its inner nature down the path of toil, punishment and reward which has been ordained for it, the path of a discipline which characteristically eschews the merely private [Besonderheit], the path which leads to the mansions and fellowship of the blessed.[30]

What essentially takes place in such religious ritual is a twofold process: On the one hand, the religious consciousness as *pure* consciousness differentiates itself from the divine essence which it portrays to itself imaginatively, and offers itself to the divinity, thus surrendering its self-consciousness to universality. On the other hand, religious consciousness as *actual* consciousness looks upon the divine being which it represents as its own possession, and even as its own accomplishment or production. These two moments are illustrated by two different forms of sacrifice prescribed by religious rituals. In the first form (the holocaust), the client of a god takes some portion of his goods and offers it up completely to the god,[31] by pouring out wine, or burning his grain or the animal which he has slain in the prescribed way. In doing this, he is merely ratifying and appropriating the sacrifice which the divine Essence has already made implicitly to him by making itself into grapes or grain (symbols of the gods of the underworld) or animals (symbols of the Olympian gods).[32] In the second form, the client of the god actually con-

---

29. "What we mean by religion is something . . . which concerns the relation of the soul to God; the sense of sin, for example, and of repentance and grace. . . . It was . . . a distinguishing characteristic of the Greek religion that it did not concern itself with the conscience at all; the conscience, in fact, did not yet exist, to enact that drama of the soul with God which is the main interest of the Christian, or at least of the Protestant faith" (Dickinson, *The Greek View*, p. 21).

30. B383, H499: . . . *es ist ein* seiendes, *eine Seele, welche ihre Äusserlichkeit mit Waschen reinigt, sie mit weissen Kleidern antut, und ihre Innerlichkeit den vorgestellten Weg der Arbeiten, Strafen und Belohnungen, den Weg der die Besonderheit entäussernden Bildung überhaupt durchführt, durch welchen sie in die Wohnungen und die Gemeinschaft der Seligkeit gelangt.*

31. Generally to underworld gods such as Ceres and Bacchus, not to the Olympians.

32. Note that animals in the stage of Art-Religion are no longer deified, but are now re-

sumes the offering which he has sacrificed to his god in the ritual feast which follows the sacrifice.

Devotion is an essential element of religious ritual, just as it is in the religious hymn, but with the difference that the devotion in the case of the ceremonies and rites we have been discussing produces results which are quite objective: the objective unity or communality of the worshippers, the works of beauty that adorn the temple and the city and the citizen during the various religious festivals, and religious treasures which can be put to use or sold in times of civic emergencies. Clearly the religious-artistic spirit at this stage has moved well beyond that feeling of separation from its works that plagued the creativity of the religious sculptor. And the work of art produced by the religious liturgist, insofar as it is an initial approximation to the *unification* of external being with self-conscious thought, is much less abstract than were its immediate predecessors.

b. The Living Work of Art

Next, the religious spirit makes a major transition to *living* art, a form of art in which the divine is presented explicitly as a living human being or beings—although still not yet as fully objectified human thought.

First of all, let us recapitulate the stages which have taken place: The Orient Light, as the Master to which all must be subservient, has freely metamorphosed itself into natural living beings. As a veritable Spirit of the Earth, it has embodied itself as grain (Ceres),[33] and as the fermenting grape (Bacchus), representing the female (nurturant) and the male (self-conscious) principles, respectively. As thus embodied, it sacrifices itself to the religious consciousness; and the religious consciousness, attaining unity with the divine in its own reenactments of this primordial sacrifice, becomes, as it were, the living night into which the Orient Sun of divinity finally sets, and the divinity now takes on the aspect of a substance subjected to religious consciousness rather than a self-possessed Master subjecting the religious consciousness.

---

lated to the gods only as their extrinsic symbols, e.g., the eagle for Zeus, the owl for Pallas Minerva, the vulture for Hermes.

33. "Bacchus" and "Dionysius" are used interchangeably by the Greeks, but "Ceres" is the Latin equivalent of the Greek "Demeter"—so this would seem to be similar to Hegel's reference to the "Penates" in the otherwise exclusively Greek context of the Ethical Substance (see *supra*, p. 17).

As religious consciousness comes to celebrate the mystery of bread and wine (the rites of Ceres and Bacchus), it is in effect giving *self-conscious* manifestation to God as *Nature*. The highest manifestations of the divine-as-Nature are to be found in both a subjective and an objective form.

In its more subjective form, the divine-as-Nature is expressed through the living beings who not merely celebrate the mysteries of the Spirit of Nature but participate in Bacchic revelries,[34] and act therein as semi-self-conscious spokesmen for the divine being by which they are overtaken and possessed.

In its more objective form, the mystery of bread and wine finally becomes the mystery of flesh and blood when the divine-as-Nature is expressed through the beautiful human bodies of athletes, gymnasts, torchbearers, etc., celebrated at the great religious festivals. These beautiful bodies, capable of portraying the divine as movement, energy and harmony, are living tableaux which effectively supplant those other stable and placid representations of the divine found in statuary.[35]

But the expression of the divine in human bodies lacks inwardness, and its expression in religious revelers lacks the clarity of thought. And the one-sidedness of both these forms thus supplies the impetus to the next stage of religious consciousness, a higher stage which is reached through the intermediary of *Language*:

> The swooning and incoherent stammering of the consciousness [of the Bacchic reveler] must be complemented with the clarity of existence found in [the beautiful living body], and the lack of spirit characterizing the latter must be complemented with the inwardness which is found in the former. The mature Element through which simultan-

---

34. The frantic, destructive, trance-like revelries (*Schwarmerei*) instigated by the cult of Dionysius are portrayed in Euripides' *The Bacchantes*.

35. Dickinson's description of the Athenian celebration of the "Panathenaea" gives us an indication of the emphasis placed in these festivals on the corporeal expression of spiritual harmony: "In this great national fête, held every four years, all the higher activities of Athenian life were ideally displayed—contests of song, of lyre and of flute, foot and horse races, wrestling, boxing, and the like, military evolutions of infantry and horse, pyrrhic dances symbolic of attack and defense in war, mystic chants of women and choruses of youths—the whole concentrating and discharging itself in that great processional act in which, as it were, the material forms of society became transparent, and the Whole moved on, illumined and visibly sustained by the spiritual soul of which it was the complete and harmonious embodiment." (*The Greek View*, p. 20) And, says Dickinson (*ibid.*, p. 18), "so numerous were these [fêtes] and so diverse in their character that it would be impossible . . . to give any general account of them."

eously inwardness is externalized and externality is interiorized is, as we have seen before, *Language*. But [the language we are referring to in this case] is not the language of the Oracle, which is completely contingent and individual in its content, nor the emotive language of the Hymn, which is concerned only with praising some individual god; nor even the contentless stammering of bacchanalian revelry. Rather, [the language we are referring to in the present instance] has broken through to a content which is both clear and universal: *clear*, because the [literary] artist has now worked his way out of those early incorporations of spirit-as-substance to a form of presentation in which existence is uniquely permeated in all its orientations with the self-conscious soul from which it is engendered; but also *universal*, because in the aftermath of the celebration of man *himself* [e.g., in the Olympic games], there disappears the one-sidedness of statuary art, which portrayed only this or that national spirit, this or that attribute of the divine.[36]

Thus literary language comes on the scene now as an objective art-form which is imbued not only with life but with the luminosity and universalizing activity of thought itself. The thrusts of ''natural'' man towards self-conscious intersubjectivity in ecstatic rituals and festive games will now be brought to perfection in *poety and drama*.

c. The Spiritual Work of Art

The first form which the new ''literary'' language takes is that of the *epic narrative*, which is an outgrowth of a particular stage in the development of the actual ethical spirit, namely, the stage at which the various national spirits begin to unite for the attainment of some common goal. This admittedly loose confederation of diverse spirits under one commander[37] is a new achievement which is celebrated in the art form of epic poetry. The self-conscious source of the Epic is the *minstrel* poet (*Sänger*), the individual who uses the particular deeds of great heroes (Achilles, etc.) as the middle term through which he gains access to the essential universality of the divinity. Thus we have here a syllogism of the form, P

36. *B*388, H505–6: *Jene Dumpfeit des Bewusstseins und ihr wildes Stammeln muss in das klare Dasein der letztern, und die geistlose Klarheit der letztern in die Innerlichkeit der erstern aufgenommen werden. Das vollkommne Element, worin die Innerlichkeit ebenso äusserlich als die Äusserlichkeit innerlich ist, ist wieder die Sprache, aber weder die in ihrem Inhalte ganz zufällige und einzelne des Orakels, noch die empfindende und nur den einzelnen Gott preisende Hymne, noch das inhaltslose Stammeln der bacchischen Raserei. Sondern sie hat ihren klaren und allgemeinen Inhalt gewonnen; ihren* klaren *Inhalt, denn der Künstler hat sich aus der ersten ganz substantiellen Begeisterung heraus zur Gestalt gearbeitet, die eignes, in allen seinen Regungen von der selbstbewussten Seele durchdrungenes und mitlebendes Dasein ist;—ihren* allgemeinen *Inhalt, denn in diesem Feste, das die Ehre des Menschen ist, verschwindet die Einseitigkeit der Bildsäulen, die nur einen Nationalgeist, einen bestimmten Charakter der Göttlichkeit enthalten.*
37. Agamemnon, the commander of the various Greek armies in the Trojan war, the history of which is narrated in Homer's *Iliad*.

is U, S is P, ∴ S is U.[38] In other words, the universality of the divine
essences becomes revealed in the deeds of certain particular heroes, and
the individual poet's subjectivity (raised beyond mere particularity to
individuality by the "Muse")[39] raises itself to, and manifests for others,
the universality of the gods, through the narration of particular heroic
deeds. The epic poet, however, is not concerned with describing the simple synthesis of the divine (universal) and the particular, and as an indi-
rect result of his artistry serves to accentuate the disparity between these
two poles. For he describes the *actions* of heroic individuals, actions
which are, as it were, "the violation of the peaceful earth, [or] the pit
which, vivified by [the libation of] blood, summons forth spirits from
the other world—spirits who, thirsting for life, appropriate some life for
themselves in the action of [the living] self-consciousness."[40] The description of the particular acts of the heroes is the stimulus by which the
epic poet seemingly rouses the latent divinities to self-actualization.
These idle divinities—mere positive representations of the various universal spirits of Nature and of nations, now portrayed by evolving
Thought as a single Pantheon[41] comprising all known and powerful divinities—are brought into play and given earthly significance by the

---

38. Here "S" signifies singularity or individuality, "P" particularity, and "U"
universality. Hegel rather frequently in the *Phenomenology* and other works compares
dialectic to the syllogisms of traditional logic, and here he implies that he appreciates the
possibility of a *diversity* of possible forms of dialectical "syllogisms," since he speaks of
this as just one form of syllogism. The form here would correspond roughly to the first
syllogistic "figure" in formal logic, in which the predicate manifests itself in the subject
through a middle term in the following manner: M is P, S is M, ∴ S is P.

39. It is not the poet that sings but his Muse: Cf. *Iliad* I, *init*: "Sing, O Goddess, the
anger of Achilles, son of Peleus, that brought countless ills upon the Achaeans." Individuality [*Einzelheit*], here as often in Hegel's later writings, is a synthesis of particularity [*Besonderheit*] and universality [*Allgemeinheit*]. The Muse endows the epic poet with
divine universality.

40. *B*390, H508: *Die Handlung ist die Verletzung der ruhigen Erde, die Grube, die durch das
Blut beseelt, die abgeschiednen Geister hervorruft, welche, nach Leben durstend, es in dem Tun des
Selbstbewusstseins erhalten.*

This is an adaptation of a passage in Ch. XI of Homer's *Odyssey* which describes Odysseus' efforts to receive prophetic illumination from the spirits of the netherworld by
pouring a libation of fresh blood into the ground.

41. This is the intellectual and spiritual Pantheon that prefigured the unification or
federation of diverse national spirits that would only be finally consummated by Romanic Legal Consciousness, and would be *architecturally* memorialized in the famous
Roman Pantheon. In speaking here of various national "spirits," Hegel seems to be using the term "spirit" in the same sense as Montesquieu, who speaks of the various col-
lective social structures as "spirits."

hero's *acts*. In fact, the divinities, although they sport the form of supreme (pure, universal) individualities, *need* such particular acts as conditions for their attaining any selfhood at all, let alone an immortalized
selfhood. But at the same time they are magnified as the solely blessed
and truly free, who are continually finding fault with the foibles of mortals—so that there develops a blatant contradiction between the ideal
independence and the real dependence of these gods. A second contradiction develops in their interrelationship among themselves, since
these supposedly serene and eternal *universal* individualities—being,
after all, particular gods standing for determinate, limited perfections
—begin through pettiness and altercations to show the imperfection of
the "universality" which they possess (i.e., the universality of the Pantheon constructed by language, which is better described as a "general-
ity" than universality in the strict sense).

As the gods are thus brought (by the epic poet) into a confrontation
with such contradictions, the idea of the rule of *Necessity* as a kind of negative, irrational nullification of the best-laid plans of gods *and* men
comes into prominence. At this point there is little recognition of the outlines of the *Self* in this Necessity which looms so large. But Necessity, as a
kind of negative unity of opposed elements, is indeed a precursor of the
Self in more explicit form. The more explicit realization of the identity of
Necessity and the Self (of the fact that the Self is its own Fate) is reserved
for later literary forms, in which the artist begins to doff the rather extrinsic narrator-role that he had as epic poet, and approximates more
and more to participation in the drama he is unfolding.[42]

Tragedy is the first major step in the direction of such greater participation. In Tragedy, we rise above the rather extrinsic fateful manipulation
of heroic individuals by the universal deities, and *vice versa*, which characterized the Epic. For Tragedy is concerned with archetypal, universal
individuals who come to grips with their Fate and in their utterances
(through the actors) recognize and declare that Fate.[43] And in a very real

---

42. For example, Aeschylus acted in his own plays, and Sophocles took an active part
in the production of his plays. Such facts symbolize the more active role that artistic-
religious Self-Consciousness now begins to take in dealing with the intricacies of Fate.

43. Hegel defines tragedy, in *Natural Law* (p. 105), as follows: "Tragedy consists in
this, that ethical nature segregates its inorganic [i.e., not yet self-conscious] nature (in
order not to become embroiled in it), as a fate, and places it outside itself; and by ac-
knowledging this fate in the struggle against it, ethical nature is reconciled with the Divine being as the unity of both." Thus Fate in its various appearances is simply an aspect

sense the "stage" upon which this dramatic action takes place is the mind and hearts of the actor-artist's fellow citizens, as represented by the spectators and in particular by the Chorus. These latter, in witnessing and commenting on the actions of the tragic hero, and in suffering with him, are led through this new form of literary language to a fuller self-conscious assimilation of the divine powers and elements in their milieu.[44]

The tragic character's self-conscious assimilation of his Fate, is, however, not unlimited; and the essential limitations with which he is fettered are aptly illustrated by the tragic mask worn by the actor, indicating man's inability to assimilate all that happens to him. For the "universal" which motivates the tragic hero springs from nature, from his role or "character," and is bound to bring this into conflict with other "universals" concomitant to other characters whose configurations are not within the parameters of his limited interests and purview. Thus the bifurcation into the "human" and "divine" law which (as regards *content*) characterizes that actual Ethical Substance which generates Tragedy as a religious art-form, is paralleled by another bifurcation (as regards the *form* of the reflection of ethical actuality in religious self-consciousness) into knowing intentions (personified by Phoebus Apollo, the lineal descendant of the Orient Light referred to earlier) and unknown consequences (personified by the Furies, who rise up to convict and punish the hero for the limitedness of his acts and rights, which

---

of the self which has not yet been assimilated, and is thus seen as something external that "happens" to its victims; and the very act of becoming reconciled with Fate is the emergence of the Divine. The references to tragedy in this subsection would lead one to believe that Hegel was thinking exclusively of Greek tragic heroes, especially Antigone and Oedipus, if it were not for the fact that there are also some very clear references to Shakespeare's *Hamlet* and *Macbeth* here (see M§737). As Maria Saldit (*Hegels Shakespeare-Interpretation*, p. 30) notes, "Macbeth and Hamlet in Hegel's early thinking stand as significant figures locked in the [tragic] circle of knowing vs. non-knowing." In his later thinking (see *Aesthetics* II, pp. 1225 ff.) Hegel more clearly distinguishes Shakespearean tragedy as portraying individuality more perfectly than Greek tragedy; but here he seems to be emphasizing the basic similarities between Shakespeare and the Greek tragedians in their conception of man's encounter with Fate. This emphasis is also found in *Difference between Fichte's and Schelling's System* (p. 89): "The works of Apelles or Sophocles would not have appeared to Raphael and Shakespeare—had they known them—as mere preparatory studies, but as a kindred force of the spirit. . . ."

44. Tragedy, like the other religious-art forms here, is not just the vehicle for the individual's reconciliation with Fate, but the intersubjective revelation of a communal encounter and reconciliation with Fate.

must necessarily infringe on acts and rights of which he is not cogni-zant).[45] But since both these powers are being transformed into each other in self-consciousness, it is fitting that Apollo, the god of the oracle, should use ambiguous language, only one facet of which will be compre-hensible to the acting and suffering tragic hero; and it is also fitting that the Furies, as embodying universal right or duties which (from the over-all viewpoint of the Concept of the unity of opposites) are *equal* in impor-tance with those espoused by the hero, should be elevated from the status of hated and misunderstood underworld deities to a position of honor along with Apollo.[46]

The figure of Zeus himself, however, presides over these incessant bi-furcations, and graphically represents the approximations of the trage-dians towards a *unified* comprehension of the *essential* conflicts in their environment, i.e., of those conflicts not simply reducible to contingent passions or dispositions of the tragic hero.

The self-consciousness which is represented in Tragedy, thus knows and recognizes only One supreme Power, Zeus; and it knows and recognizes Zeus alone [indifferently] as the "guardian of the State" *or* as the "protector of the family"; and with regard to the oppositions [between consciousness of particular determinations and unawareness of universals outside the scope of these determinations] within knowledge, the tragic self-consciousness knows and recognizes Zeus alone *both* as the Father of particular knowl-edge tending towards definition, and as "Zeus of the oath and of the avenging Furies,"[47] i.e., of the universal implications lying concealed within the [determinate choices of individuals].[48]

---

45. Cf. Kierkegaard, *Fear and Trembling*, p. 93: "In Greek tragedy concealment (and consequently recognition) is an epic survival grounded upon a fate in which the dra-matic action disappears from view and from which it derives its obscure and enigmatic origin. . . ."

46. Aeschylus' *Eumenides* (l. 776 ff.) relates the story of the transformation of the ob-noxious underworld Furies, who had been humiliated by Apollo at the trial of Orestes, into benignant and honored deities. The goddess Athena assures them that: "Justice gives thee a realm to share, a rich inheritance, and nothing of thine honour takes away . . . [a mansion] where Grief cometh not" (l. 890 ff.). And in Sophocles' *Oedipus at Colo-nus*, produced a few decades later, the Furies are no longer just three dreadful sisters but benignant deities to whom a shrine is built, and whose transformation seems to be a sym-bol of Oedipus' own redemption from, and through, his Fate. See also *Natural Law*, p. 105.

47. This title and the two others mentioned here were all official religious epithets manifesting different aspects of Zeus.

48. B396, H516: *Das Selbstbewusstsein, das in ihr vorgestellt ist, kennt und anerkennt deswegen nur Eine höchste Macht, und diesen Zeus nur als die Macht des Staats oder des Herdes, und im Gegensatze des Wissens nur als den Vater des zur Gestalt werdenden Wissens des* Besondern, —*und als den Zeus des Eides und der Erinnye, des* Allgemeinen, *im Verborgnen wohnenden Innern.*

Thus the imaginative depiction of Zeus is the literary parallel to the efforts made by ancient philosophers to synthesize conceptually the thought of the contingent or particular with that of the universal or essential. But on the purely artistic-religious level of Tragedy, the highest form of synthesis or "reconciliation" that can be brought about under the auspices of Zeus is not a fully conceptual reconciliation, but only the reconciliation of *forgetfulness*, the *Lethe* of those netherworld gods who rescue the hero and his witnesses from the contradictions of life by the sacred repose of death, and that other (less obvious) "lethe" of the Olympian heaven, according to which the hero and his tragic empathizers are at least absolved by a friendly deity from crime and its punishment, if not from guilt itself.[49]

The ultimate reconciliation in the stage of Art-Religion, however, emerges from the development of *Comedy*.[50] In Comedy, the abstract attributes and prerogatives that were formerly associated with the gods and projected onto them are now reappropriated. (*a*) The divine substance as Nature is now consciously represented merely as an object of enjoyment, and this conscious representation brings to a fitting culmination the partial and unconscious representations of this sort which were found earlier in certain aspects of the religious rituals, such as in the communion of feasting on that which had been sacrificed to a god. (*b*) The divine substance as *ethical* essence is identified primarily with the State (sacred to Zeus) and the individuality of the Family (sacred to Hera and the Penates). And this aspect of the divine substance is now also made the subject of conscious reappropriation: For example, the

---

49. In Greek mythology, "*Lethe*" is not actually used with reference to the *Olympian* realm. Hegel's reference to "Lethe" in this sense is a figurative way of expressing a second and sublimated form of forgetfulness which is an alternative to, and/or a complement of, that "forgetfulness" which issues from death itself. Still, this higher form of forgetfulness cannot bring about freedom from *guilt*. Only Christianity, as we shall see, can accomplish this.

50. Here we proceed from the artistry of Aeschylus, Sophocles and Euripides, who grappled manfully with the enigmas of the Divine, to the artistry of Aristophanes, who in subjecting all things, the gods included, to his wit, in effect asserts the divinity of man—man the blessed or Happy Self-Consciousness, who in concert with his fellows has managed completely to "mediate" that otherness that plagued its opposite, the "Unhappy (Self-)Consciousness" (in Part I). The confrontation between these two "types" of Self-Consciousness will be the necessary and sufficient impetus to the stage of Revealed Religion (see next section).

state which prides itself on being its *own* ''Lord and Ruler'' is shown to be actually at the mercy of this or that individual.[51]

While thinking in the form of ''Reason''[52] busies itself with disentangling the simple Ideas of the Good and the Beautiful from the mass of maxims and customs that these Ideas were connected with in the Ethical Substance, the spirit of Comedy follows suit by directing its barbs at the various gods who had been used as sanctions for the former customs— and then even focuses its devastating wit on the power of dialectical Reason itself, as a tool of *sophistry* which can be used to pander to youthful caprices and to confuse the aged.[53]

Thus, with Comedy, the spirit of Religious Art jettisons (in both a literal and a figurative sense) the *mask*, which had been an essential accoutrement in performances of Tragedies.[54] The player in the comedy of life

---

51. Greek democracy, parallel to Comedy itself, had supposedly reappropriated the prerogatives of Zeus and became its own divine ruler; but as Aristophanes shows in his satire *The Knights*, the Greek people (personified in the play by the slave master Demus) end up continually trading off one tyrannical ''servant of the people'' for another more tyrannical.

52. E.g., Socrates.

53. Aristophanes' *The Clouds* is an extended satire of dialectical sophistry as caricatured in Socrates. And in *The Frogs*, the Chorus reflects the view of what Hegel calls the ''Comic'' Consciousness when, with tongue in cheek, it contrasts the intellectual ''seriousness'' of Aeschylus (who in the play is about to return from the netherworld to life in the world above) with the sophistry of ''dialectic'':

> ''Blest the man who possesses a
> Keen intelligent mind.
> This full often we find.
> He, the bard of renown [Aeschylus],
> Now to earth reascends,
> Goes, a joy to his friends,
> Just because he possesses a
> Keen intelligent mind.
> *Right* it is and befitting,
> Not, by Socrates sitting,
> Idle talk to pursue,
> Stripping tragedy-art of
> All things noble and true.
> Surely the mind to school
> Fine-drawn quibbles to seek,
> Fine-set phrases to speak,
> Is but the part of a fool!''

54. As Lowenberg (*Hegel's Phenomenology*, p. 330) notes, comedy shows that the gods portrayed by masks in tragedy were just masks; only the actors are real. (The actors themselves are the realities which gave rise to the gods.)

no longer feels subject to the great divine essentialities as externalities, no longer feels the instinctive need to effect some kind of reconciliation between man's individuality and divine universality through the negative unity of Fate—because the uninhibited, fearless "happy" self-consciousness, with its own power of reconciling oppositions, now shows that *it itself* is the Fate that had previously taken on the aspect of a great void of negation. Thus the culmination of Art-Religion shows us the new face of a Fate which does not just appear surreptitiously and then disappear, but remains within itself, preserves itself, and endures.

C. REVEALED RELIGION
[INTERSUBJECTIVE SELF-CONSCIOUSNESS THROUGH CHRISTIANITY]

Introductory Remarks:

Emil Fackenheim in his interpretation of the Phenomenology *aptly characterizes the progression of religion there as a swing from the transcendence of the Nature-Religions, which had only a modicum of immanence; to the immanence of the Art-Religions, with their minimal transcendence; and then finally to the dynamic equipoise of both transcendence and immanence in Revealed Religion:*

Divine-human inwardness already *exists in the religion of light. Divine-human otherness* still *exists in its extreme opposite, historically actual in the Greek "religion of art,"*. . . . *For all the commensurateness of the human acquired in its aesthetic immanence, the Divine retains transcendence, infinity, and incommensurability with all things human, [while] the religion of art, oblivious to transcendence, is confined to idolatrous worship of finite gods. But as the ignored or abandoned truth at length enters into consciousness these gods, their worship, and the worshiping nation are all destroyed.*

*The Christian religion is the absolute religion because it contains, preserves and reconciles the depth of the "religion of light" with the self or spirit of the religion of art. Here the Divine is the depth of an Infinity incommensurable with all things finite and human, and it has yet become absolutely commensurate with human selfhood, so radically as to enter into actual human finitude and to suffer actual human death. (*The Religious Dimension, *pp. 55–56.)*

In Revealed Religion, or Christianity, the transcendent God becomes incarnate, manifests himself to men, sacrifices himself for mankind, and identifies himself so thoroughly with his followers that thenceforth hardly any strong and significant distinction between God's Spirit and that of religious consciousness can be made. In fact, the identification is so close that the "Revelation" of God to man is ipso facto *and* pari passu *the revelation of God to himself. This is but one of a whole series of paradoxes that results, in Hegel's estimation, from the essential Christian stand-*

point. The theologian Hans Küng sums up at length some of the more salient consequences and paradoxes of this standpoint, and tries to defend Hegel against over-hasty reactions from the camps of theological orthodoxy:

The standard reflections in the light of classical theology will here be . . . re-flected by the theologian of the schools: One could say that Hegel avails himself of a new, quite philosophical terminology ("'moment," "Consciousness," "in-itself," "for-itself" . . .). However, one must respond, was not the Christological terminology that we are so used to today (ϑύσις, ὑπόστασις, "natura," "persona") once a non-biblical philosophical "innovation" which was employed sometimes heretically, sometimes in orthodox fashion, and thus became extremely suspect? Hegel prefers expressions like "Father," "Son," "generation," and "maternity" to be developed in their speculative significations—but must not these words even in traditional theology be understood as highly equivocal (more dissimilar than similar to their referent) and thus subject to a process of reinterpretation through the [trifold] path of "affirmation, negation and supereminence"? Hegel's distinction between the act of generation and the act of creation, between Logos and world, is rather weak—but must not both be seen as a unity, if the Scriptural passages about "creation through the Logos" (ἐν χριστῷ) are to make any sense? Hegel identifies sin with the Absolute—but was not the Son of God made sin according to Paul, or according to John a "sin-offering" [Sündenlam]? Hegel teaches that the reconciliation of men is the self-reconciliation of God—but does not the whole idea of reconciliation depend on its not taking place in some privileged man but through God in God's Son? Hegel teaches a distancing from Christ-the-individual through the universal Christ as mankind but is it not the wont of all believers to be impelled by their spirit to form the one body of Christ, to "make up for what is still lacking in Christ"? Hegel teaches a "becoming" of God—but has not the eternal Logos become a God-Man? Hegel teaches a necessary development of the divine—but is the knowledge of the necessity of the δεῖ in sacred history not to be found in Scripture? And finally, Hegel teaches a panentheism which places the creature in unity with God—but according to the Christology we are familiar with is not God man, and the Creator a creature, in one and the same Jesus Christ?—Every theologian feels the problems which crop up in the wake not only of Hegel's responses but also of those of classical Christology and under often diverse formulations oppress us even today in their insolubility. (Menschwerden Gottes, p. 284.)

If we recall that the happy, Comic [*komische*] Self-Consciousness, the irreligious denouement of Art-Religion that learned to treat the gods as familiars and to insist that it itself was the source of the gods and of external verities, is an outgrowth of that state of actual Spirit that we called the Ethical Substance, it becomes obvious what a turnabout has been produced. In the Ethical Substance, the self-conscious subject is a predicate of the *Substance*, which is the essential thing; with the advent of the Comic Self-Consciousness, however, the Substance itself, with all of the divine personifications of its attributes, has itself become a predicate of the self-conscious subject. So now, instead of the proposition "Substance is Subject," we have a converse proposition: "the Self is Absolute Being." This latter proposition does not completely exclude the significance of the former, however, since one could still say even here that

"Substance is Subject"—as long as it is clearly understood that the "Substance" in this case is specifically and exclusively religious consciousness' *own* substance, or the substantial elements whose sacrifice has been recognized and *consummated* in this ultimate way by this final form of religious-irreligious consciousness.[55]

It should be obvious that the Comic Self-Consciousness shows only remote affinity with the roots whence it came; and, in fact, it provides a motive force on the religious (Self-Conscious) level for the transition to the next stage of *actual* (Conscious) Spirit—the stage (already discussed, pp. 30 ff.) of abstract personhood and Legal Status,[56] which by the power of abstract thought inflates the self to the proportions of an abstract being, and gradually comes to conceive of *its* divinity in accord with this intense and unified focus on abstract personhood. The extreme subjectivity which began with the Comic Consciousness correspondingly follows the path we have already outlined in our discussions of Stoicism, Scepticism, and the Unhappy Consciousness. In other words, parallel to the development from Stoicism to the Unhappy Consciousness in Part I (see K90 ff.), and to the corresponding development from Abstract Personhood to contingent personhood at the mercy of the "Lord and Master of the World" (see *supra*, pp. 32 ff.), there is a development now in Religion from the individualistic aftermath of the Comic Self-Consciousness to the final stages of Judaism, which provided the proximate prerequisites for the emergence of early Christianity.[57] The ironic result of its progress down this path will be that the

---

55. As in the holocaust which completely consumed the offerings to Ceres and other gods, now all the divine gifts and values are sacrificed to the all-consuming wit of the Comic Self-Consciousness, which has made *itself* the Absolute. This apparently antireligious stance, however, has positive significance in the evolution of Religion, since, as we shall see, it conditions and necessitates a confrontation with its dialectical counterpart, the Unhappy Consciousness.

56. Hegel had previously discussed the development of this stage of personhood in its own right, but now recapitulates, showing how those changes in the "Actual" Spirit took place in, and presupposed, a certain religious context. This is a recurring point in Hegel. Major changes or advancements in the social or political sphere require parallel changes in the religious viewpoint.

57. At this point, Hegel's probable reference to Judaism at the beginning of Nature-Religion (*supra*, p. 134) should be recalled. In primitive Judaism, religious consciousness was characterized by a comparatively external Master–Slave relationship to God conceived as Creator of the world. But now, as the emergence of the Comic Self-Consciousness marks the zenith and the demise of the (Greek) spirit that gave birth to it, and supplies the transition to the new (Roman) spirit of Legalism and abstract personhood, the final stages of (Old Testament) Judaism are seen in the Roman context, i.e.,

happy consciousness of comedy, which incorporated all substantiality into itself to consummate the sacrifice of Substance is, because of its very extremism, transformed into an Unhappy Consciousness groping about for some objective expression of its substance, losing that self-certainty which it guarded so jealously, and exclaiming with a genuine sense of bereavement that "God is dead."[58]

Concomitant with this "death of God" is the "death of art," at least insofar as the sense of wonder, mystery and transcendence that had permeated the great productions of the stage of Art-Religion is now but a dim and unsubstantial memory:

> The statues now are cadavers from which the living soul has departed; the hymns are words no longer vivified by belief; . . . The literary works inspired by the Muse now lack spiritual force. . . . In short, all these works are [in the stage of Revealed Religion] what they are for us even now [in the modern world]—namely, beautiful fruits detached from their tree. Just as a maiden might offer choice fruits to us, an amiable Fate offers us these fruits [of Art-Religion]. . . . But with those products of that art, Fate does *not* also give us the *world* [that made them possible]. . . . *Our* enjoyment of them is thus *not* a form of worship through which *our* consciousness might find fulfillment and perfect truth. . . . But just as the maiden who offers us the picked fruits is greater than that Nature which directly provides them (insofar as she epitomizes Nature's entirety in the sparkle of her *self*-conscious eyes and in her manner of presenting its fruits), so also the Spirit of the

---

with emphasis on the fact that Judaea at the time of the emergence of Christianity was a province in the Roman Empire (although it cannot properly be identified with the Roman World [see *Philosophy of History*, p. 321]), and with additional emphasis on the fact that the transition from Stoicism/personhood, to Scepticism/contingency, to Unhappy Consciousness/subservience to *internal* Lord and Master—which took place in the Roman context as a whole—also, and even paradigmatically, took place in the province of Judaea. In other words, the Jews were considered by Hegel to be the forerunners of the Unhappy Consciousness, which was also to become endemic in the Roman Empire as a whole (see *ibid.*, pp. 278, 318, 321 ff., 329, 383, 424). And as was the case in the Roman version, the relationship of the Jewish Unhappy Consciousness to God was not just an intellectual abstraction or an attitude of subservience to an external "Lord and Master of the World," but a kind of Master–Slave relationship to the Absolute himself, who seemed to more intangible and more distant as the Jews become more and more anxious for the concrete objectification of God in the form of a Messiah (see Pöggeler, *Hegels Idee einer Phänomenologie des Geistes*, p. 79; Plant, *Hegel*, Ch. III).

58. "God is Dead" is a quote from a Lutheran hymn: "*Gott selbst ligt todt!*" The feeling that "God is dead" is shared in different ways by the Greeks disillusioned with their gods in the aftermath of the Comic Self-Consciousness, by the Romans in the aftermath of Scepticism, by the Jews after centuries of waiting in vain for God to fulfill his scriptural promises, by the Jewish Christian converts after the crucifixion of Jesus, and in more modern times by Pascal's sense of a "lost God" (*Faith and Knowledge*, p. 190). But paradoxically, this sense of the death of God is "the starting point of holiness and of elevation to God" (*History of Philosophy* III, p. 5).

[amiable, no longer dire] Fate[59] which offers us these works of art is greater than the ethical life and actuality of those people [who produced that art]—since [this new Spirit] is the inner recollection (*Er-Innerung*)] of what in them had been the external expression of their Spirit.[60]

Thus, as a result, Religion at this point finds itself at a crossroads where the old meets the new and looks about confusedly for some sort of synthesis or reconciliation. This reconciliation will take place in a Bethlehem of religious Self-Consciousness in which

these forms just mentioned [the now lifeless artistic creations: statuary, ritual celebrations, religious dramas, etc.] stand on one side; and, on the other, the world of Personhood and Right, that devastating wilderness of [formal] elements set free from their content, the Stoical person-as-thought-about and the ceaseless unrest of the sceptical consciousness bring to completion the full circle of figures which stand by and press close around the birthplace of Spirit arriving at self-consciousness; and the grief and longing of the Unhappy Consciousness which permeates *all* these figures constitutes their center and the communally shared birthpangs of Spirit's advent[61]—since the Unhappy Consciousness [here represents] the simplest form of that pure Concept which contains all the other figures as constituent "moments."[62]

---

59. Fate is no longer conceived as something external to the self, at this stage, but has been unmasked as a form of one's own self-projection. In *Early Theological Works* (pp. 228 ff.), Hegel depicts Jesus as one who had finally disarmed and nullified the dreadfulness of Fate which had stalked the Greek world.

60. *B402, H523-4: Die Bildsäulen sind nun Leichname, denen die belebende Seele, sowie die Hymne Worte, deren Glauben entflohen ist. . . . Den Werken der Muse fehlt die Kraft des Geistes . . . . Sie sind nun das, was sie für uns sind—vom Baume gebrochne schöne Früchte, ein freundliches Schicksal reichte sie uns dar, wie ein Mädchen jene Früchte präsentiert. . . . So gibt das Schicksal uns mit den Werken jener Kunst nicht ihre Welt. . . . Unser Tun in ihrem Genusse ist daher nicht das gottesdienstliche, wodurch unserem Bewusstsein seine vollkommne es ausfüllende Wahrheit würde. . . . Aber wie das Mädchen das die gepfluckten Frucht darreicht, mehr ist als die . . . ausgebreitete Natur derselben, welche sie unmittelbar darbot, indem es auf eine höhere Weise dies alles in den Strahl des selbstbewussten Auges und der darreichenden Gebärde zusammenfasst, so ist der Geist des Schicksals, der uns jene Kunstwerke darbietet, mehr als das sittliche Leben und Wirklichkeit jenes Volkes, denn er ist die Er-Innerung des in ihnen noch veräusserten Geistes. . . .*

61. In one sense the Unhappy Consciousness is just one of the forms of (Self-) Consciousness in which Revealed Religion will emerge; but in another sense it sums up the situation that they all have in common, that loss of objective coordinates which is suffered by Consciousness in a state of extreme immersion in self.

62. *B403, H525: Diese Formen, und auf der andern Seite die* Welt *der* Person *und des Rechts, die verwüstende Wildheit der freigelassenen Elemente des Inhalts, ebenso die gedachte* Person *des Stoizismus und die haltlose Unruhe des skeptischen Bewusstseins, machen die Peripherie der Gestalten aus, welche erwartend und drängend um die Geburtsstätte des als Selbstbewusstsein werdenden Geistes umherstehen; der alle durchdringende Schmerz und Sehnsucht des unglücklichen Selbstbewusstseins ist ihr Mittelpunkt und das gemeinschaftliche Geburtswene seines Hervorgangs, —die Einfachheit des reinen Begriffs, der jene Gestalten als seine Momente enthält.*

The reconciling birth that is awaited is the genesis of a state of Religion which will combine simultaneously the sense of *conscious* immersion in objective substance that was characteristic of Nature-Religion and the early stages of Art-Religion, and is now demanded by the Unhappy Consciousness, with the *self-conscious* certainty that has been so anxiously pursued by the Comic Consciousness and its melancholy successors.

The "birth" in this case is not just something imaginary or metaphorical, but factual. This stage is the culmination of that long evolution of the divine Essence from the external immediacy of luminous Numinosity, through the gropings of Nature-Religion and the self-discoveries of Art-Religion to the point where it can both appear and be recognized as a concrete, existing self-consciousness. It can *appear* because the substance of the divinity has become self-conscious in the world. It can also be *recognized* as the transcendent Essence which it is, because the Unhappy Consciousness, which has been searching after just such an Essence in objective form, will not fail to recognize and even welcome it.

Thus a God-man appears in the world and is recognized as such. This God-man has an actual and explicit "mother"—self-consciousness itself, that Unhappy Consciousness which has attained the requisite depth and interiority to be able to recognize the appearance of its God; but only a concealed or implicit "Father"—the universal Essence which has evolved through all manner of intermediate and imperfect reflections to a stage of ultimate *abstraction*, where this Essence makes a clean break with all its embodiments in Nature and appears as it is in itself, i.e., as an individual *Self*. Thus what might appear at first blush to be "stooping" on the part of the divinity—becoming a living, publicly perceptible human being—is actually an elevation (elevation to the greatest possible abstraction from, detachment from, Nature); in other words, in sharp contrast to the situation in Sense-Certainty where the "richness" of sensuous presence proved to be the poorest and most abstract state of being, here the "lowliness" of specific corporeal existence proves to be the highest attainment of thought, the most extreme alienation of universal thought from its *merely* natural antecedents, the most concentrated focusing of thought into one simple and determinate revelation. Thus with the coming of this single individual,[63] Nature becomes

---

63. Hegel does not mention Jesus Christ by name here because his emphasis is entirely on the developments in Religion that lead necessarily to the phenomena of revelation and incarnation. But as Küng (*Menschwerden Gottes*, p. 262) notes, there can be no doubt

conscious of its own divinity; while self-consciousness, which had gradually appropriated divinity to itself, finally receives its longed-for confirmation of the presence of that divinity in the natural world also.

This unity of Nature and self-conscious thought in the Incarnation is an *immediate* unity, insofar as it is a sensuous presence; but also a mediated unity, insofar as it is created by, and dependent on, an act of recognition on the part of self-consciousness, which constantly nullifies all alien otherness in the divine being who is perceived. This latter, mediated unity is an approximation to a true speculative, conceptual unification of Being and Thought, self and other—but *only* an approximation, because the stark, sensuous presence of the Absolute is a hindrance to its being conceptually comprehended. A further stage of mediation takes place when the Absolute withdraws its sensuous presence but is retained in memory (by the religious community) as a presence which "has

---

that Jesus Christ is the exemplar in this case: "Hegel names various names in the *Phenomenology*, but he also often refrains from naming, even in passages where the allusions are quite obvious—e.g., the references to Schelling, to Napoleon, to Louis XIV. And so here also Hegel treats of Jesus Christ in great detail, without actually mentioning 'Jesus' or 'Christ.' "

From Hegel's philosophical-phenomenological viewpoint, the Incarnation is of great interest because it epitomizes that synthesis of self-and-other that is the essence of Spirit in all of its concrete forms. (It is only Spirit in a very abstract form that sees itself as detached or alienated from otherness.) A preliminary condition for man's *perception* of the Incarnation is that man (i.e., the Comic Self-Consciousness) appropriate divinity to himself, and thus make the initial but necessary connection (in his own psyche) between the natural, the finite, on the one hand, and the Absolute on the other. But perception of the divine as incarnate can also inspire man to become divine (*Aesthetics* I, 534). From an even more comprehensive viewpoint, these two processes are reciprocal, complementary and mutually corroborating, and this is what Hegel especially wants us to realize.

As Hegel notes in his introduction to Nature-Religion (*supra*, p. 133), Incarnation is essential to the Christian religion, while it is only a peripheral element in other religions. For example, Vishnu, one of the chief gods of Hinduism, is thought by the Hindus periodically to incarnate himself under diverse forms: as Krishna, as Buddha, and as Rama. But with respect to the Hindu who believes in such incarnations, it could not be said that his belief is centered on incarnation (especially since it is a doctrine of Hinduism that all matter, including any empirical ego that may appear, is *Maya*, cosmic illusion). Christianity, on the other hand, is *essentially* a belief in incarnation, and in the unique and unrepeatable Incarnation of the Son of God.

Finally, it should be noted that Hegel, in equating the "Revelation" of God with the Incarnation, differs somewhat from standard Christian usage. For in the Christian tradition, God's revelation of himself is thought to have begun with the Jews, and the Old Testament Scriptures are generally considered the "revealed word of God" alongside of, and on an almost equal footing with, the New Testament. But in Hegel's *Phenomenology*, revelation is a New Testament Phenomenon.

been.'' This imaginative representation of the divine Being as One who was once among us is simultaneously a spiritual death (the loss of a vivifying sensuous presence) and a spiritual resurrection (reinstatement of the divine Self as a universal self-consciousness which still remains and pervades the religious community as the Spirit which animates it). This form of mediation, however, is still defective insofar as it implies a split between the present and the past, the Here and the Beyond; and those in the religious community who try to overcome this split by trying to trace back their present state to some original state of the community (which they would like to recapture or reinstate), or to the original acts or words of the God-man himself, are thoroughly misguided.[64] For the unity of the human and divine is not to be found by harking back to the past, but by a constant making-present of this unity in and through the spiritual self-mediation of the community.

Let us now examine in some detail the necessary moments according to which this ultimate stage of religious communality develops. (It should be realized that in talking about ''necessity'' here, we are already assuming a viewpoint above and beyond the stage we are considering here. For the religious viewpoint essentially involves imaginative representations, and tends to see the conceptual necessities we will discuss here as free or contingent events, or ''happenings.'')[65] Three essential moments must be considered: (1) The interior interrelationships of the Trinitarian conception of the Absolute, which forms the basis for the ultimate community; (2) the external relationships of the Absolute; and (3) the fusion of the Absolute with the world, brought about in and through the religious community.

[a. The Trinity Conceived in Its Interiority[66]]

As will be recalled, the Unhappy Consciousness (see K95 ff.) represented in its imagination an unchangeable, universal, essential self, and

---

64. This criticism would seem to be directed at those Protestants who want to base their faith solely on the actual words of Scripture, and at any Christians who think that the key to the Christian spirit is in determining the acts and characteristics of ''the historical Jesus'' (to use the contemporary expression).

65. A similar observation was made in the case of Faith (see *supra*, p. 60).

66. Parallel conceptual expositions of the Christian doctrine of the Trinity are to be found *supra*, p.59, and in *Philosophy of History*, p. 324.

Just as Hegel sees in the Incarnation both a conformity to, and a confirmation of, his own speculative doctrine of Reason (as the unity of Thought and Being, self and other), groped for some objectification of this idea as the terminus in which alone it could find satisfaction. Then, in Faith (see *supra*, p. 58 ff.), the unchangeable became a "Being" posited just beyond reality. But if we examine its abstract concept, we find that (*a*) this Being is imbued with negativity from the start; (*b*) it must express this negativity in the *essentially* negative moment of existence-for-self; and (*c*) this latter expression is a reflection of the Essence which generated it. This necessary process of revelation is now understood, but is represented *pictorially* by the Religious Self-Consciousness in the present as an eternal "happening" "before" the creation of the world; i.e., (*a*) the emergence of the Father out of his eternal identity, (*b*) the Father's generation of the Son as his expression, and (*c*) the emergence of the Spirit as the communal bond of similarity (or, better, identity) uniting Son with Father in spite of their differentiation.

[b. The Relations of the Triune Absolute *ad extra*]

From the conceptual viewpoint, the necessary and sufficient instigation for an externalization of this essential divine life is the *otherness* which is an essential concomitant of the interior interrelationships just described. The otherness of the divine expression from the divine Essence, and the other aspects of otherness, must at some point reach a degree of absolute abstraction:[67] and the absolute abstraction of otherness

----

so also he sees in the Trinity both conformity to, and confirmation of, his own triadic dialectic. Hegel's philosophy is speculative Christianity, and Christianity is an imaginative embodiment of speculative (Hegelian) idealism.

It goes without saying that Hegel considered the complex interrelationships of the divine Persons of the Trinity to be *the* concept of God *par excellence*. It is the key to the perfection of the Christian religion over other religions. Other monotheistic religions like Islam (see *Philosophy of Mind*, §393) may emphasize the unity of God, and polytheistic systems may emphasize the diversity in God; but it is only Christianity that finally synthesizes both unity and diversity in its God-concept. Given Hegel's insistence that the forms of religion and theology condition actual or political forms of Spirit, this fact is of the utmost practical importance for understanding Hegel's later political philosophy. For example, Hegel says (*ibid.*) that the lack of differentiation in the Islamic concept of God is reflected in the tendency towards monolithic political structure in Muslim countries. He also considers Protestant Christianity (including its Trinitarian theology) an indispensable basis for a free political State (see *Philosophy of History*, p. 435).

67. One is reminded here of Plato's argument in the *Sophist* (255) that once one admits of admixtures of otherness, he also must, because of the very nature of *otherness*, allow for a special category of Otherness as something remaining and perduring in its own right, outside of, and other than, the other categories.

conceived (*a*) *as* an abstraction, is what is called "Nature." But Nature, insofar as it retains from the divine Essence the negative moment of *existence-for-self*, also comes into existence (*b*) as an individual self. This self, if it is to express its selfhood, must then (*c*) depart from its innocent immersion in Nature to *alienate* itself from Nature—and this very act of alienation sets up (*d*) an antinomy between good and evil. (The achievement of self-consciousness is initially perceived as an "evil" because of its disruption of Nature, although as an emergence of Thought in its simplicity it would have to be viewed as "good." This initial perception of oneself as evil is complemented by the initial perception of the Essence externalizing itself in Nature as "good," although insofar as the Essence thus particularizes and *limits* itself it *could* be called "evil.")[68] Since self-consciousness in its immediate state cannot bear the ascription of "evil" either to itself or to the divine Essence, it (*e*) humbly ascribes evil only to the element of otherness associated with the divine Essence; and it may also (*f*) contrast this element with its counterpart, the other-otherness which remains good in spite of its differentiation; then, since the very idea of otherness (whether good or evil) is inimical to *precise* differentiation, it may speak of the differentiations of otherness (*g*) as an indefinite number. Finally, since the divine Essence is recognized as "the essential" by the "evil" consciousness, and on its pure conceptual level is compelled to express its essence, it must itself (*h*) take the initiative and repair the damage brought about by the dichotomization into good and evil. It does this by (*i*) clothing its expression with sensuous existence-for-self, thus becoming both "unessential" and "evil"; and then (*j*) by consciously sacrificing this sensuous existence-for-self, cancelling its own inessentiality and evil, and by implication (*k*) re-creating finite self-consciousness as universal (i.e., essential) and reunited with the divine Essence (i.e., good). By doing this, it (*l*) paves the way for the unessential and evil self-consciousness to become universal and good by following the same path.

The "believing" consciousness, we have already seen, tends to represent imaginatively divine attributes and actions as immanent in, or taking place in, the external world. In accord with this fundamental orientation, it thus perceived the necessary developments described above as the following "happenings": (*a*) Creation of the world out of nothing;

---

68. Compare *Philosophy of Mind*, §382, where "evil" in general is ascribed to that which, in tending to an extreme of particularity, departs from universality.

(*b*) creation of man (Adam); (*c*) Adam's loss of innocence; (*d*) Adam's confusion concerning the knowledge of good and evil;[69] (*e*) Eve's ascription of the evil to the tempter, Satan (the serpent); (*f*) the contrast of this evil spirit with its counterpart (possibly the proto-redeemer prophesied in Genesis III, 15); (*g*) the idea that the number of spirits (good and evil) is a host of infinite magnitude; (*h*) the decision by the Father to send a Messiah; (*i*) the incarnation of the Son; (*j*) the passion, death and resurrection of the Son; (*k*) the Atonement or reconciliation of the human race now accomplished in principle by the Son; and (*l*) the consequent establishment of the new covenant, the "order of grace" by which man can be "restored" to friendship with God.

[c. Synthesis of the Divine and the Human in a Religious
     Community after the Protestant Pattern]

Introductory Remarks:

Jesus for the Christian is the symbol and the pledge not only of the union of the finite self with its absolute Other but also of the finite self with other finite selves. Plant* offers evidence that Hegel interpreted Jesus primarily as one who was trying to inculcate a sense of community among his followers, while these followers themselves seemed to be more interested in attaining personal immortality and preeminence in the afterlife than in fostering community. If one would understand Hegel's interpretation of Christianity, the relationship of Christianity to the development of community or intersubjectivity seems to be the indispensable interpretative key.

---

69. In *Philosophy of History* (p. 321) Hegel explains in greater detail the story in *Genesis* about the "Tree of the Knowledge of Good and Evil:" Man, created in the image of God, lost, it is said, his state of absolute contentment, by eating of the Tree of Knowledge of Good and Evil. Sin consists here only in Knowledge: this is the sinful element, and by it man is stated to have trifled away his natural happiness. This is a deep truth, that evil lies in consciousness: for the brutes are neither evil nor good; the merely Natural Man quite as little. Consciousness occasions the separation of the Ego, in its boundless freedom as arbitrary choice, from the pure essence of the will—i.e., from the Good. Knowledge, as the dismantling of the unity of mere Nature, is the 'Fall,' which is no casual conception, but the eternal history of Spirit. For the state of innocence, the paradisiacal condition, is that of the brute. Paradise is a park, where only brutes, not men, can remain. For the brute is one with God only implicitly. Only Man's Spirit (that is) has a self-cognizant existence. This existence-for-self, this consciousness, is at the same time separation from the Universal and Divine Spirit. If I hold to my abstract Freedom, in contraposition to the Good, I adopt the standpoint of Evil. The Fall is therefore the eternal Mythus of Man—in fact, the very transition by which he becomes man."
*Hegel, chap. II.

Gray** shows how Hegel's early theological thought was marked by a growing conviction that Christianity had degenerated into a Privatreligion, *the purpose of which was "to cultivate the morality of isolated individuals," and needed to return to the sort of* Volksreligion *found in Greek culture, which "is by its very nature a public phenomenon which cannot even be thought of apart from other phases of a people's life." Hegel's feelings about the proper expression of religion become evident in his criticism of the somber and melancholy Christian mode of celebrating the Lord's Supper:*

"At our greatest public festival one approaches the celebration of the sacred gift in the clothes of mourning and with lowered eyes. At the festival which should be the celebration of universal brotherhood, many a one feels that he may become infected by the brotherly cup [of sacramental wine] from which one diseased drank before him. And in order that one's spirit may not be attentive, not maintained in its sacred emotion, one must get the offering out of one's pocket and place it on the [collection] plate during the celebration. In contrast, the Greeks approached the altars of their gods, laden with the friendly gifts of nature, crowned with garlands of flowers, garbed in colors of gladness, their open countenances inviting to friendship and love and disseminating cheer."†

Nevertheless, Hegel did not advocate a simple return to pagan spontaneity and festivity in Christianity. The essential thing which he found present in the Greek model and lacking in Christianity was a synthesis of religious and secular life. And the way to inculcate this *dimension into Christianity—if we may be allowed to consider the hints in the very incomplete discussion here in the context of the later developments in Hegel's thought—was not simply to devise warmer, more sociable and more spontaneous celebrations of the Lord's Supper and other Christian liturgies, but to inaugurate a change which on the one hand was plain and undramatic but on the other was quite radical: the simple extension of the Christian spirit over all the ordinary areas of everyday existence. Changes to be made in formal Church organization or liturgical practices (in addition to the reforms already introduced by Protestantism) did not seem to be of any great importance to Hegel; we have little evidence that he put any great stock in such ecclesiastical changes. But the extension of the Christian message throughout the world was indispensable for Christianity. In* Philosophy of History *(p. 327) Hegel observes that adherence to the counsels of the Gospel would lead to social revolution; and there is no doubt that (as Plant and others have shown) Hegel's ever-continuing interest in social and political philosophy to the end of his life was a direct offshoot of his special and un-Kierkegaardian vision of the secular congruity of the Christian religion.*

Now the closest approximation to Christianity in this *sense was (in Hegel's*

***Hegel and Greek Thought*, p. 23.
†*Ibid.*, p. 27 (*Jugendschriften* cited here).

*opinion) Protestantism, and especially Lutheranism as Hegel understood it—
perhaps idealized it. For Hegel thought that the great genius of Protestant Christianity was that (in contrast to a sheltered, provincial ambivalence towards the
world found in Catholicism) it managed to synthesize the Christian spirit with
worldly concerns, and establish the sort of community that Christ had in mind* in the
world. *Thus in* Aesthetics I *(p. 509), Hegel remarks that: "In religion the
Dutch were Protestants, an important matter, and to Protestantism alone the important thing is to get a sure footing in the prose of life, to make it absolutely valid in
itself independently of religious associations, and to let it develop in unrestricted freedom." And in* Philosophy of Mind *§552 ad. fin.) he portrays the proper "province" of the Protestant religion as the ethical life (*Sittlichkeit*) of a nation rather
than specifically ecclesiastical activity: "In the Protestant conscience the principles
of the religious and of the ethical conscience come to be one and the same: the free spirit
learning to see itself in its reasonableness and truth. In the Protestant state, the constitution and the code, as well as their several applications, embody the principle and
the development of the moral life, which proceeds and can only proceed from the truth
of religion." Hegel sums up the general thrust of such observations in* Philosophy
of History *(p. 422), where he contrasts Catholicism, which "does not claim the
essential direction of the secular," with the spirit of the Reformation, which, "having . . . gained the consciousness of its Freedom through that process of mediation
which takes place between man and God—that is, in the full recognition of the objective process as the existence [or revelation] of the Divine essence—now takes it up
and follows it out in building up the edifice of secular relations."*

    *Hegel does not want simply to identify religion with ethical and political life: he
is quite careful to say, for example, in* Philosophy of Right *(§327, Remark),
that: "In religion there lies the place where man is always assured of finding a consciousness of the unchangeable, of the highest freedom and satisfaction, even within
all the mutability of the world and despite the frustration of his aims and the loss of his
interests and possessions. Now if religion is in this way the groundwork which includes the ethical realm in general, and the state's fundamental nature—the divine
will—in particular, it is at the same time only a groundwork; and it is at this point
that state and religion begin to diverge." However, the actual "divergence" or distinction of religion from the state in Hegel's schema is weakened by three factors: (1)
The State he primarily has in mind is a Protestant State; (2) more specifically, his
preference is for a German Lutheran state, and German Lutheranism because of
historical accidents (the need for protection, etc.) has always (even into the early
twentieth century) had the closest conceivable ties with the State; and (3) Hegel is
speaking within the context of idealistic–systematic political philosophy (as ex-*

pounded by Fichte et al.), one of whose important tenets is that the ideal state (cf. also the "Ethical Substance" in the Phenomenology) *is one which is perfectly responsive to the will of the citizens who constitute it.*

In a word, religion (Protestantism) is, in spite of the weak distinction which Hegel makes between it and the state, the very soul of social and political existence, organically united with the latter. For it is in this religion that the essential reconciliation of man with God, and man with man, is established in human hearts; and this in turn is the essential foundation for extending such a spirit of reconciliation throughout "external" or secular life.[††]

As Küng (Menschwerdung Gottes, *p. 296) remarks, Hegel's solution to the traditional dichotomy between religion and secular existence and other dichotomies is a new synthetic paradoxical formula: "God in the* world, *transcendence in* immanence, *the 'beyond' in the 'here and now'." Questions about the afterlife, about ritual practices, ecclesiastical organization, become very insignificant in the light of this formula.*

As mentioned above (p. 56) Hegel seems to "solve" the traditional problem about how the Christian can be "in" the world without being "of" the world by simply denying the existence of any important distinction between the two spheres, the "distinction" between the Protestant religion and its Protestant state being conceived as very complementary and certainly not in dialectical opposition. Thus, in the Hegelian sense, the Christian mission to "spread the Kingdom of God" is interpreted simply as the extension of the spirit of love, mutual reconciliation and community throughout social and political life, in proportion to one's powers, and preferably in emancipation from the "imaginative" elements of religiosity. The alternative to this, in Hegel's estimation, was Faith, or Catholic consciousness, which tried to be "in" and "of" two worlds. One wonders, however, whether in fact there is not such a close tie between Christianity and the world, or Protestantism and the free state, in Hegel that the ability of the Christian to affect the world in any creative or innovative way might be hindered. With the benefit of hindsight, we may question the overly close cooperation of Protestant or Catholic authorities with various oppressive regimes in recent decades. Surely even the dialectical requirement of a unity-in-distinction would call for something between the extreme "dual alle-

---

†† Hegel's notes in his 1805/06 "Philosophie des Geistes" (Hamburg: 1976) are often cryptic, but sometimes revealing: He writes, "This universal Spirit, or the spirit of the Christian community, is the 'state' of the Church"; and he adds in the margin, "[This Spirit] is the synthetic connection of the State and the Church" (p. 283). Then he goes on to observe (p. 284): "The State is the actuality of heaven—In thought a reconciliation, the essence of which with each other through the Church—They are unreconciled—thus is the State, and the Church, imperfect. . . ."

giance'' dichotomy that Hegel associates with Faith or Catholic consciousness and the emphasis on civic participation of Protestantism in government that Hegel gravitated towards, especially in his middle and late years, after he had completely given up the idea of a simple return of Christianity to the Greek ideal of folk religion.^{†††}

In Hegel's discussion here of the communal spirit of the Revealed Religion, one finds no mention of priests, masses, religious rituals, or devotional objects; and religion has clearly gone as far as religion can go beyond the alienated, "Catholic" kind of Faith spoken of in the earlier sections of the Phenomenology. *Hegel concentrates here only on the essential and important synthetic elements of Christianity which had been present from its beginnings, but (at least, in Hegel's opinion) had become explicit only in Protestantism.*

Here again we must distinguish between the conceptual, philosophical viewpoint and the quasi-conceptual imaginative representations or picture-thinking of the religious consciousness.

From the conceptual point of view the religious community in the Revealed Religion emerges in the following moments: (*a*) The Unhappy Consciousness which witnesses or experiences the "death of God" in effect interiorizes the divine substance and consequently begins to become divinized in its own subjectivity; (*b*) this consciousness reactivates, and returns to, the consciousness of evil, to become *conscious* of this *consciousness* in a new way (and thus negate the previous negation); (*c*) it relives the forsaking of natural existence (which was formerly perceived as evil) and now sees this as a forsaking of certain aspects of Nature which, because of their abstraction, were evil in the first place, so that the forsaking of them becomes a good and reconciling act; and (*d*) it responds to the death of the God-man by creating a community[70] not only to

---

†††However, in view of the fact that Hegel appears to have discountenanced any possibility of personal immortality (cf. Reardon, *Hegel's Philosophy of Religion*, pp. 137-8), subjected man's inner life to the State (*Philosophy of Right*, §270, Addition), and ascribed both man's "eternal life" and the external life of God to the state as an "actual God" or "earthly deity" (cf. Reardon, *ibid.*, and *Philosophy of Right*, §272, Addition), it would seem inconsistent and inconceivable that Hegel himself *could* make the distinction between religion and secular life any clearer and more definite.

70. The creation of this community is the explication of God's "Concept," i.e., an eminently *concrete* revelation. And this Concept of God or Absolute Spirit—according to Küng (*Menschwerden Gottes*, p. 298), who is undaunted by the possible secularistic overtones we have alluded to with relation to Hegel's idea of community—is suggestive as regards the development of a new and viable post-Hegelian concept of a God who "is

memorialize that death but also to perpetuate it spiritually by the constant mutual sacrifices of the individuals who compose that community:

> The death of the divine man *qua* death is an abstract negativity, the immediate result of the process which merely terminates in a "natural" universality. But death loses this merely natural meaning in the spiritual milieu of self-consciousness; or, better, it becomes elevated to its Concept, which we referred to above [as that which raises natural existence to universality]. From its initial connotation as "the annihilation of this individual" [Christ], death now becomes transformed in meaning into a "universalization of Spirit," insofar as Spirit abides within the [Christian] community, dies there daily, and rises daily from death again.[71]

However, as perceived *imaginatively* by the religious consciousness, there is an element of alienation hovering over all these developments. (*a*) The "death of God" is perceived primarily as a historical event, the Crucifixion; (*b*) consciousness of original sin is perceived primarily as repentance for some fault committed by a distant ancestor; (*c*) natural existence is perceived simplistically as intrinsically evil and hence something to be renounced;[72] and (*d*) the religious community is perceived as one which is based on some *past* reconciliation (the historical Atonement of the God-man), and must achieve its own corresponding reconciliation in the distant *future* (the Parousia), the attainment of which is prefig-

----

no longer that (Feuerbachian) 'Essence' that dispossesses man of his creativity and makes him indolent; nor that (Marxian) opiate, which leads man to abdicate his own actuality and prevents him from responding socially to the changes in his environmental context; nor the (Freudian) projection of our physical–psychic anxiety and wishes; nor that which epitomizes the emotionally and existentially superfluous, even the harmful or the deadly, for the sophisticated human consciousness." Rather, says Küng, the God that Hegel is preparing the way for is the God "who in the midst of, and by means of, the very conditions of our life and our relations to others stands as the Unconditioned, whose concern for us is unconditioned, who is the depth and the ultimate meaning of our life, and who is both infinitely distant from us and our surface existence and at the same time nearer to us than we are to ourselves. . . ."

71. *B*418, H545: *Der* Tod *des göttlichen Menschen* als Tod *ist die* abstrakte *Negativität, das unmittelbare Resultat der Bewegung, die nur in die* natürliche *Allgemeinheit sich endigt. Diese natürliche Bedeutung verliert er im geistigen Selbstbewusstsein, oder er wird sein soeben angegebner Begriff; der Tod wird von dem, was er unmittelbar bedeutet, von dem Nichtsein* dieses Einzelnen *verklärt zur* Allgemeinheit *des Geistes, der in seiner Gemeine lebt, in ihr täglich stirbt und aufersteht.*

72. "Evil" has been presented in this section, and in the *Phenomenology* as a whole, under multiple guises: as the finite, as the particular, as differentiation, as "the merely natural," as the contingent, as the unessential, as that which does not conform to its Concept or is not seen in the context of its Concept. What is common to all of these senses is a departure-from-"universality," in either the usual or the special second-order Hegelian usage of that term.

ured imaginatively in "the coming of the Spirit" (Pentecost). Thus if we take into account this self-perception on the part of the religious community, its present phenomenal state may be described as the *converse* of the God-man:

> Just as the individual God-man had a virtual [*ansichseienden*] Father, and only an "actual" mother [73]; so in converse manner the universal man-God, i.e., the religious community, has its own action and knowledge as its "father,"[74] but for a "mother" has *eternal love*; a love which it only *feels*, but does not [yet] encounter as an actualized immediate *object* of its consciousness.[75]

Just as the Spirit of God the Father had to be made explicit in the "Son of Man" only in and through his crucifixion, so the perfection of the religious community can only be attained when eternal love is made explicit as an essential aspect conceptually woven into the makeup of the social life of the "adopted sons of God," and not just a contingency subject to the vagaries of feeling. But this final explication is hindered by the fact that the actual world which the religious Self-Consciousness confronts is divided and disintegrated [*gebrochen*]. And thus, as a result,

> The Spirit of the community, as far as regards its Consciousness [i.e., this objective condition of the actual world] is cut off from its religious [Self-]Consciousness, which insistently assures it that in *itself* [i.e., in principle], it is *not* "cut off,"[75] although as an "in-itself" [as something merely implicit] it is not yet realized, i.e., has not arrived at absolute existence-*for*-itself.[76]

---

73. Hegel has already explained (M§755, H526) that the God-man's "mother," *conceptually* speaking, is self-consciousness, while his "father" is the in-itself of substance. Picture-thinking presents this as the "virgin birth."

74. Cf. Kierkegaard, *Fear and Trembling* (p. 38): "In the world of spirit . . . only he who works gets the bread. . . . Here it is of no use to have Abraham for one's father . . . , but he who is willing to work gives birth to his own father."

75. B421, H548: *So wie der* einzelne *göttliche Mensch einen* ansichseienden *Vater und nur eine* wirkliche *Mutter hat, so hat auch der allgemeine göttliche Mensch, die Gemeinde, ihr eignes Tun und Wissen zu ihrem Vater, zu ihrer Mutter aber die* ewige *Liebe, die sie nur* fühlt, *nicht aber in ihrem Bewusstsein als wirklichen unmittelbaren Gegenstand* anschaut.

75. Cf. the Gospel of John XVI, 33, where Jesus tells his disciples, "Fear not, for I have overcome the world."

76. B421, H548: *Der Geist der Gemeinde ist so in seinem unmittelbaren Bewusstsein, getrennt von seinem religiösen, das zwar es ausspricht, dass sie an sich nicht getrennt seien, aber ein* Ansich, *das nicht realisiert, oder noch nicht ebenso absolutes Fürsichsein geworden.*

Because religious Self-Consciousness operates in the realm of imagination, it interprets its own origins in terms of past historical events, and perceives its own goal as a future state of victory in heaven; and it is constitutionally maladapted to accomplish its mission, the extension of love and community, in the actual, present world of Spirit. As we saw above (p. 166), the ultimate practical solution to Religion's dilemma will be worked out in Hegel's later works by his positing the State as that which assists and directs the religious self-consciousness to attain actual fulfillment, and in its turn depends on religion to prepare men dispositionally or emotionally for that maximal participation in the State's endeavors that will assure ultimate intersubjective harmony. But in the context of the *Phenomenology* (to the despair of Marx and other critics) the solution is not in the practical sphere, but involves a change of conscious perspective: a raising of our sights from the mutual sacrifices of members of the religious community to the great passion-play taking place in the world as a whole, and the theoretical groundwork that is necessary for understanding and interpreting this latter. The attainment of this final vantage point is the subject of the last chapter, "Absolute Knowledge."

VIII.

Absolute

Knowledge

[The Dialectical Comprehension of the Content of Religion]

Introductory Remarks:

The Phenomenology *was completed in Hegel's Jena period just as Napoleon invaded Jena (October 13, 1806), and shortly before an absolute deadline set by Hegel's publisher. (If Hegel did not have the entire manuscript in the publisher's hands by October 18, 1806, Hegel's friend Niethammer would have to buy up all the publisher's copies, according to an agreement the publisher had insisted on.) No doubt because of such factors, this last chapter is highly condensed (twelve pages in the Hoffmeister edition, as compared with 76 pages for the chapter on Religion and 160 pages for the chapter on Spirit) and difficult. The difficulty seems to stem largely from Hegel's more than usual neglect of supplying editorial hints as to the overall structure of the chapter, a structure which, as is usually the case, is triadic. The triadic subdivisions of this chapter given at the end of the Hoffmeister edition are rather unenlightening. The reader of the text may find the following structural hints of some value: The first paragraph (M§788) gives an introduction to the general character of Absolute Knowledge as synthesis of Spirit's Consciousness and Self-Consciousness. But the* development *of this form* (Gestalt) *of Spirit must first be clarified. Thus (1) M§789–793, H550-553 features a rather lengthy recapitulation of Spirit-as-Consciousness (i.e., of the long chapter entitled "Spirit"), and this begins with an introduction (M§789) which compares the three moments of Spirit-as-Consciousness to the three stages of Consciousness Proper in Part I (see K62 ff.), and thence proceeds into a second set of comparisons: (a) a comparison of the Ethical Substance of Spirit to the earlier sections on Rational Observation (M§240 ff.), (b) a comparison of Spirit-as-Culture to the sections on Rational Individualization (M§347 ff.), after which begins (c) a discussion of the synthesis of thought and being in Spirit-as-Morality-and-Conscience (cf. the similar discussion in the sections on* die Sache selbst, *M§394 ff.). (2) The ensuing comparison of Spirit with Religion (§794–797) is complicated by the fact that Hegel (a) concentrates here on the* self-conscious *moment of Spirit-as-*Consciousness *(cf. e.g., M§792), in contrast to the objective (imaginative) aspects of Religious* Self- Consciousness *(cf. e.g., M§794f.); and (b) also refers here to the "Beautiful Soul" (cf. M§655 f) as "divinity's self-intuition" (M§795), so that the reader might interpret these references as pertaining to the chapter on Religion. (3) Next Absolute Knowledge is demonstrated to be a unification of the reconciliations achieved (a) by conscious Spirit and (b) by self-conscious Spirit (religion), respectively (see M§798-800, H556-557). Then (4) A treatment of Absolute Spirit as the "content" of Absolute Knowledge extends from M§801 to the second sentence of M§803. Finally (5) now that the* groundwork *for Absolute Knowledge has been illuminated, the discussion of Absolute Knowledge proper begins at the third sentence of M§803, H559 (starting with "Not until . . ." in the Miller translation, "Not till . . ." in the Baillie, and* "Erst nachdem . . ." *in the German editions) and continues to the end of the book.*

Previews of the character of Absolute Knowledge have already been given in several places in the Phenomenology, *notably: in the Preface (M§37), where it is emphasized that the distinctions between knowing and truth, essence and existence, Subject and Substance will disappear when the progress of Spirit has been completed; in the Introduction (M§89), where a final point is described at which consciousness will not only become identical with its "other," appearance with essence, but will also* explicitly *comprehend this identity and the convergence of this comprehension with the stage actually reached by Science; in the section on Enlightenment (M§568), where the final solution to the dichotomy between the immediacy of Faith and the mediation of Enlightenment is adumbrated as a state of "mediation in which the immediate is itself the third term [i.e., Spirit] through which it mediates itself with the 'other,' viz. with its own self''; and finally, in the introduction to Religion, where Absolute Knowledge is described (a) as a stage in which Spirit in the world conceptualizes Religion's proper object and Religion concerns itself with the actual world, so that the split between the "secular" and the "religious" is finally overcome (M§678), (b) as the final synthesis of Consciousness and Self-consciousness, certainty and truth (M§682), and (c) as the Notion or Concept (Begriff) which finally comprehends its own opposite (M§683). The type of knowledge alluded to in all these characterizations is distinctive both as regards its form and as regards its content.*

(1) As regards form, *(a) this knowledge is not engendered by representations of external reality or sensory qualities (colors, etc.), but by the "Concept"; but (b) the "Concept," in the special Hegelian usage, is not an abstract or subjective idea, but an eminently concrete synthesis of the self and "nature" (including not only external Nature, but also human nature and society as "second nature"); and (c) this concrete Hegelian "Concept" is not a simple unity, but a dialectical comprehension, which will not just "synthesize" oppositions between subject and object (and other corollary oppositions) but will grasp and present the self-movement of every difference out of unity and back into unity, so that apparently inactive contemplation becomes quite active (M§804). The dialectical development of this Concept is often triadic, and often proceeds from universal to particular to individuality; but Hegel was no formalist, and often produces variations on this pattern.*

(2) As regards content, *Absolute Knowledge is concerned with the* philosophical *comprehension of the truths of religion, especially of the Christian religion—but freed from mythical and imaginative overtones, and from that sense of alienation from the actual world which has always and unavoidably characterized the religious consciousness. Thus as Absolute Knowledge is developed into a scientific system, it goes beyond the intuitive perception of spirit in Nature by Nature-Religion to a reasoned and rational comprehension of the development of spirit in Nature; it will go beyond the immediate unity of spirit and human nature in Art-Religion to a conceptual comprehension of this unity in philosophical anthropology; it will go beyond the pictorial presentation of the Trinity in Christianity to an understanding of the essential triadic development of the Concept which is revealed in this religious doctrine; it will go beyond the doctrine of the incarnation of the God-man, to a wide-ranging demonstration of the synthesis of universal and particular in many areas of philosophical investigation; and it will go beyond the Christian notion of the universal infusion of the Holy Spirit throughout the religious community, to a more philosophical comprehension of community which does away with the alienation from the actual world present in the Christian notion.*

Absolute Knowledge in the latter "material" aspects must be understood as a so-

lution finally worked out by Hegel to the problems, with which he wrestled in his youth, concerning the contemporary significance of Christianity (see supra, *pp. 165 ff.). But Absolute Knowledge in the above-mentioned "formal" aspects is probably best understood in its historical context as Hegel's immediate response to the "Absolutes" propounded by Fichte and Schelling. Hegel shared with Fichte and Schelling the notion that the vocation of philosophy was to present the idea of synthesis rather than analysis* (Difference between Fichte's and Schelling's System, *p. 177), and show the relation of all things to the Absolute (ibid., p. 99). But Hegel, along with Schelling, took exception to Fichte's absolute synthesis of ego and non-ego (see K136) as being excessively subjective (ibid., pp. 81,117), unable to account for finite determinations (Rosen,* G. W. F. Hegel, *pp. 58 ff.), and lacking "System"* (Difference . . ., *pp. 113,118). Hegel found Schelling's Absolute (the "indifferent" equilibrium of Subject and Object [see K21,137,152,157]) more compatible than Fichte's, especially because it gave due regard to the objective (*Difference . . ., *p. 82), and to Nature and the empirical in general (Plant,* Hegel, *Ch. IV). But Hegel eventually judged Schelling's Absolute empty and sterile—a "night in which all cows are black" (M§16, H19)—and Schelling's reliance on intuition of the Absolute (rather than demonstration and conceptual mediation) unphilosophical. Thus in the* Phenomenology *Hegel, in contrast with both Fichte and Schelling (as Hegel perceived them), sets out to establish an adequately* mediated *cognition of the synthesis of Subject and Object, a cognition which is adequately grounded in phenomenal* experience, *which comprises the finite and the* determinate *without forcing them into the mold of an abstract Absolute, and which avoids* both *the extreme of Fichtean Subjectivism* and *the extreme of Schellingian overemphasis on Nature and Art and Imagination.*

But, if Hegel's concept of a "Phenomenology" is to be taken seriously, our merely "external" knowledge (see K134) of the historical context of German idealism (particularly the intellectual currents in Fichte and Schelling), which gave rise to the idea of "Absolute Knowledge," will not help one to see the immanent, "internal necessities" leading up to Absolute Knowledge in the Phenomenology. *It was Hegel's intent that the reader of the* Phenomenology *should be brought gradually "on his own" to the vision of the Absolute synthesis as he proceeded through the stages of the* Phenomenology. *The one thing Hegel wanted to avoid was the presentation of an Absolute that is, as it were, "shot from a gun."*

If a reader does get the impression that "Absolute Knowledge" comes on the scene abruptly in this chapter rather than emerging out of the groundwork Hegel has been laying, this may be due to the reader's misunderstanding of the nature of dialectical "proof." Dialectical proof for the validity of the Absolute standpoint does not, in

Hegel's estimation, include presenting evidence that this standpoint explains phenomena better than other possible standpoints, and/or refuting those who criticize it—but is simply showing *that "the subjective signifies the transformation of itself into the object, and that the objective signifies its not remaining such, but making itself subjective"* (History of Philosophy *III, p. 526). Now, in the* Phenomenology, *the primary object (the in-itself) has been Consciousness, while Self-Consciousness (the for-itself) has been the subjective pole. No one can accuse Hegel of not relentlessly tracing the transformations of* this *object into* this *subject, and vice versa, throughout the* Phenomenology, *and in an especially intense way in the lengthy recapitulations in this final chapter. If a reader follows Hegel's arguments and still fails to see the validity of Absolute Knowledge, this may be due to the fact that he does not accept Hegel's canons for dialectical "proof." But, of course, one of the main problems is to follow the very tightly woven arguments.*

Briefly, the arguments here take the form of a recapitulation of Part II of the Phenomenology, *beginning with Spirit. First he follows the development of Spirit-as-*Consciousness, *i.e., Spirit proper or the spirit of the "actual world," and points out how it has led up to a state of absolute freedom and communal self-certitude (especially exemplified in the final reconciliation of the Beautiful Soul and the Acting Conscience) towards the end. Next he recalls the obverse development of Spirit-as-Self-Consciousness, i.e., Religion proper, to a final state of community based on highly sophisticated, although overly* objectified, *symbolic or pictorial representations and rituals organized around the belief in the passion, death, and resurrection of the God-man. Finally, he tries to give a brief idea of how a highly developed philosophical system based on the premise of the dialectical unification of opposites brings together in a more satisfactory, conceptual manner both the excessively abstract absolute self-certainty achieved by Spirit-as-Consciousness, and the excessively abstract* and objectified religious truth achieved especially in the Christian elaboration of the dogmas of the Trinity, the Incarnation, the Passion and Resurrection of Christ, and the "coming of the Holy Spirit" upon the religious community.*

How faithfully does Hegel adhere, in his later work, to the formal and material aspects of Absolute Knowledge developed in the Phenomenology? *As will be shown below, Hegel himself underwent some vicissitudes after the publication of the* Phenomenology *regarding the most suitable approach for presenting "Absolute Knowledge." It could be shown that Hegel's later* Logic, Philosophy of Spirit, *and other parts of his System conform to the basic concept of "Absolute Knowledge" propounded at the end of the* Phenomenology. *However—if we may*

---

*"Abstract" in the usual Hegelian sense: "not yet situated in its proper conceptual context."

bypass the (still ongoing) discussions about whether, and just how, Hegel's post-humously published lectures on the philosophy of history fit into his published "System"—the Philosophy of History *offers a good example in Hegel's later work of what, in the* Phenomenology, *is characterized as "Absolute Knowledge."*

The Philosophy of History, *unlike the* Phenomenology, *does not need to demonstrate the necessity of, and justify the assumption of, the dialectical-conceptual standpoint of "Absolute Knowledge." It begins with this as its presupposition, and proceeds to analyze the spiritual evolution of mankind in terms of the necessary progression of its dialectical "moments." Likewise, the* Philosophy of History *not only (in Hegel's estimation) overcomes the basic defect of Religion mentioned in the* Phenomenology, *namely, religion's lack of* conceptual *explicitness, its need for supervening conceptual formulation if its true meaning is ever to be brought out, but overcomes the basic defect of the Ethical Spirit (which reached an absolute vantage point in "Conscience") namely, its inability to find a suitably absolute content. We can also point to more specific grounds for the claim that the Philosophy of History exemplifies Absolute Knowledge in the Hegelian sense: For is it not the basic thesis of* Hegel's *philosophy of history that the peoples of the world pass through the conceptual-dialectical moments of universal unity, antithetical diversification and synthetic individualization (*Philosophy of Right, *§353 ff.)? Is not the* necessary *evolution of these peoples to a state in which* freedom *permeates the whole mass of mankind (see* Philosophy of History, *pp. 18, 19, 456) remarkably homologous with the foreordained development of the "Mystical Body of Christ" in the world, in Pauline theology? And is it not also the case that Hegel in his philosophy of history considers himself to be taking over the role of the Christian theologian in justifying the ways of God and* scientifically *demonstrating the existence of a Divine Providence in the world (*Philosophy of History, *pp. 12 ff. and 457)? In short, if one examines Hegel's* Philosophy of History *closely, he will see that it is a good example of what* Hegel *must have meant by Absolute Knowledge as a synthesis of the mundane and religious, "conscious" and "self-conscious" aspects of Spirit.*

In commenting above (Religion, n. 5) on Hegel's omission of the deeper forms of Oriental *religion from his sections on Religion, I suggested that these religions might more properly be classified as "philosophy" than as "religion," in Hegel's usage of that term. I could go further than this and say that, when one considers the emphasis on the unity of opposites—Yin and Yang in Taoism, subject and object in Buddhism, Consciousness and Space in Hinduism—these philosophical religions would seem to have a* prima facie *claim to inclusion under the rubric of "Absolute Knowledge." But this claim is only* prima facie. *Hegel would exclude these*

Oriental philosophies from this category for the same reason he disqualifies Fichte and Schelling: because the vision they contain of the "unity of opposites" is not "Scientific" enough, not empirically based, and insufficiently subjected to conceptual mediation. And this is just to emphasize that Hegel's idea of Absolute Knowledge is thoroughly Westernized, *influenced by the Enlightenment ideals of reason, scientific observation, and recourse to experience (of course in ways, and for a purpose, that would never have occurred to Galileo or Bacon or Newton).*

One final remark: it should be obvious from the preceding observations that the emphasis in Hegel's "Absolute Knowledge" is not on a quantitative *assimilation of knowledge (such that, as some have interpreted Hegel, one emerges literally "knowing everything"), but on* qualitative *perfection of the viewpoint. As Hegel indicates in the Preface and Introduction to the* Phenomenology, *one who forges in a conceptually mediated and experientially based way to the vision of the dialectical unity of opposites does so in order to avoid the Kantian epistemological problems of the "thing-in-itself," the solipsism of intuitionism, etc. —and not to achieve a gnostic expansion of knowledge to infinite proportions.*

As was mentioned in the Introduction (M§89), the final goal at which these phenomenal transitions will end will be the Absolute Concept, that ultimate unity-in-distinction of thought and being, self-consciousness and consciousness, at which all disparity between subjective certitude and objective truth will have finally disappeared, such that the object of consciousness will be thoroughly imbued with self-consciousness (i.e., no longer alien), and the activity of self-consciousness will be thoroughly manifest to all consciousnesses (i.e., no longer merely private, or arcane).

In order to understand how this ultimate Concept is developing, let us now recapitulate the developments which have taken place in the phenomenology of Spirit:

[A. SPIRIT'S RECONCILATION OF CONSCIOUSNESS AND SELF-CONSCIOUSNESS IN CONSCIENCE]

The initial stages of Spirit,[1] i.e., the early development of the Ethical

___
1. See *supra*, pp. 20 ff.

Substance, were somewhat analogous to Sense-Certainty in the phenomenology of Consciousness, since the development in these initial stages of Spirit emphasized immediate objective consciousness to such an extent that self-consciousness, and the concomitant concept of the Self, were only implicit then. These stages can also be compared to the sections on Rational Observation,[2] insofar as they were concerned with exploring the "thing-like" character of the Ethical Substance to trace the emergence of the ego (as self-identical Person, and eventually Soul). In the subsequent substages (the early states of Culture)[3] a disruption of this immediacy develops, analogous to the antithesis that developed[4] in the phenomenology of Perception. And just as the insight into the perceptual object as a combination of existence-for-self and existence-for-another defused those antitheses in that early phenomenology, so also the insight into Utility[5] as objective actuality which received its significance and essence solely from a subjective source—consciousness itself—was the beginning of the defusion of the great antitheses which peaked in the stage of Culture. (This final insight of utilitarianism is comparable to the earlier insight of Individualizing Reason[6] into the fact that its claim to individuality consisted mainly in the application of its own factual, thing-like productions [i.e., sentimental nostrums and moral platitudes] to the world; but in utilitarianism, the application is less abstract and less arbitrary, since the philosophy of utility actually infuses external objects with values that are publicly recognized.) Finally, just as the phenomenology of Understanding[7] revealed the presence of the universal Essence within consciousness, and as the product of consciousness, so also in the phenomenology of Spirit the Absolute Concept gradually emerges when Spirit-as-consciousness becomes Spirit-as-self-consciousness in the sections on Morality,[8] which culminated in Conscience.[9] In Reason, this latter corresponds to the final sections on Subjective/Objective Individuality (*die Sache selbst*),[10] in which the com-

---

2. See K103 ff.
3. See *supra*, pp. 35 ff.
4. See K68.
5. See *supra*, pp. 78 ff.
6. See K116–25.
7. See K69 ff.
8. See *supra*, pp. 92 ff.
9. See *supra*, pp. 107 ff.
10. See K92 ff.

plete identity of self and (Ethical) Substance, and *vice versa*, was attained for the first time; but here (with Conscience) that basic insight is extended further, to grasp explicitly and produce this identity through a community of Consciences reconciled to one another in mutual understanding, and mutual confirmation of self-certainty.[11]

This latter stage, Conscience, is a truly historical seminal manifestation of the Absolute Concept; but the emphasis there is on self-certainty. As will be recalled, Spirit as Conscience manifested itself as the individual who was immediately and connaturally conjoined with universal Essence, or the Self who was immediately synthesized with existence. Thus we have in the attitude of Conscientiousness the unmistakable synthetic characteristics of the Absolute Concept.[12] But the Absolute Concept is not just a unity, but also a distinguishing of the synthesized elements; and Conscience similarly distinguished itself into (*a*) a pole exemplifying Consciousness oriented towards universality through solitary religiosity (the Beautiful Soul), and (*b*) a pole exemplifying Self-Conscious individuality and actual dynamic, practical existence (the Acting Conscience). Then finally, just as the Absolute Concept proves itself to be the unity-*in*-distinction of its opposed elements, so also the Beautiful Soul and the Acting Conscience, through the mediating activities of Confession and mutual forgiveness, manifest their true character as simply disparate manifestations of one and the same divine Spirit expressing itself in and through finite consciousnesses. The state of recognition reached in this final stage, insofar as it produces in the World-Spirit the state of dialectical self-consciousness prerequisite for a Science of Spirit, brings to a close Spirit's historical impulsion towards this state, and supplies the necessary (formal) conditions for the development of Absolute Knowledge.

[B. RELIGION'S RECONCILIATION OF SELF-CONSCIOUSNESS WITH CONSCIOUSNESS IN THE CHRISTIAN COMMUNITY]

When we say that the state of dialectical Self-consciousness just mentioned supplies the conditions for the development of Absolute Knowledge, this statement must be understood in the context of the temporal progressions of actual Spirit in the world, according to which consideration various partial manifestations (Ethical Substance, Culture, Abso-

---

11. See *supra*, pp. 122 ff.
12. I.e., the Hegelian "Concept" as a concrete unity-in-distinction of oppositions.

lute Freedom, etc.) preceded the full and adequate revelation of Spirit (as the transcendent self-certainty produced by the community of Consciences). But from another point of view, one could also say that this same revelation of Spirit in a complete and adequate fashion preceded the various historical and partial approximations to this viewpoint on the part of Spirit itself (which only became conscious of *itself* as Spirit, i.e., Self-Conscious, in the stage of Conscience). In other words, we could point to the *intensive* development of *Religious* Self-Consciousness as containing *all along* that basic insight into the unity of self-and-otherness that has only become the subject of *Scientific* knowledge[13] in the modern age. For that very insight has been the guiding light of Religion from its earliest stages[14] (although Religion, as has been shown, held onto, and re-presented that insight through feeling and imagination, in an objectified fashion, not in a conceptually mediated fashion, even in the most advanced stages of Revealed Religion). And so, because of the preconceptual and prephilosophical formulations of religious truths, we must emphasize that:

. . . the religiouus community, insofar as it is primordially the "substance" of Absolute Spirit, is that raw or unsophisticated species of consciousness whose real existence is the more stark and barbaric, and whose unexpressible [*dumpfes*] self has the harder struggle with its estranged content the deeper its inner Spirit is.[15]

The Religious Self-Consciousness, with its evolving notions of community and Spirit, has had, admittedly, an uncanny knack for intuiting the preconceptual *content* of Absolute Spirit at all times. But we must now unite content and intuition with form and systematic scientific cognition.

[C. UNIFICATION OF THE TWO RECONCILIATIONS IN ABSOLUTE KNOWLEDGE]

The realization that Religion itself, in spite of the noble and essential

---

13. For example, in Fichte's *Science of Ethics* (already discussed above in the Commentary on the section on Conscience, pp. 107 ff.).

14. In other words, Religion in all of its various manifestations had been preaching the union of the self and otherness, of subject and substance, from time immemorial, albeit in prescientific form.

15. *B*430, H559: *Die religiöse Gemeine, insofern sie zuerst die Substanz des absoluten Geistes ist, ist das rohe Bewusstsein, das ein um so barbarischeres und härteres Dasein hat, je tiefer sein innerer Geist ist, und sein dumpfes Selbst eine um so härtere Arbeit mit seinem Wesen, dem ihm fremden Inhalte seines Bewusstseins.*

synthesis it had made in the realm of imagination and feeling, would never be able adequately and intelligibly to *express* its "revelation" publicly and scientifically has caused a kind of reversal, a negation of negation in our modern era. The modern heirs of the Unhappy religious Consciousness finally have turned against their religious manner of expressing a "reconciliation" which (because of its preconceptual form) was for all practical purposes an estrangement; and they have begun to give true *Scientific* formulation to that idea of Spirit which has already made its appearance in the cultural-literary milieu in the form of the dialectical unity of the Beautiful Soul and the Acting Conscience. But the primary thrusts in the direction of a new Scientific formulation have come from a succession of modern philosophers who have tried to forge *both* the subjective dialectical self-consciousness manifested by the community of Consciences *and* the syntheses of subject and substance foreshadowed in the imaginative projections of Religious Self-Consciousness, into more and more sophisticated and explicit conceptual expressions of the unity of self and otherness, or thought and being. This general trend or tendency can be seen in the following series of modern philosophical positions: (*a*) an initial reaction to the Unhappy Consciousness of Religion, and Reason's initial discovery of the world as Self-Consciousness' own possession (e.g., Bacon); (*b*) the development of rational scientific Observation, through which one finds the world in the shape of thought and simultaneously synthesizes its thinking with existence (e.g., Newton); (*c*) *die Sache selbst*—the insight that thinking, the *cogito*, immediately implies existence (Descartes); (*d*) the explication of this immediate unity into Spirit's sophisticated unity of thought with the extended world (Spinoza);[16] (*e*) a reaction against this universal synthesis, in the name of individuality, and its replacement with a "personal" synthesis of perception and being (Leibniz); (*f*) subsequent development of the philosophy of utility, which united the in-itself with the for-itself (Helvétius); (*g*) Absolute Freedom, which looked to the will itself as the source of political and moral existence (Rousseau, Kant); (*h*) the interpretation of the Absolute as a negative movement between self-

---

16. "The only attributes of the infinite Substance that were recognizable by men were, according to Spinoza, thought and extension. The *Phenomenology* extends Spinoza's doctrine on this somewhat further insofar as in it *time* in the form of history is added to thought and to extension, or Nature" (Bonsiepen, *Der Begriff der Negativität*, p. 175).

identical ego and the temporal expression of self-differentiation (Fichte);[17] (*i*) the converse emphasis on the Absolute's identity with its immediate spatial expressions in Nature (Schelling); and finally (*j*) the presentation of the latter two views as simultaneous and reciprocal, i.e., of Spirit as *both* the constant negative withdrawal from the externalities of substance into itself *and* the equally constant positive immersion in a developing spiritual Substance without any fear of losing itself in this process of development.[18] Spirit in this latter sense, bringing former stages to their natural conclusion, is "Absolute Knowledge," as has already been indicated; and it has been the purpose of this *Phenomenology of Spirit* to lead up to this state of Absolute Knowledge by reorganizing the various moments in the history of (individual and social) consciousness according to the reciprocities and antitheses of subject and object that they give rise to.

Having arrived at the threshold of Absolute Knowledge, we should recall that the generator of *this* knowledge is the Absolute Concept—the paradigmatic synthesis of all potentially one-sided determinations, and the presentation of these determinations as a unity of opposites. What still remains to be accomplished now is the further systematic examination of the development of this Absolute Concept *in its own right*. This further examination, insofar as it transcends the one-sided attitudes and half-truths criticized by the *Phenomenology*, and insofar as it presents the system of knowledge systematically, is Science in the strict sense of that word. In the system of Science that results,[19] we will no longer en-

---

17. In the philosophy of Fichte, as Findlay puts it (M, p. xxix), "the pure self necessarily opposes itself to, yet also identifies itself with, the flux of time, and is further opposed to the frozen differentiation of space."

18. Hegel writes in *Difference between Fichte's and Schelling's System*, p. 161: "The science of the subjective Subject–Object [Fichte] has hitherto been called transcendental philosophy: that of the objective Subject–Object, philosophy of nature [the early Schelling]. . . . The higher standpoint from which the one-sidedness of both sciences is truly suspended is the standpoint which recognizes the same Absolute in both of them [i.e., Hegel's projection in this 1801 essay about what Schelling's later system would be like—a projection that he finally decided to implement himself in the *Phenomenology*, after he became dissatisfied with Schelling's attempts to do so]."

19. As Otto Pöggeler shows in "Selbstbewusstsein und Identität" (*Hegel-Studien* XVI, p. 191), Hegel seems to have in mind here his projected system of philosophy as it had been worked out in his 1805/6 Realphilosophie. The System of "speculative philosophy" at that time was envisioned as consisting of six parts: 1) Being; 2) Relation; 3) Life and Cognition; 4) Knowing Knowledge [*wissendes Wissen*]; 5) Spirit; and 6) the Self-Knowledge of Spirit. These initial plans underwent major revisions in the later versions

counter the sort of problems we have encountered in this *Phenomenology*: for example, Selfhood will no longer appear as the external Necessity of Fate, but will be immanent in the explicit negativity of the content; and "determination" will no longer be a by-product of one-sidedness, but an already balanced distinction which leads organically to the totality of conceptual determinations. And, of course, the disparity between subject and object, between certitude and truth, will have been overcome. But this is not to imply that Science, having wrested its fundamental Concept out of the multiple mediations exemplified in the *Phenomenology*, might now, forgetful of its origins out of Sense-Certainty, simply repose in the intuition of the Absolute Concept in its various abstract aspects. On the contrary, Science, although capable of conducting the examination and presentation of the dialectical unity of opposites on an abstract intellectual or logical level, must still, because of the very *negativity* implied in its status as a "unity-in-*difference*," return again to its origins in immediacy to replenish itself with the differentiations of consciousness.[20] And dialectical Science, as the unity of opposites, comprehends in itself its own opposite: namely, the outer boundaries of Spirit

---

of the System which were published. See *Jenaer Systementwürfe III* (Hamburg: Felix Meiner Verlag, 1976), p. 286.

20. "The Absolute must posit itself in the appearance itself, i.e., it must not nullify appearance but must construct it into identity" (*Difference between Fichte's and Schelling's System*, p. 115). One way of clarifying the relationship between the *Phenomenology* as an introduction to Science, and the Science of the identity-of-opposites, would be to say that while the *Phenomenology* emphasizes unity-in-*difference*, the System of Science emphasizes *unity*-in-difference (see K13–14), and the two complementary views together contribute to, and insure the integrity of, Absolute Knowledge as comprehension of the unity-*in*-distinction of opposites. It is only by some such complementarity that Hegel could avoid succumbing to the mistake that he himself warns against (*op. cit.*, p. 156): "[In a philosophy maintaining an identity of opposites] the claims of separation must be admitted just as much as those of identity. When identity and separation are placed in opposition to each other, both are absolute, and if one aims to maintain identity through the nullification of the dichotomy, the [identity and dichotomy] remain opposed to each other. Philosophy must give the separation into subject and object its due. By making both separation [which is emphasized in the *Phenomenology*] and the identity [emphasized in the *Encyclopedia*], which is opposed to it, *equally* absolute, however, philosophy has only posited separation *conditionally*, in the same way that such an identity—conditioned as it is by the nullification of its opposite—is also only *relative*. Hence, the Absolute itself is the identity of identity *and* non-identity; being opposed and being one are both together in it" [italics added]. Similar admonitions against losing contact with phenomenal reality by exclusively propounding a philosophy of identity are found (*op. cit.*, pp. 89,91,127). As applied to the relationship of the 1807 *Phenomenology* to the then-contemplated *Logic*, this would mean that an integral and balanced view of the "identity

sacrificing itself spatially throughout Nature and temporally throughout history (the recollection of which latter progression has been the task
of this *Phenomenology of Spirit*). But in Science itself, the immediate "giv-
ens" of consciousness, the characteristics of the Self, the basic Concept
of Nature and the Self-Revelation of Spirit in history—all will be presented in terms of the various ways in which they exemplify the dialecti-
cal-speculative Concept.

The groundwork for this System of Science was thus prepared by this
Phenomenology of Spirit, in the course of which we have retraced the stages
of Spirit's Way of the Cross in the world, and reenacted the sacrifices
that Spirit has made in attaining to Absolute Knowledge in and through
human self-consciousness, which has, on its own side, attained mature
spiritual development only in recent times. The final recollective interiorization we have arrived at is "absolute" in so far as (1) Spirit itself has
been forging ahead to this knowledge, as its final goal; (2) human consciousness has progressed beyond abstract and arbitrary philosophical
syntheses to a concrete and communal immersion in the passion of Spirit
taking place throughout space and time; and (3) the imaginative, mythical and devotional awareness of Spirit, which has been present in religious self-consciousness from time immemorial, has now been elevated
to a dialectical–conceptual comprehension, making possible its systematic dialectical–conceptual presentation:

The goal, Absolute Knowledge, i.e., Spirit which cognizes itself *as* Spirit, has to tread
the path of a re-collective interiorization of [discrete world-]spirits, as they are in themselves and as they consummate the organization of the realm of spirit. The enshrinement
of these spirits according to the aspect of their appearance as independent existents in
the form of contingency, is History; their enshrinement according to the aspect of their
relationship to the emergence of the Concept, on the other hand, is the "Science of
Knowledge as a phenomenon" [i.e., Phenomenology];[21] the two together—history as

---

of opposites" could be maintained only by seeing the *Phenomenology* and the "System" in
conjunction with each other.

Hegel's claim (M§805) that there would be a one-to-one correspondence between
the abstract moments of his System of Science and various forms (*Gestalten*) in the *Phenomenology* is best understood with reference to the six-part inchoate System that Hegel
was planning at the time of the writing of the *Phenomenology* (see n. 19, *supra*). Pöggeler (*op. cit.*) interprets the precise correspondences as follows: "Being" corresponds to
"Sense Certainty" in the *Phenomenology*; "Relation" to "Perception" and "Understanding"; "Life and Cognition" to "The Truth of Self-Certainty"; "Knowing
Knowledge" to "Reason"; "Spirit" to "Spirit"; and "The Self-Knowledge of Spirit"
to "Religion" and "Absolute Knowledge."

21. The sort of history that one finds in the *Phenomenology*, says Pöggeler in *Grund-*

[phenomenologically] comprehended—offer us a depiction of the process of Absolute Spirit's own commemorative interiorization [of its phenomenological forms] and of its [actual, historical] Calvary[22]—in other words, the actuality, truth and certainty of its throne, without which it would be lifeless lonesomeness: for only "out of the chalice of this kingdom of spirits does his own infinity foam up to [the Absolute.]"[23]

---

probleme . . . (p. 168), "does not give us real history with all of its contingencies, but is history considered from the side of its conceptualized organization," i.e., insofar as it has an aspect of necessity about it.

22. Cf. *Faith and Knowledge*, pp. 190–1: "The pure concept . . . must re-establish for philosophy the Idea of absolute freedom and along with it the absolute Passion, the speculative Good Friday in place of the historic Good Friday. Good Friday must be speculatively re-established in the whole truth and harshness of its God-forsakenness. . . . The highest totality can and must achieve its resurrection solely from this harsh consciousness of loss, encompassing everything, and ascending in all earnestness and out of its deepest ground to the most serene freedom of its shape."

23. B443–4, H564: *Das Ziel, das absolute Wissen, oder der sich als Geist wissende Geist hat zu seinem Wege die Erinnerung der Geister, wie sie an ihnen selbst sind und die Organisation ihres Reiches vollbringen. Ihre Aufbewahrung nach der Seite ihres freien in der Form der Zufälligkeit erscheinenden Daseins, ist die Geschichte, nach der Seite ihrer begriffnen Organisation (aber) die Wissenschaft des erscheinenden Wissens: beide zusammen, die begriffne Geschichte, bilden die Erinnerung und die Schädelstatte des absoluten Geistes, die Wirklichkeit, Wahrheit und Gewissheit selnes Throns, ohne den er das leblose Einsamne wäre; nur—aus dem Kelche dieses Geisterreiches schäumt ihm seine Unendlichkeit.*

The end is an adaptation of Schiller's *Die Freundschaft*. The original verses read: *Aus dem Kelch des ganzen Seelenreiches Schäumt ihm—die Unendlichkeit.*

APPENDIX

LITERARY WORKS USED BY HEGEL TO TYPIFY VARIOUS
"FORMS OF THE WORLD" IN PART II OF THE
PHENOMENOLOGY*

*The following are brief summaries of these works with emphasis on those elements or parts of the plot or structure which are foundational to, or alluded to in some detail in, various sections of Part II of the *Phenomenology*.

1. *Antigone*, by Sophocles (495–406 B.C.)

This play, performed about 443–1 B.C., opens with a quandary: The two sons of Oedipus the King, who had been deposed from his native Thebes some years previously, and had recently died, had just killed each other in battle. The youngest son, Eteocles, who had been king of Thebes, was buried with due solemnities. But Polynices, who as the eldest son had asserted a natural right to the throne and had persuaded the armies of Argos to help him acquire the kingship by force, was technically an "enemy"; and to impress this fact on the ambivalent sentiments of Polynices' fellow countrymen, the new king, Creon, decreed that it would be considered a capital crime for anyone to presume to bury Polynices. Antigone, the sister of Polynices, in spite of pleas from her sister Ismene, decided to disobey Creon's edict in order to obey the higher, divine law that one should bury one's kinsman so that his deceased spirit may not wander aimlessly but find his true repose with his ancestors and friends in Hades. Antigone eluded the guards stationed about her brother's body, and performed the sacred rites. She was discovered by a guard, taken to Creon, and, in spite of the protests of

Creon's son, Haemon, who was in love with Antigone, was sentenced by Creon to be buried alive. While she was being taken to receive her sentence, however, the blind prophet Teiresias came to Creon to warn him that he would lose one of his own children if he went through with the execution. Creon repented, and sent his men to free Antigone. But it is too late. Antigone had already hanged herself, and Haemon, seeing what had happened, also slew himself. Creon's wife, Eurydice, hearing what had happened, also committed suicide.

Creon, although an antagonist in this play, is portrayed throughout as one who is primarily interested in the common good and in the impartial administration of the positive laws within his jurisdiction.

2. *Oedipus the King,* by Sophocles

The basic plot of this play, which was written and performed sometime after Antigone, is rather well known. Oedipus' father, Laius, King of Thebes, was warned by an oracle that his son would murder him. In order to avoid this doom, Laius gave his newborn son to a herdsman and told him to kill the child. Instead of doing this, the herdsman gave Oedipus to others who raised him in another land. When Oedipus attained adulthood, he was warned by an oracle that he was destined to kill his father and marry his mother. As it happened, he was ill-treated by his father on the road one day, and killed him in self-defense without knowing his identity. He also eventually came into the good graces of Laius' widowed wife, and married her—his mother. Finally, an oracle announced that a grave disaster impended for the whole country unless it was purified of some nameless infamy within its midst. Oedipus, now king of the country, earnestly and relentlessly sought information from oracles and witnesses until he came face-to-face with the source of the pollution: himself. His mother–wife, realizing the truth, committed suicide. Oedipus, aghast at, and inconsolate for, what he considered to be his own incomparably enormous crimes, pulled out his eyeballs so that he would never again have to look on his fate in the light of day, and insisted that he be sent to a solitary place at the outskirts of Thebes to live out the rest of his days, and that his uncle, Creon, take his throne.

3. *Oedipus at Colonus,* by Sophocles

This is Sophocles' last play, and portrays the last days of Oedipus.

Oedipus, with the assent of his two sons, has been expelled from the solitary sanctuary he was given at the end of the story narrated in *Oedipus the King*, and was compelled to roam distant lands as a vagrant accompanied only by his daughter, Antigone. His other daughter, Ismene, remains at Thebes as a kind of "contact," but remains faithful to her father. Oedipus, now much chastened and relieved of the burden of his guilt, finally hears from an oracle that he is destined to spend his last days at the shrine of the Eumenides in Colonus near Athens, and that his presence and burial there would bring great blessings to that state. After some encounters with the elders at Colonus, Oedipus, while a suppliant at the shrine of the Eumenides, is received kindly by Theseus, king of Athens, who promises to provide for him and protect him for the rest of his days. Thereupon Creon arrives from Thebes, and tries to persuade Oedipus to return to his native land. Oedipus, still smarting from his earlier banishment by Creon, refuses, and hurls curses at Creon. Creon seizes both daughters of Oedipus, who are present at the shrine, and sends them away with his men, as hostages to assure that Oedipus will follow them. He then tries to seize Oedipus by force. Theseus, who had been offering sacrifices at the nearby sanctuary, reappears, sends his men to track down the captors of Antigone and Ismene, and puts Creon in custody. Oedipus' two daughters are returned to him, and all three are then advised by Theseus that Oedipus' eldest son, Polynices, who had conspired with Creon for Oedipus' previous ouster from Thebes, is now a suppliant at the shrine seeking an audience with his father. Oedipus consents to hear Polynices only reluctantly. Polynices asks Oedipus to use his influence to establish him on the throne, and promises as king to bring him back to Thebes. Oedipus, however, curses his son and predicts that he will kill and be killed by his own brother. Polynices leaves with a sense of impending doom. Oedipus then receives some mysterious intimations of his impending death, and, though blind, leads Theseus away privately to show him the spot where he is to be buried secretly. He prophesizes that as long as his burial place remains a secret with Theseus and his successors, all will be well with Athens, and then dies.

It should be noted that in this play Creon is a selfish and vile character, while in *Antigone* (see Appendix, #1), Creon is portrayed in a much more favorable light. If one considers that the present play, even though it narrates events prior to the events in *Antigone*, was apparently written long *after Antigone*, the change in the characterization of Creon in the two plays may be taken to imply that Sophocles himself had had some second thoughts about, and had changed his attitude towards, the actions of Creon narrated in *Antigone*. It would seem that one who considered *Antigone* and *Oedipus at Colonus* in their interconnection would come up with a less favorable interpretation of Creon than Hegel apparently has in his oblique references to Creon as a protagonist of "human law" in the sections on the "Ethical Substance."

4. *Eumenides*, by Aeschylus (525–456 B.C.)

The background of this play is the recent murder of Clytaemnestra by her son Orestes, after Clytaemnestra had murdered her husband and Orestes' father, Agamemnon, with the help of her lover Aegisthus.

Because Orestes had intended to avenge his father against an impious act, all the gods seem to be on the side of Orestes after the murder. But the Furies [*Erinyes*], the avenging deities of the underworld, whose task it is to punish crimes against parents, are unwilling to allow Orestes to go unpunished.

A heated dialogue takes place between Apollo, the divine judge of the upper (Olympian) world, who had been defending Orestes, and the Furies. Apollo excoriates the Furies for having been lax in the punishment of Clytaemnestra for murdering her husband, so that Orestes had to take revenge into his own hands.

At a subsequent heavenly hearing presided over by the goddess Athena, the Furies claim that Orestes' killing of one of his own blood was a more serious crime than his mother's slaying of her husband (who was not of her own blood).

Apollo as a witness explains that Orestes' deed was the will of Zeus, the supreme god. But the Furies object that the will of Zeus is not to be trusted in a situation like this, since Zeus himself had come into power only by dethroning his own divine father (Cronos) and putting him in chains.

Orestes then pleads that he has been purified from his guilt by all the prescribed ritual purifications; and Athena finally passes judgment in favor of Orestes.

The Furies are at first incensed at this verdict, but are won over by the persuasive words of Athena; and in fact are won over so completely that they are henceforth depicted as "The Benignant Ones" (*Eumenides*).

5. *Rameau's Nephew*, by Denis Diderot (1713–1784)

This 18th century novel consists simply of a fast-moving dialogue between a French philosopher-moralist and a sensualist, court parasite and professional flatterer, called "Rameau," who is the nephew of the famous French composer, Jean Phillipe Rameau. The conversation takes place in a cafe amidst the background of a chess tournament. It begins in a low key, gradually comes to incorporate references to a multitude of artistic, literary and political figures noteworthy in French intellectual and social circles, and eventually builds up to a crescendo of feeling about the human predicament and what we might call now "alienation." The general thrust of the dialogue is such a mighty satire of the then prevalent manners and morals that it is no wonder Diderot, perhaps with an eye to the government censors, never even attempted to publish the novel during his lifetime. This posthumous book, however, is considered by many literary critics to be Diderot's greatest work.

The tension and the "action" in the novel result not only from the obvious antithesis between the moralist and the sensualist, but in the extraordinary welter of complex contradictions that emerge from the character of Rameau as he speaks, sings and acts (Rameau is a talented mime who at certain points in the novel is lost for words and resorts to pantomime). In his own existential situation (at the time of the novel, he is an "unemployed" courtier who has lost favor with his patrons by some honest but injudicious remarks), he draws a stark contrast between resignation to poverty and outlandish greed, the need for recognition and the need for self-respect, morality as "principle" and morality as "prudence," morality as socially determined and morality as individually contrived, sensuality as animality and sensuality as a prerequisite for humanity, art and genius as boons to humanity and as inimical to basic human relationships, etc. The novel ends with the question as to whether a philosopher also has to take a "position" (i.e., play an obsequious role) like everyone else who wants to remain on good terms with the king.

6. *"Confessions of a Beautiful Soul"* *(Bekenntnisse einer schönen Seele)*

This is a somewhat independent narrative which constitutes the rather long "Book Six" of *Wilhelm Meister's Apprenticeship*, a novel by J. W. von Goethe (1749–1832).

The novel in which this narrative is embedded is a philosophical–edu-cational "romance" concerned with the aesthetic, psychological and social development of one Wilhelm Meister, the son of a wealthy Ger-man businessman. At the outset of the novel, Wilhelm, who has a love for women, drama, and poetry (in that order) is disillusioned about the apparent infidelity of his beloved Mariana, and subsequently appears to settle into a business career in accord with his father's wishes. Some-time afterwards, however, on a business trip, his old predilections begin to assert themselves. He becomes involved with various dramatic com-panies, various women, and exposes himself to sundry adventures and misadventures in multiple places and social circumstances.

At one juncture in the story, Wilhelm brings a physician to visit the severely ill wife of the actor–director in a theatrical group he is working for at the time. The physician in his conversation with the woman men-tions a manuscript that has come into his hands, and to which he has af-fixed the title "Confessions of a Beautiful Soul." He promises to send the manuscript, and then leaves. The manuscript arrives shortly there-after; the woman reads it, and is visibly influenced and consoled by it be-fore she dies. The manuscript is then inserted in its totality at this point in the novel.

These "Confessions" are a private autobiography of a fairly well-to-do woman who in the mature years of her life became a Canoness and was widely reputed to be a saint or mystic. She had been very sickly as a young girl, was exposed as an adolescent to the frivolities of courtly life and "polite" society, and then, at the dawn of adulthood, made a deci-sion that for the rest of her life she would absolutely refuse to be led by the prevailing norms and expectations of family and society. She would be "her own person," resolutely faithful to her inner feelings, no longer drawn this way and that by merely external and superficial enticements, fashions, etc. This resolve, which was finally tolerated by her family and friends, led to an extended period of withdrawal from society. This withdrawal from old relationships and circumstances, however, grad-ually led to the formation of new social connections, based on mutual spiritual and religious interests. The extremity of the withdrawal was also much mitigated when she befriended a nobleman named "Philo." Philo both respected her high religious and moral sentiments and through their frequent conversations kept her thoroughly informed about events taking place in the world. As Philo became more familiar with her, he also began to offer insights into his own life and background. At one point Philo said just enough to indicate his past involvement in something that his saintly friend considered dreadful. She was repelled by the revelation, but at the same time because of her empathy for the man began to see that she herself would be capable of the same or greater sins. This led to intensification of her fideistic efforts to achieve spiritual and religious perfection, efforts which had the side-effect of temporarily alienating Philo. In a final episode in the narrative, both she and Philo are present for her sister's wedding at her uncle's castle, and it is there that she is awakened, through her uncle's instrumentality, to the necessity of combining the aesthetic, moral and religious dimensions of her life.

Towards the end of her story, the narrator relates some sad events in her family life and also describes her relationship to some individuals who, as it turns out, will play roles in the novel *Wilhelm Meister*. (The most important of these latter characters is Natalia, who will eventually become Wilhelm's wife in the novel.)

BIBLIOGRAPHY

Avineri, Shlomo. *Hegel's Theory of the Modern State*. Cambridge, 1972.

Becker, Werner. *Hegel's Phänomenologie des Geistes: Eine Interpretation*. Stuttgart, 1971.

Bierwaltes, Werner. *Platonismus und Idealismus*. Frankfurt am Main, 1972.

Bonsiepen, Wolfgang. *Der Begriff der Negativität in den Jenaer Schriften Hegels*. Bonn, 1977.

Butler, Clark, *G. W. F. Hegel*. Boston, 1977.

Debrock, Guy. "The Silence of Language in Hegel's Dialectic," *Cultural Hermeneutics* III, 1973.

Dickinson, G. Lowes. *The Greek View of Life*. New York, 1961.

Diderot, Denis. *Rameaus Neffe*, in *Goethe's Werke*. Ermatinger (Hsgb.) Leipzig, 1907–1926. Vol. XXXIII.

———. *Rameau's Nephew*. Barzun-Bowen (trans.) New York, 1956.

———. *Dictionnaire encyclopédique*, in *Oeuvres complétes*, Vols. XIII-XVII. Paris, 1876.

Fackenheim, Emil. *The Religious Dimension in Hegel's Thought*. Bloomington, Ind., 1967.

Fichte, Johann Gottlieb. *The Vocation of Man*. Chisholm (ed.). Indianapolis, 1956.

———. *The Science* [sic] *of Ethics*. Kroeger (trans.). London, 1907.

———. *Science of Knowledge*. Heath and Lachs (trans., eds.). New York, 1970.

Findlay, J. N. *Hegel: A Re-examination*. New York, 1962.

Gadamer, Hans-Georg. *Beiträge zur Deutung der Phänomenologie des Geistes*. Bonn, 1966.

Goethe, Johann Wolfgang von. *Wilhelm Meister's Apprenticeship*. Thomas Carlyle (trans.), Nathan Haskell Pole (ed.). Boston, 1901.

Gray, Glen. *Hegel and Greek Thought*. New York, 1968.

Harris, H. S. *Hegel's Development: Towards the Sunlight*. Oxford, 1972.

Hegel, G.W.F. *Aesthetics*. Knox (trans.). Oxford, 1971.

_____. *The Difference between Fichte's and Schelling's System of Philosophy*. Harris-Cerf (trans.). Albany, N. Y., 1977.

_____. *Faith and Knowledge*. Albany, New York, 1977.

_____. *Lectures on the History of Philosophy*. Haldane (trans.). London, 1968, Vol. III.

_____. *The Logic of Hegel*. Wallace (trans.). Oxford, 1931.

_____. *Natural Law*. Knox (trans.). Philadelphia, 1976.

_____. *Phänomenologie des Geistes*. Bonsiepen, Hsgb. Hamburg, 1980.

_____. *Phänomenologie des Geistes*. Hoffmeister, Hsgb. Hamburg, 1948.

_____. *The Phenomenology of Mind*. Baillie (trans.). London, 1961.

_____. *The Phenomenology of Spirit*. Miller (trans.). Oxford, 1977.

_____. *La phénoménologie de l'esprit*. Hyppolite (trans.). Paris, 1939.

_____. *Philosophische Propädeutik*. "Sämtliche Werke." Stuttgart, 1961, Dritter Band.

_____. *The Philosophy of History*. Sibree (trans.). New York, 1956.

_____. *Philosophy of Mind*. Wallace (trans.). Oxford, 1971.

_____. *Philosophy of Nature*. Miller (trans.). Oxford, 1970.

_____. *The Science of Logic*. Miller (trans.). New York, 1969.

_____. *System of Ethical Life*. Harris-Knox (trans.). New York, 1979.

Heidegger, Martin. *Hegel's Concept of Experience*. New York, 1970.

Heiss, Robert. *Hegel, Kierkegaard, Marx*. E. B. Garside (trans.). New York, 1975.

Helvetius, C. A. *De l'Esprit, or Essays on the Mind and Its Several Faculties*. ("Albion Press: Printed for James, Cundee, Ivy-Lany; and Vernor, Hood and Sharpe, 31, Poultry, 1810").

Hirsh, Emanuel. "Die Beisetzung der *Romantiker* in Hegel's Phänomenologie," in Hans F. Fulda and Dieter Henrich (Hsgb.) *Materialien zu Hegel's Phänomenologie des Geistes*. Frankfurt, 1973.

Hulin, Michel. *Hegel et l'orient*. Paris, 1979.

Hyppolite, Jean. *Genesis and Structure of Hegel's Phenomenology of Spirit*. Evanston, 1974.

Janicaud, Dominique. *Hegel et le destin de la Grèce*. Paris, 1975.

Kainz, H. P. *Hegel's Phenomenology, Part I: Analysis and Commentary*. Tuscaloosa, Ala., 1976.

Kaminsky, Jack. *Hegel on Art*. Albany, New York, 1970.

Kant, Immanuel. *Critique of Practical Reason*, Beck (trans.). Indianapolis, 1956.

———. *Religion within the Limits of Reason Alone*. T. Greene and H. Hudson (trans.). Chicago, 1934.

———. *Fundamental Principles of a Metaphysic of Morals*. Abbot (trans.). Indianapolis, 1949.

Kaufmann, Walter. *Hegel: A Reinterpretation*. London, 1966.

Kierkegaard, Sören. *Fear and Trembling and The Sickness unto Death*. Lowrie (trans.). Princeton, 1968.

Kojeve, Alexandre. *Introduction to the Reading of Hegel*. Bloom ed. Nichols (trans.). New York, 1969.

Köningson, Marie-Jeanne. "Hegel, Adam Smith et Diderot," in *Hegel et le siècle des lumières*. Hondt ed. Paris, 1974.

Küng, Hans. *Menschwerdung Gottes: Eine Einführung in Hegel's Theologisches Denken als Prolegomena zu einer Künftigen Christologie*. Freiburg, 1970.

Labarierre, Pierre-Jean. *Structures et movement dialectique dans la phénoménologie de l'Esprit de Hegel*. Paris, 1968.

———. *Introduction a une lecture de la Phénoménologie de l'Esprit*. Paris, 1979.

Lamb, David, *Hegel—from Foundation to System*. The Hague, 1980.

Lange, Erhard (Hsgb.). *Hegel und Wir*. Berlin, 1970.

Lauer, Quentin. *A Reading of Hegel's "Phenomenology of Spirit."* New York, 1976.

Loewenberg, Jacob. *Hegel's Phenomenology: Dialogues on the Life of the Mind*. La Salle, Ill., 1965.

Lukacs, Georg. *The Young Hegel: Studies in the Relations between Dialectics and Economics*. Livingstone (trans.). Cambridge, 1976.

Maier, Josef. *On Hegel's Critique of Kant*. New York, 1966.

Marx, Karl. *The Economic and Philosophic Manuscripts of 1844*. Milligan (trans.). Struik ed. New York, 1964.

Marx, Werner. *Hegel's Phenomenology of Spirit: Its Point and Purpose.—A Commentary on the Preface and Introduction*. New York, 1975.

Maurer, Reinhart. *Hegel und das Ende der Geschichte*. Stuttgart, 1965.

Mol, Hans. *Identity and the Sacred*. New York, 1976.

Navickas, Joseph. *Consciousness and Reality: Hegel's Philosophy of Subjectivity*. The Hague, 1976.

Niel, Henri. *De la médiation dans la philosophie de Hegel*. Paris, 1945.

Nietzsche, Friedrich. *Twilight of the Idols*. Hollingdale (trans.). Middlesex, England, 1968.

Norman, Richard. *Hegel's Phenomenology: A Philosophical Introduction*. New York, 1976.

O'Brien, George. *Hegel on Reason and History*. Chicago, 1975.

Plant, Raymond. *Hegel*. London, 1973.

Planty-Bonjour, Guy. "L'Esprit general d'une nation selon Montesquieu et le 'Volksgeist hegelien'," in *Hegel et le siècle des Lumières*. Paris, 1974.

Pöggeler, O. *Hegels Idee einer Phänomenologie des Geistes*. München, 1973.

Randall, John Herman. *The Making of the Modern Mind*. New York, 1976.

Reardon, Bernard. *Hegel's Philosophy of Religion*. London, 1977.

Robinson, Jonathan. *Duty and Hypocrisy in Hegel's Phenomenology of Mind: An Essay in the Real and Ideal*. Toronto, 1977.

Rosen, Stanley, *G.W.F. Hegel: An Introduction to the Science of Wisdom*. New Haven, 1974.

Royce, Josiah. *Basic Writings*. Chicago, 1969.

Saldit, Maria. *Hegels Shakespeare-Interpretation*. Berlin, 1927.

Scheier, Claus-Artur. *Analytischer Kommentar zu Hegels Phänomenologie des Geistes*. Freiburg, 1980.

Schelling, F.W.J. *System of Transcendental Idealism*. Meath (trans.). Charlottesville, Va., 1978.

Schiller, Friedrich. *On the Aesthetic Education of Man*. Snell (trans.). New York, 1954.

Schleiermacher, Friedrich. *Reden über Religion*, in *Werke* Vol. IV, Aalen, 1967.

Schneider, Helmut (Hsgb.). "Hegels Notizen zum absoluten Geist," in *Hegel Studien*, Band IX (Sonderdruck, 1974).

Schubert, Johannes. *Goethe und Hegel*. Leipzig, 1933.

Seidel, G. J. *Activity and Ground: Fichte, Schelling and Hegel*. Hildesheim, 1976.

Shklar, Judith. *Freedom and Independence: A Study of the Political Ideas of Hegel's "Phenomenology of Mind."* Cambridge, 1967.

Simon, Josef. *Das Problem der Sprache bei Hegel*. Stuttgart, 1966.

Steinkraus, Warren E. (ed.). *New Studies in Hegel's Philosophy*. New York, 1971.

Taylor, Charles. *Hegel*. Cambridge, 1975.

Thulestrup, Niel. *Kierkegaards Verhältnis zu Hegel*. Stuttgart, 1970.

Viereck, Peter. *Metapolitics: The Roots of the Nazi Mind*. New York, 1965.

Voltaire, Francois Marie Arrouêt de. *A Philosophical Dictionary*. New York, 1932.

Westphal, Merold. *History and Truth in Hegel's "Phenomenology of Spirit."* New York, 1978.

Wilkins, Burleigh. *Hegel's Philosophy of History*. Ithaca, N. Y., 1974.

NAMES AND AUTHORS

Hegel's *Phenomenology of Spirit* is considered by many philosophers to be one of the most difficult Western philosophical masterpieces. Its difficulty is matched by its importance not only in the development of Hegel's own thought but also by its fundamental impact on later thinkers.

Kainz's book is an analysis and commentary on the second half of Hegel's *Phenomenology of Spirit*. It follows his earlier exposition of *Hegel's Phenomenology, Part I: Analysis and Commentary* (University of Alabama Press, 1976) and continues where that work left off. Kainz's work provides the reader with a very useful guidebook through the wandering mazes of Hegel's difficult work. It follows the text closcly, clarifying important ideas in a refreshing way and shedding light on obscure passages without giving the impression that the original is simple, for it recognizes the persistence of key problems in Hegelian interpretation.

Howard P. Kainz, professor of philosophy at Marquette University, is a well-known Hegel scholar and a widely published author. Some of his other publications include *Hegel's Philosophy of Right with Marx's Commentary: A Handbook for Students* (Nijhoff, 1974), *Ethical Dialectica: A Study of Ethical Oppositions* (Nijhoff, 1979), and *The Philosophy of Man, Revisited* (University of Alabama Press, 1981), and articles in *Idealistic Studies, The American Philosophical Quarterly, Hegel-Studien, The Owl of Minerva, Journal of the History of Ideas,* and other journals.

0–8214–0738–4